Early
Black American Poets

Early
Black American Poets

Selections with Biographical
and Critical Introductions

by

William H. Robinson, Jr.

Howard University

WM. C. BROWN COMPANY PUBLISHERS
Dubuque, Iowa

A Question

Shall my hand lie cold on the strings of my lyre,
And the heart that is warm lose its pathos and fire,
Ere my countrymen hear my song?
Shall the bard who sang in the tents of the slave,
And now wakes his harp for the free and the brave,
Unheeded wander along?

A.A. Whitman

Contents

II. FORMALIST POETS

III. ROMANTIC POETS

General Introduction

This book was written for two specific reasons: to try to meet some of the growing demands of anxious teachers and students curious to know much more about black American poets than the ordinary anthologies of Negro literature afford; and in so doing, to display generous samplings from the little known diversity and quality of poetic writings by early black American poets of the eighteenth and nineteenth centuries. I have confined myself, wherever possible, to those poets who have produced at least a volume of verse.

Having lectured on and taught American Negro Literature for many years at Southern Negro colleges and white Northern colleges and universities, including Harvard University Extension, I know firsthand the vexations and embarrassments faced by teachers of the literature who have been unable conveniently to refer to more than the usual one, or perhaps two, poems by early black poets. Into the twentieth century, such writings become increasingly available, and anthologies are most helpful there (although more in-depth attention to the literature of the Harlem Renaissance would prove helpful). Too, the chronological formats of most anthologies, beginning in prose with Chestnutt, and in poetry with Phillis Wheatley and going to George Moses Horton to Paul Laurence Dunbar, suggest that no other Negroes were writing at the time. Although there are reasons enough to suspect as much, such is decidedly not the case. In both prose and poetry, Negroes have been writing for some time. In prose, Herbert Aptheker traces written Negro protest back to the seventeenth century. Prose sermons by Negro ministers in the eighteenth and nineteenth centuries are plentiful. There were short stories by

Mrs. Ada N. Harris, "Elsie," (*A.M.E. Review*) (Philadelphia, 1890-1891); "Victoria Earle" (i.e., Mrs. A.E. Matthews) with *Aunt Lindy* (N.Y., 1893, in hard covers); James T. Franklin and George Mcllelan (q.v.) both in 1895; and by Mrs. F.E.W. Harper (q.v.) in *Sketches of Southern Life* (1896). Besides the more well-known William Wells Brown's *Clotel, or The President's Daughter* (London, 1853; revised for American publication as *Clotelle: A Tale of the Southern States*, Boston, 1864, and again as *Clotelle: Or the Colored Heroine, a Tale of the Southern States*, Boston, 1867), and Martin Delany's *Blake, or The Huts of America* (N.Y., 1859), some other early novels would include Frank J. Webb's *The Garies and Their Friends* (London, 1857); Mrs. Clarissa M. Thompson, *Treading the Winepress* (Boston, 1885-1886); Mrs. K.D. Tillman', *Beryl Weston's Ambitions,* etc., (Philadelphia, 1888); Mrs. A.E. Johnson's widely hailed *Clarence and Clorine, or God's Way* (Philadelphia, 1889-1890), and "Sanda's" (i.e., W.H. Stowers and W.H. Anderson) *Appointed, an American Novel* (Detroit, 1894). Nineteenth century plays written by Negroes would include William Wells Brown's *The Escape, or Leap for Freedom,* in five acts (Boston, 1858); J.D. Sampson's *The Disappointed Bride; or, Love at First Sight,* in three acts (Hampton, Virginia, 1883) and William Edgar Easton's *Dessalines* (N.Y., 1893).

Similarly, there is a surprising diversity and number of early versifiers who spoke in a range of voices in English, French, Negro dialect, translations from Greek and Latin, with varying degrees of competence, and in a variety of forms from the predictable hymnal-inspired quatrain to the technical virtuosity of Spenserian stanzas, ottava rima and other original stanzas by Albery A. Whitman. The themes focus, commonly and understandably enough, on American racial injustices, or temperance, idealized Christianity, piety, morality; refreshingly, they sometimes considered other matters such as love, humor, death, the array of nature in successive seasons, etc. Although they had been in Africa different peoples with different backgrounds, American racist urgencies hammered them all into a brand new race: The American Negro. Yet their various voices came through. Some were angry or sarcastically ironic (e.g., Whitfield, Rogers, Bell), but others were genteel, deferential or, as with Whitman, conciliatory.

Even for white writers, commercial America was never nationally disposed to cultivate broadcast concern for such a "non-negotiable item" as poetry; for Negro poets, the problems of publishing were immense and could easily have proven to be downright intimidating. But they insisted. Eager to counter racist charges of inability or inferiority, some Negro writers contributed, however unwittingly, to the protraction of the cherished stereotyped comic darky of the white press, for when they wrote for the white publications, there was often a failure on the part of white readers to distinguish between the black artistic creator and the black artistic creation in fiction or in poetry. Conversely, when they wrote for Negro publications—and Negro journalism gets under way in 1827—they often had to satisfy Negro readers' demands for counter caricatures. Thus many Negro characters in early Negro publications are often unbearably upright, morally straight and in daily pursuit of virtue or Christian morality as they exert their every effort towards middle-class notions of respectability. Also, again however unwittingly, some of them displayed embarrassing immaturity in both thought and technique. Many of them had been born and reared in one variety or another of slavery, some had only the barest rudiments of formal education, and the few who managed to enter or to complete college were usually kept busy as preachers, teachers or on endless fund raising efforts for their colleges, hospitals, churches. In a solution of sorts, many black poets often accommodated their truest feelings about whatever by privately printing their works. It is from such productions that perhaps the best examples of authentic early black poetry can be gleaned. While their themes overlapped, often into sentimentalism, their work can be grouped, roughly, as versified oratory, "Formalism," romanticism and dialect poetry.

Encountering the works of the declamatory orator-poets, such as Whitfield, Bell, Rogers, Mrs. Harper, with their cling-clang meters, extravagant patriotism, often cloying sentimentality, their bombast and naive optimism, modern readers may become quickly impatient. But that would fail to consider the context in which such verse flourished; that would be to ignore the speaking tradition among Negroes. These lines were usually most effective when they were read aloud, or, more accurately, when they were "rendered" on platforms of convention halls or opera houses or church pulpits across the country; sometimes freely participated in by audience responses, laughter, applause, these lines were close to the sermons. Mrs. F.E.W. Harper's *Poems on Miscellaneous Subjects,* for instance, reached its twentieth edition as early as 1874, but this was not due to the conventional notion of poetic excellence, Mrs. Harper was fully aware of her limitations in that kind of poetry, it was due more to the sentimental, emotion-freighted popularity that she had given the lines with her disarmingly dramatic voice and gestures and sighs and tears. The impact of her histrionics, of her "acting," on both black and white audiences, has been recorded by several of her listeners. The so-called "Formalists" (Phillis Wheatley, Cordelia Ray, Mcllelan and others) reveal formal influences of classical propriety and restraint and conscious control; typically, they seem self-consciously dutiful in their infrequent and intellectualized choices of "non controversial" topics. The "Romanticists" (John Boyd, The Creole Poets, and especially A.A. Whitman) versify idealities, not the real world around them; as with many so markedly romantic writers, there can be found in their lines an implied self-righteousness, a concealed compulsion for conservatism. Welcome in this collection for the great variety of poetic and emotional ranges they display, almost all of their lyrical thrusts might have benefitted from more discipline or kindly editorial concern. For comments on the Dialect Poets, see pages 229-231.

Finally, it must be kept in mind that "American Literature" of the eighteenth and much of the nineteenth centuries was long regarded as undefinable or non-existent or of inconsequential worth. Self-respecting literary historians, unwilling to live with such a maligned past, did something about the matter. Just as white American writers contorted in intimidating, self-conscious imitation of their literary kin on the Continent until the likes of Ralph Waldo Emerson in his "American Scholar" (1837) began to make them aware of their own American peculiarities that required American sensibilities shaped by American, not European, experiences to evaluate their literature knowingly, so black American writers might recognize that they too may require peculiar criteria for the faithful evaluation of their literature which reflects what has most certainly been a peculiarly American experience. Through the pioneering critical efforts of Henry James, Van Wyck Brooks, J.E. Spingarn, and others, "American Literature" now regards much—perhaps too much—early writings more sympathetically than had been true before. But if today a college textbook in "American Literature" can include such diverse writings as excerpts from travelogues (Christopher Columbus, Jacques Cartier, Claude Dablan, etc.), letters, journals and diaries (John Winthrop, Sarah Kemble Knight, Cotton Mather, Samuel Sewall), and if the verse of the likes of Philip Pain, John Josselyn, Edward Coote Pinkney can be included in the *Oxford Anthology of American Literature,* which went through ten (10) printings by 1956, then clearly many of the efforts of early black American poets deserve student attention also. Hopefully, this collection will supply some of the justification for such expectation, for the following selections are, in their strengths and weaknesses, exactly what early black American poets said and how they said it. They might be accepted or rejected, but they ought at least be listened to as they speak.

My thanks are due and hereby tended to many people including my students and colleagues, in the North and in the South, but I especially want to single out the invaluable assistance given to me by Mrs. Dorothy Porter, curator of the Spingarn-Moorland collections of Afro-American Life and Letters here at Howard University; she and her cooperative staff greatly expedited my work professionally and personally. I was heartened along the way by the special encouragement of the late Dr. Ulysses Lee of Morgan State College in Baltimore, and by the geniality of Dr. Arthur P. Davis, my colleague here at Howard. Both scholars are two of the three editors of the classic in the field, *The Negro Caravan,* a fruitful source for anyone concerned with American Negro letters from the beginnings to 1941. I am also indebted to Mrs. Coleman for permission to use the selections of the Creole poets, and to Dr. Richard Allsop, of the University of West Indies, 1968-1969 visiting professor in Linguistics at Howard University, for his help in translation of these French speaking poets.

Benjamin Brawley's *Early Negro American Writers* (Chapel Hill, 1935), an anthology of early poetry and prose, was helpful, as was Vernon Loggins' *The Negro Author* (New York, 1931), although this work is a *discussion of* rather than a collection of early works. Biographical information on the poets, whenever available, was gleaned and deduced from various, unnumbered cross references, and works such as William W. Brown's *The Rising Son* (Boston, 1874); Henry Northrup et. al., *The College of Life* (Chicago, 1895); Hallie

Q. Brown's *Homespun Heroes and Other Women of Distinction* (Xenia, Ohio, 1926), and many others such race books which make up an entire genre of repositories of race pride. Finally, I want to acknowledge in print what my wife, Doris Carol, already knows in other ways.

English Department   William H. Robinson
Howard University, 1969

Early
Black American Poets

*Selections with Biographical
and Critical Introductions*

I

Orator Poets

Lucy Terry
(1730-1821)

Lucy Terry is easily as important for her long, Yankee life as she is for being presently regarded as America's first Negro poet, although her single known poem was composed in 1746 and not published until 1893. Like many other New England black servants and slaves, she was kidnapped as a child and brought to Rhode Island, where she was bought as a servant to Ebenezer Wells, who had her baptized in 1744 in his Deerfield, Massachusetts, home. She married the very capable Abijah Prince in 1756 and was a decided asset to that free Negro entrepeneur, who was born about 1706 probably in Wallingford, Connecticut. It was Abijah Prince who shrewdly parlayed a gift of land into extensive real estate holdings in Northfield, Massachusetts, and, six children later—their names were Cesar, Duroxa, Drucilla, Festus, Tatnai and Abijah, Jr.—in the towns of Guilford and Sunderland, Vermont. He is named in the Sunderland, Vermont, charter as one of its founders. Across the creek neighbors to Colonel Ethan Allen, Abijah and Lucy combined to fight off a land encroachment claim, arguing all the way up to the Federal Supreme Court, and winning against the likes of Royall Tyler, valedictorian at Harvard, class of 1766, poet and author and, later, chief justice of Vermont. Lucy also harrangued authorities of Williams College for the admission of one of her sons, but although she cited Biblical and legal chapter, verse and statute, she lost. In her last years, when she was in her late eighties, she was a familiar sight as annually she made her way on horseback from her home in Sunderland, through the Green Mountains, to Guilford, the burial site of her husband who had died in 1794, and back to Sunderland—a thirty-six mile round trip. Her sing-song versification of an actual Indian raid is a simple enough affair, but it is said to represent the best contemporary account of that assault. A biography of Mrs. Prince is under way, but see George Sheldon, *A History of Deerfield, Massachusetts* (Deerfield, 1895).

Bars Fight, August 28, 1746

August 'twas, the twenty-fifth,
Seventeen hundred forty-six,
The Indians did in ambush lay,
Some very valient (sic) men to slay,
The names of whom I'll not leave out:
Samuel Allen like a hero fout,
And though he was so brave and bold,
His face no more shall we behold;
Eleazer Hawks was killed outright,
Before he had time to fight,
Before he did the Indians see,
Was shot and killed immediately;
Oliver Amsden, he was slain,
Which caused his friends much grief and pain;
Simeon Amsden they found dead,
Not many rods off from his head;
Adonijah Gillet, we do hear,
Did lose his life, which was so dear;
John Saddler fled across the water,
And so escaped the dreadful slaughter;
Eunice Allen see the Indians comeing (sic),
And hoped to save herself by running,
And had not her petticoats stopt her,
The awful creatures had not cotched her,
And tommyhawked her on the head,
And left her on the ground for dead;
Young Samuel Allen, oh! lack-a-day,
Was taken and carried to Canada.

* * * * * * * *

Jupiter Hammon
(1720?-1806?)

As is the case with so many Negroes in Colonial America, the birth and death dates and places of Jupiter Hammon are not exactly known. Oscar Wegelin, earliest authority on Hammon, published a letter from a Mr. George Muirson, date May 19, 1730, from his Long Island estate, St. George. It is a reply to a letter from Hammon's owner, Henry Lloyd, who had evidently asked for medical advice about Jupiter's illness, which was affecting the boy's legs; the letter was written, says Wegelin, when Hammon "must have been a child of ten or twelve years." In his own *Address to the Negroes of the State of New York,* composed on September 24, 1786, Hammon admits to being "now upwards of seventy years old." Wegelin reports that a copy of this address was printed in New York in 1806, "after the poet ceased to be a slave," but the biographical information on this edition is a paragraph long attestation of the character of the Negro, and the authenticity of its writing, and it is signed by three white men subscribers. As they refer to Hammon in the past tense throughout, it seems clear that Hammon was likely dead by that time.

It seems just as clear that Jupiter Hammon[1] was an obedient, conservative minded servant, caught up in the fervor of Methodist preached piety and Christianity; as several have suspected, he may well have been a minister of sorts, as there were black and Indian churches on Long Island, where he lived as a slave to the influential

---

[1] There may be some connection between Jupiter Hammon's name and the ancient Egyptian-African deity called Jupiter Ammon. See Frank A. Rollin (Mrs. Francis Whipper) *Life and Public Services of Martin R. Delany* (Boston, 1883), p. 16.

Lloyd family of Lloyd's Neck. There were even Indian and Negro ministers then, including the Connecticut born Samson Occom, Dartmouth trained and ordained in 1759 by the Suffolk Presbytery (he was known by Phillis Wheatley also); and there was Paul Cuffee (1757-1812) Indian-Negro pastor at Wading River. Although Hammon recognized and stated in his *Address* the cruel paradox of Colonial slavery, especially for recent black and white veterans of the Revolutionary War; and although he urged freedom for young Negroes, the predominant tone of the essay is one of personal resignation and adjustment to the system of slavery with frequent supplications for the ultimate rewards of the Christian heaven.

Revealing as much about the white world in which he moved as anything else, Hammon's broadside verses have historical, socio-logical and some literary interest. His first effort seems to have been "An Evening Thought. Salvation by Christ, with Penetential Cries: Composed by Jupiter Hammon, a Negro belonging to Mr. Lloyd of Queen's Village, on Long Island, the 25th of December, 1760," which is likely the first poetical composition by an American Negro published in this country. His next broadside was "An Address to Miss Phillis Wheatly (sic), etc.," dated Hartford, August 4, 1778, with a note that says "The above lines are published by the Author, and a number of his friends, who desire to join with him in their best regards to Miss Wheatley (sic)." Beneath the lengthy title is the heading: "Miss Wheatly (sic); pray give (us?[2]) leave to express as follows:" and the poem begins its twenty-one stanzas that show marked hymnal influence in stanzaic pattern, meter, rime, diction and imagery. "An Essay on the Ten Virgins," (1779) was printed at Hartford also, but no copy seems to be preserved. "A Winter Piece," a prose sermon with a two page poem, "A Poem for Children, with Thoughts on Death," appended was published in 1782. Finally, "An Evening's Improvement./ Shewing,/ The Necessity of Beholding/ The Lamb of God./ To which is added,/ A Dialogue./ entitled/ The Kind Master and/ Dutiful Servant./ Written by Jupiter Hammon, a Negro/ Man belonging to Mr. John Lloyd, of Queen's/ Village on Long Island, now in Hartford./" appeared, dated "Hartford,/ printed for the Author, by the assistance of his friends;" it was likely written in the mid-1780's.

---

[2]The broadside is creased where a word ("us"?) seems to have been printed.

Helpful in grasping some of Hammon's thinking is the afore-mentioned *Address,* but see also Oscar Wegelin, *Jupiter Hammon, American Negro Poet; Selections from his Writings and a Bibliography* (N.Y., 1915). For extensive accounts of the Lloyd family, see Benjamin Thompson, *The History of Long Island,* 2nd edition (N.Y., 1843). Benjamin Brawley's remarks in his *Early Negro American Writers* (Chapel Hill, 1935) are especially worthwhile.

An Evening Thought: Salvation by Christ with Penetential Cries

Salvation comes by Christ alone,
  The only Son of God;
Redemption now to every one,
  That loves his holy Word.

. . . . . .

Dear Jesus, give thy Spirit now,
  Thy grace to every Nation,
That han't the Lord to whom we bow,
  The Author of Salvation.

Dear Jesus, unto Thee we cry,
  Give us the Preparation;
Turn not away thy tender Eye;
  We seek thy true Salvation.

. . . . . .

Lord, hear our penetential Cry:
  Salvation from above;
It is the Lord that doth supply,
  With his Redeeming Love.

Dear Jesus, by thy precious Blood,
  The World Redemption have:
Salvation now comes from the Lord,
  He being thy captive slave.

Dear Jesus, let the Nations cry,
  And all the People say,
Salvation comes from Christ on high,
  Haste on Tribunal Day.

We cry as Sinners to the Lord,
  Salvation to obtain;
It is firmly fixed, his holy Word,
  Ye shall not cry in vain.

· · · · · ·

Lord, turn our dark benighted Souls;
  Give us a true Motion,
And let the Hearts of all the World,
  Make Christ their Salvation.

· · · · · ·

Lord, unto whom now shall we go,
  Or seek a safe abode?
Thou hast the Word, Salvation Too:
  The only Son of God.

"Ho! every one that hunger hath,
  Or pineth after me,
Salvation be thy leading Staff,
  To set the Sinner free."

Dear Jesus, unto Thee we fly;
  Depart, depart from Sin,
Salvation doth at length supply,
  The glory of our King.

Come, ye Blessed of the Lord,
  Salvation greatly given;
O, turn your hearts, accept the Word,
  Your Souls are fit for Heaven.

Dear Jesus, we now turn to Thee,
  Salvation to obtain;
Our Hearts and Souls do meet again,
  To magnify thy Name.

Come, holy Spirit, Heavenly Dove,
  The Object of our Care;
Salvation doth increase our Love;
  Our Hearts hath felt thy fear.

Now Glory be to God on High,
  Salvation high and low;
And thus the Soul on Christ rely,
  To Heaven surely go.

Come, Blessed Jesus, Heavenly Dove,
  Accept Repentance here;
Salvation give, with tender Love;
  Let us with Angels share.

                              1760

                    Finis
            * * * * * * *

An Address to Miss Phillis Wheatly (sic), Ethiopian Poetess, in Boston, who came from Africa at eight years of age, and soon became acquainted with the gospel of Jesus Christ.

                    1.

O, come, you pious youth! adore
  The wisdom of thy God,
In bringing thee from distant shore,
  To learn His holy word,

                    2.

Thou mightst been left behind,
  Amidst a dark abode;
God's tender mercy still combined,
  Thou hast the holy word.

                    3.

Fair Wisdom's ways are paths of peace,
  And they that walk therein,
Shall reap the joys that never cease,
  And Christ shall be their King.

                    4.

God's tender mercy brought thee here;
  Tossed o'er the raging main;
In Christian faith thou hast a share,
  Worth all the gold of Spain.

5.

While thousands tossed by the sea,
  And others settled down,
God's tender mercy set thee free
  From dangers that come down.

6.

That thou a pattern still might be,
  To youth of Boston town,
The blessed Jesus set thee free
  From every sinful wound.

7.

The blessed Jesus, who came down,
  Unveiled his sacred face,
To cleanse the soul of every wound,
  And give repenting grace.

8.

That we poor sinners may obtain
  The pardon of our sin,
Dear Blessed Jesus, now constrain,
  And bring us flocking in.

9.

Come, you, Phillis, now aspire,
  And seek the living God,
So step by step thou mayst go higher,
  Till perfect in the word.

10.

While thousands moved to distant shore,
  And others left behind,
The blessed Jesus still adore;
  Implant this in thy mind.

11.

Thou hast left the heathen shore;
  Through mercy of the Lord,
Among the heathen live no more;
  Come magnify thy God.

12.

I pray the living God may be,
    The shepherd of thy soul;
His tender mercies still are free,
    His mysteries to unfold.

13.

Thou, Phillis, when thou hunger hast,
    Or pantest for thy God,
Jesus Christ is thy relief,
    Thou hast the holy word.

14.

The bounteous mercies of the Lord
    Are hid beyond the sky,
And holy souls that have His word
    Shall taste them when they die.

15.

These bounteous mercies are from God,
    The merits of His Son;
The humble soul that loves His word
    He chooses for his own.

16.

Come, dear Phillis, be advised
    To drink Samaria's[1] flood;
There nothing that shall suffice
    But Christ's redeeming blood.

17.

While thousands muse with earthly toys,
    And range about the street,
Dear Phillis, seek for heaven's joys,
    Where we do hope to meet.

---

[1] Samaria was the ancient capitol of Israel.

18.

When God shall send his summons down,
  And number saints together,
Blessed angels chant (triumphant sound),
  Come live with me forever.

19.

The humble soul shall fly to God,
  And leave the things of time,
Start forth as 'twere at the first word,
  To taste things more divine.

20.

Behold! the soul shall waft away,
  Whene'er we come to die,
And leave its cottage made of clay,
  In twinkling of an eye.

21.

Now glory be to the Most High,
  United praises given,
By all on earth, incessantly,
  And all the host of heaven.

1778

* * * * * * *

Gustavus Vassa
(1745-1801?)

While there is some question about the exact date of his death, there is a fully detailed and engagingly narrated account of the extraordinary life of Gustavus Vassa, or Olaudah Equiano, to use his African name, in *The Interesting Narrative/ of/ The Life/ of Olaudah Equiano,/ or/ Gustavus Vassa,/ The African./* Written by Himself, in two volumes, (London, 1789). He was born, the seventh and youngest son of a chieftan father in Essaka (in present Eastern Nigeria), which was under "nominal subjection of the King of Benin." Kidnapped when he was ten with his sister by local slave traders, he was taken to America, where he slaved on a Virginia plantation until he was purchased, for forty pounds sterling, by Michael Pascal, who imposed the name Gustavus Vassa on him, and used his services on several Atlantic voyages before he served in the Mediterranean during the Seven Years War. He was sold again to Robert King, a Philadelphia born, Quaker slave-owner, from whom he was able to buy his freedom in 1766 with wages saved from his meager earnings. Adept at picking up the English language and making the most of his mastery of elementary mathematics, he was able to serve as an amateur navigator and shipping clerk, which skills were helpful as he sailed with an Arctic expedition that, aboard *The Race Horse* in 1773, set a new world's record when it reached "nearly as far towards the Pole as 81 degrees north, and 20 degrees east longitude, being much farther by all accounts than any navigator had ever ventured before," (further than Henry Hudson's trip to New Zemlya in 1608, Ed). He married late, in 1792, by which time he was a tireless petitioner for the abolition of African slavery, for a while contributing to the efforts to colonize poor blacks of England in

13

Sierra Leone. His efforts took their toll, for too many speaking efforts cost him his voice. His prose, the authenticity of which has been demonstrated, is much more lively than the slight verse he composed,[1] and yet the poem has its value as one more documentation of the feelings of a most unusually interesting black man of the eighteenth Century. There is a useful abridged edition of his two volumes in *Equiano's Travels* by Paul Edwards (New York, 1967).

Miscellaneous Verses

Well may I say my life has been
One scene of sorrow and of pain;
From early days I griefs have known,
And as I grew my griefs have grown:

Dangers were always in my path;
And fear of wrath, and sometimes death;
While pale dejection in me reign'd
I often wept, by grief constrain'd.

When taken from my native land,
By an unjust and cruel band,
How did uncommon dread prevail!
My sighs no more could I conceal.

To ease my mind I often strove,
And tried my trouble to remove:
I sung, and utter'd sighs between —
Assay'd to stifle guilt with sin.

But O! not all that I could do
Would stop the current of my woe;
Conviction still my vileness shew'd;
How great my guilt—how lost from God!

Prevented, that I could not die,
Nor might to one kind refuge fly;
An orphan state I had to mourn—
Forsook by all, and left forlorn.

---

[1] And published in his autobiography.

Those who beheld my downcast mien
Could not guess at my woes unseen:
They by appearance could not know
The troubles that I waded through.

Lust, anger, blasphemy, and pride,
With legions of such ills beside,
Troubled my thoughts while doubts and fears
Clouded and darken'd most my years.

Sighs now no more would be confin'd—
They breath'd the trouble of my mind:
I wish'd for death, but check'd the word,
And often pray'd unto the Lord.

Unhappy, more than some on earth,
I thought the place that gave me birth—
Strange thoughts oppress'd—while I replied
"Why not in Ethiopia died?"

And why thus spared, nigh to hell?—
God only knew—I could not tell!
A Tott'ring fence, a bowing wall,
I thought myself e'er since the fall.

Oft times I mused, nigh despair,
While birds melodious fill'd the air:
Thrice happy songsters, ever free,
How bless'd they were compar'd to me!

Thus all things added to my pain,
While grief compell'd me to complain;
When sable clouds began to rise
My mind grew darker than the skies.

The English nation call'd to leave,
How did my breast with sorrows heave!
I long'd for rest—cried "Help me, Lord!
Some mitigation, Lord, afford!"

Yet on, dejected, still I went—
Heart-throbbing woes within were pent;
Nor land nor sea, could comfort give,
Nothing my anxious soul relieve.

Weary with travail, yet unknown
To all but God and self alone,
Numerous months for peace I strove
And numerous foes I had to prove.

Inur'd to dangers, griefs, and woes,
Train'd up 'midst perils, deaths, and foes,
I said, "Must it thus ever be?—
No quiet is permitted me?"

Hard hap, and more than heavy lot!
I pray'd to God "Forget me not—
What thou ordain'st willing I'll bear,
But O! deliver from despair!"

Strivings and wrestlings seem'd in vain;
Nothing I did could ease my pain:
Then gave I up my works and will,
Confess'd and own'd my doom was hell!

Like some poor pris'ner at the bar,
Conscious of guilt, of sin and fear,
Arraign'd, and self-condemn'd I stood—
Lost in the world, and in my blood!

Yet here, 'midst blackest clouds confin'd,
A beam from Christ, the day-star, shin'd;
Surely, thought I, if Jesus please,
He can at once sign my release.

I, ignorant of his righteousness,
Set up my labors in its place;
Forgot for why his blood was shed,
And pray'd and fasted in its stead.

He dy'd for sinners—I am one!
Might not his blood for me atone?
Thou I am nothing else but sin,
Yet surely he can make me clean!

Thus light came in and I believ'd;
Myself forgot, and help receiv'd!
My Saviour then I know I found,
For, eas'd from guilt, no more I groan'd.

O happy hour, in which I ceas'd
To mourn, for then I found a rest!
My soul and Christ were now as one—
Thy light, O Jesus, in me shone!

Bless'd by thy name, for now I know
I and my works can nothing do;
The Lord alone can ransom man—
For this the spotless Lamb was slain!

When sacrifices, works, and pray'r,
Prov'd vain, and ineffectual were,
"'Lo, then I come!" the Saviour cry'd,
And, bleeding, bow'd his head and dy'd!

He dy'd for all who ever say
No help in them, nor by the law:—
I this have seen; and gladly own
"Salvation is by Christ alone!"[2]

* * * * * * * *

---

[2] Acts iv, 12.

George Moses Horton
(1797?-1883?)

Born in Northampton County, North Carolina, George was the slave of three generations of Hortons, which did not deter him much, if at all, from doggedly learning to read and write and launching a career as America's first professional black poet. He began early, earning twenty-five and seventy-five cents per poem on the Chapel Hill Campus of the University of North Carolina, where students, smitten or rejected in love, turned for relief to his readily declaimed appropriate verses. Encouraged, he arranged with his master to rent himself out, moved to the campus and began something like full time support of himself by dictating until he could write and then by writing occasional verses, some of which found their way into local newspapers. He was helped in his reading and writing by various students and even the president, Joseph D. Caldwell, but especially helpful was Mrs. Caroline Lee Hentz, New England born and reared poet and novelist and wife of a new professor at Chapel Hill. It was she who had helped him prepare his first volume, *Hope of Liberty,* (Raleigh 1829), and it was she who had his "Liberty and Slavery" published in her hometown newspaper, the *Lancaster Gazette,* where it was noticed and reprinted as "Slavery" in William Lloyd Garrison's *Liberator,* March 29, 1834, with another of his poems.

For most of his life, Horton had begged in person, in letters and in verse for his liberty. As the title makes clear, *Hope of Liberty* was written to secure money enough for him to purchase his freedom and sail to Liberia, but he was sorely disappointed, even though the volume was twice reprinted as *Poems by a Slave* (Philadelphia, 1837, and Boston, 1838). Finally, as an old man, he was freed by mandate of occupying Union forces, after which he moved to Philadelphia where it is thought he hacked out a survival writing short stories for Sunday school publications until 1883, when he died. Besides the *Hope of Liberty,* he also produced the *Poetical Works of George M. Horton, the Colored Bard of North Carolina* (Hillsborough, N.C., 1845), which has added value for its prefatory autobiography, "The Life of George M. Horton, the Colored Bard of North Carolina." Copies are extremely rare, but see Benjamin Brawley, *Early Negro American Writers,* and Richard Walser, *The Black Poet* (New York, 1967). There was a final volume, *Naked Genius* (Raleigh, 1865), also very rare, and there may exist somewhere the manuscript for a projected fourth volume, *The Black Poet.*

Horton's poetry has engendered a considerable bibliography.— Collier Cobb's *An American Man of Letters, George Moses Horton* (Chapel Hill, 1886) is an early concern—which documents his poetic virtues and faults that include obvious imitation of some of his bookish sources, Byron, Wesleyan hymnal stanzas, meter, rime scheme and vocabulary. There is much stock posing also in several of his pieces and he seems always aware of his unique role as an early black American poet in a world of white unbelievers. There is not much thought in most of his work, his best pieces being those that plead for his freedom with a sincerity that is believable, despite the conventionally stilted syntax and the abstract language. At best a minor American poet of the nineteenth century, Horton still deserves more than passing attention. "The Art of a Poet" is from *Naked Genius,* the other selections, except "Slavery" are from *Hope of Liberty.*

The Lover's Farewell

And wilt thou, love, my soul display,
And all my secret thought betray?
I strove, but could not hold thee fast,
My heart flies off with thee at last.

The favorite daughter of the dawn
On love's mild breeze will soon be gone;
I strove, but could not cease to love,
Nor from my heart the weight remove.

And wilt thou, love, my soul beguile,
And quell thy favorite with a smile?
Nay, soft affection answers nay,
And beauty wings my heart away.

I steal on tip toe from these bowers,
All spangled with a thousand flowers;
I sigh, yet leave them all behind
To gain the object of my mind.

And wilt thou, love, command my soul,
And waft me with a light control?
Adieu to all the blooms of May,
Farewell—I fly with love away!

I leave my parents here behind,
And all my friends—to love resigned—
'Tis grief to go, but death to stay:
Farewell—I'm gone with love away!

* * * * * * *

To Eliza

Eliza, tell thy lover why
Or what induced thee to deceive me?
    Fare thee well—away I fly—
I shun the lass who thus will grieve me.

Eliza, still thou art my song,
Although by force I may forsake thee;
    Fare thee well, for I was wrong
To woo thee while another take thee.

Eliza, pause and think awhile—
Sweet lass! I shall forget thee never:
    Fare thee well: although I smile,
I grieve to give thee up forever.

Eliza, I shall think of thee—
My heart I shall ever twine about thee;
    Fare thee well—but think of me,

Compell'd to live and die without thee,
  "Fare thee well!—and if forever,[1]
"Still forever fare thee well!"

Slavery

When first my bosom glowed with hope,
  I gazed as from a mountain top
    On some delightful plain;
But oh! how transient was the scene—
It fled as though it had not been,
    And all my hopes were vain.

How oft this tantalyzing blaze
  Has led me through deception's maze;
    My friends became my foe—
Then like a plaintive dove I mourned;
To bitter all my sweets were turned,
    And tears began to flow.

Why was the dawning of my birth
Upon this vile, accursed earth,
    Which is but pain to me?
Oh! that my soul had winged its flight,
When I first saw the morning light,
    To worlds of liberty!

Come, melting Pity, from afar,
And break this vast, enormous bar
    Between a wretch and thee;
Purchase a few short days of time,
And bid a vassal rise sublime
    On wings of liberty.

Is it because my skin is black,
That thou should'st be so dull and slack,
    And scorn to set me free?
Then let me hasten to the grave,
The only refuge for the slave,
    Who mourns for liberty.

---

[1] "Fare thee well!... fare thee well!" from Byorn's "Fare Thee Well," lines 1-2.

The wicked cease from troubling there;
No more I'd languish or despair—
    The weary there can rest!
Oppression's voice is heard no more,
Drudg'ry and pain and toil are o'er,
    Yes! there I shall be blest!

(*The Liberator,* March 29, 1834)

* * * * * * * *

The Slave's Complaint

Am I sadly cast aside,
On misfortune's rugged tide?
Will the world my pains deride
            Forever?

Must I dwell in Slavery's night,
And all pleasure take its flight,
Far beyond my feeble sight,
            Forever?

Worst of all, must hope grow dim,
And withold her cheering beam?
Rather let me sleep and dream
            Forever!

Something still my heart surveys,
Groping through this dreary maze;
Is it Hope?—then burn and blaze
            Forever!

Leave me not a wretch confined,
Altogether lame and blind—
Unto gross despair consigned,
            Forever!

Heaven! in whom can I confide?
Canst thou not for all provide?
Condescend to be my guide
            Forever:

And when this transient life shall end,
Oh, may some kind, eternal friend,
Bid me from servitude ascend,
     Forever!

* * * * * * *

On Hearing of the Intention of a Gentleman to Purchase the Poet's Freedom

When on life's ocean first I spread my sail,
I then implored a mild auspicious gale;
And from the slippery strand I took my flight,
And sought the peaceful haven of delight.

Tyrannic storms arose upon my soul,
And dreadful did their mad'ning thunders roll;
The pensive muse was shaken from her sphere,
And hope, it vanished in the clouds of fear.

At length a golden sun broke through the gloom,
And from his smiles arose a sweet perfume—
A calm ensued, and birds began to sing,
And lo! the sacred muse resumed her wing.

With frantic joy she chaunted as she flew,
And kiss'd the clement hand that bore her through;
Her envious foes did from her sigh retreat,
Or prostrate fall beneath her burning feet.

'Twas like a proselyte, allied to Heaven—
Or rising spirits' boast of sins forgiven,
Whose shout dissolves the adamant away,
Whose melting voice the stubborn rocks obey.

'Twas like the salutation of the dove,
Borne on the zephyr through some lonesome grove,
When Spring returns, and Winter's chill is past,
And vegetation smiles above the blast.

'Twas like the evening of a nuptial pair,
When love pervades the hour of sad despair—
'Twas like fair Helen's sweet return to Troy,
When every Grecian bosom swell'd with joy.

The silent harp which on the osiers hung,
Was then attuned, and manumission sung;
Away by hope the clouds of fear were driven,
And music breathed my gratitude to Heaven.

Hard was the race to reach the distant goal,
The needle oft was shaken from the pole;
In such distress who could forbear to weep?
Toss'd by the headlong billows of the deep!

The tantalizing beams which shone so plain,
Which turned my former pleasures into pain—
Which falsely promised all the joys of fame,
Gave way, and to a more substantial flame.

Some philanthropic souls as from afar,
With pity strove to break the slavish bar;
To whom my floods of gratitude shall roll,
And yield with pleasure to their soft control.

And sure of Providence this work begun—
He shod my feet this rugged race to run;
And in despite of all the swelling tide,
Along the dismal path will prove my guide.

Thus on the dusky verge of deep despair,
Eternal Providence was with me there;
When pleasure seemed to fade on life's gay dawn,
And the last beam of hope was almost gone.

* * * * * * * *

The Art of a Poet

True nature first inspires the man,
But he must after learn to scan,
    And mark well every rule;
Gradual the climax then ascend,
And prove the contrast in the end,
    Between the wit and fool.

A fool tho' blind, may write a verse,
And seem from folly to emerge,
   And rime well every line;
One lucky, void of light, may guess
And safely to the point may press,
   But this does not refine.

Polish mirror, clear to shine,
And streams must run if they refine,
   And widen as they flow;
The diamond water lies concealed,
Till polished it is ne'er revealed,
   Its glory bright to show.

A bard must traverse o'er the world,
Where things concealed must rise unfurled,
   And tread the feet of yore;
Tho' he may sweetly harp and sing,
But strictly prune the mental wing,
   Before the mind can soar.

* * * * * * *

Frances E. W. Harper
(1825-1911)

Frances Watkins was born an only child of free parents in Baltimore, Maryland, but, her mother dying three years later, she was reared by an aunt and educated by her abolition-minded uncle, William Watkins in his school for free colored children until she was thirteen years old. She later moved to Ohio, taught at Little York, Pennsylvania, where she saw her first fleeing fugitive slave; she was also moved by the true story of the ultimate death of a free Negro who unwittingly violated Maryland's laws that forbade free Negroes from entering that state, upon pain of imprisonment and sale into slavery. These and other such brutalities galvanized her into a life-long anti-slavery crusade.

She set out at once, lecturing in Boston, Philadelphia and New Bedford, where in 1852 she was engaged by the Anti-Slavery Society of Maine as permanent lecturer and proved to be an extremely effective platform speaker. In 1860 she married Fenton Harper in Cincinnati, and they became the parents of a daughter, Mary. When Mr. Harper died four years later, Mrs. Harper resumed her lecture tours and again with great success, despite the hooting and jeering insults from racists unbelievers, drunks and constitutional cranks. So zealous and attractive was she on the platform that she once lectured in twenty different cities and towns throughout Maine, sometimes twice an evening, and on Sundays—all on consecutive nights. She lectured in every southern state except Texas and Arkansas and once, in Darlington, South Carolina, she drew such an immense crowd that she was obliged to speak from the doorway of a packed church so that the swarm outside could also hear her. She visited fugitives in Canada, contributed some of her earnings from sales of her writings to the cause, wrote to and comforted Mrs. John Brown for the two weeks before the martyr's execution. She led an inspired and dedicated life, speaking to black and whites, mayors and peasants, always with the same message—"Let my people go."

Likewise were her writings, letters, short stories, essays, a novel, and poetry, designed for racial enlightenment and religious edification, feminist and temperance sympathy. Her literary output poses problems for the exacting bibliographer, for she might make selections from earlier volumes and print them under different titles that might include newer poems not listed in the table of contents. Her first work, *Forest Leaves,* does not seem extant, but her *Poems of Miscellaneous Subjects* (Philadelphia, 1854) reached many editions, at least twenty by 1874. *Moses, a Story of the Nile,* reached a third edition by 1870; *Poems* was printed in 1871 and 1900; *Sketches of Southern Life* (1872 and enlarged 1896) includes several clumsy attempts at southern Negro dialect in the mouth of Aunt Chloe. *Iola Leroy, or Shadows Uplifted* (1892) is a novel involving the racial pride of an octoroon. Some of her letters can be found in William Still's *The Underground Railroad* (Philadelphia, 1872). Her essays are scattered in various Negro literary and religious publications of the time.

William Still reports that "Fifty thousand copies at least of her small books have been sold to those who have listened to her eloquent lectures." This figure can be believed for while her verse may reveal many faults to the reader, her listeners must have been impressed. But even read, her lines sometimes show her earnestness and zeal and determination and sincerity.

A Double Standard

Do you blame me that I loved him?
   If when standing all alone
I cried for bread, a careless world
   Pressed to my lips a stone?

Do you blame me that I loved him,
   That my heart beat glad and free,
When he told me in the sweetest tones
   He loved but only me?

Can you blame me that I did not see,
   Beneath his burning kiss,
The serpent's wiles, nor even less hear
   The deadly adder hiss?

Can you blame me that my heart grew cold,
   That the tempted, tempter turned—
When he was feted and caressed
   And I was coldly spurned?

Would you blame him, when you drew from me
   Your dainty robes aside,
If he with gilded baits should claim
   Your fairest as his bride?

Would you blame the world if it should press
   On him a civic crown;
And see me struggling in the depth,
   Then harshly press me down?

Crime has no sex and yet today
   I wear the brand of shame;
Whilst he amid the gay and proud
   Still bears an honored name.

Can you blame me if I've learned to think
   Your hate of vice a sham,
When you so coldly crushed me down,
   And then excused the man?

Yes, blame me for my downward course,
   But oh! remember well,
Within your homes you press the hand
   That led me down to hell!

I'm glad God's ways are not your ways,
   He does not see as man;
Within his love I know there's room
   For those whom others ban.

I think before His great white throne,
   His theme of spotless light,
That whited sepulchres shall wear
   The hue of endless night.

That I who fell, and he who sinned,
   Shall reap as we have sown;
That each the burden of his loss
   Must bear and bear alone.

No golden weights can turn the scale
   Of justice in His sight;
And what is wrong in woman's life
   In man's cannot be right.

* * * * * * *

Death of the Old Sea King

'Twas a fearful night—the tempest raved
   With loud and wrathful pride,
The storm king harnessed his lightning steeds,
   And rode on the raging tide.

The sea-king lay on his bed of death,
   Pale mourners around him bent;
They knew the wild and fitful life
   Of their chief was almost spent.

His ear was growing dull in death,
   When the angry storm he heard;
The sluggish blood in the old man's veins
   With sudden vigor stirred.

"I hear them call," cried the dying man,
   His eyes grew full of light;
"Now bring me here my warrior's robes,
   My sword and armor bright.

"In the tempest's lull, I heard a voice;
   I know 'twas Odin's call.
The Valkyrs are gathering round my bed
   To lead me unto his hall.

"Bear me unto my noblest ship,
　　Light on the funeral pyre;
I'll walk to the palace of the braves
　　Through a path of flame and fire."

Oh, wild and bright was the stormy light
　　That flashed from the old man's eye,
As they bore him from the couch of death
　　To his battle-ship to die.

And lit with many a mournful torch
　　The sea-king's dying bed,
And like a banner fair and bright,
　　The flames around him spread.

* * * * * * *

Songs for the People

Let me make the songs for the people,
　　Songs for the old and young;
Songs to stir like a battle-cry,
　　Wherever they are sung.

Not for the clashing of sabres,
　　For carnage nor for strife,
But songs to thrill the hearts of men
　　With more abundant life.

Let me make songs for the weary,
　　Amid life's fever and fret,
Till hearts shall relax their tension
　　And care worn brows forget.

Let me sing for little children,
　　Before the footsteps stray,
Sweet anthems of love and duty,
　　To float o'er life's highway.

I would sing of the poor and aged,
　　When shadows dim their sights;
Of the bright and restful mansions,
　　Where there shall be no night.

Our world, so worn and weary,
  Needs music, pure and strong,
To hush the jangle and discords
  Of sorrow, pain and wrong.

Music to soothe all its sorrow,
  Till war and care shall cease;
And the hearts of men grown tender
  Girdle the world with peace.

* * * * * * *

The Slave Mother

Heard you that shriek? It rose
  So wildly in the air,
It seemed as if a burdened heart
  Was breaking in despair.

Saw you those hands so sadly clasped—
  The bowed and feeble head—
The shuddering of that fragile form—
  That look of grief and dread?

. . . . . .

She is a mother, pale with fear,
  Her boy clings to her side,
And in her kirtle vainly tries
  His trembling form to hide.

He is not hers, although she bore
  For him a mother's pains;
He is not hers, although her blood
  Is coursing through his veins!

He is not hers, for cruel hands
  May rudely tear apart
The only wreath of household love
  That binds her breaking heart.

* * * * * * *

The Slave Auction

The sale began—young girls were there,
  Defenceless in their wretchedness,
Whose stifled sobs of deep despair
  Revealed their anguish and distress.

And mothers stood with streaming eyes,
  And saw their dearest children sold;
Unheeded rose their bitter cries,
  While tyrants bartered them for gold.

And woman, with her love and truth—
  For these in sable forms may dwell—
Gazed on the husband of her youth,
  With anguish none may paint or tell.

And men, whose sole crime was their hue,
  The impress of their Maker's hand,
And frail and shrieking children, too,
  Were gathered in that mournful band.

Ye who have laid your love to rest,
  And wept above their lifeless clay,
Know not the anguish of that heart,
  Whose loved are rudely torn away.

Ye may not know how desolate
  Are husbands rudely forced to part,
And how a dull and heavy weight
  Will press the life-drops from the heart.

* * * * * * *

Nothing and Something

It is nothing to me, the beauty said,
With a careless toss of her pretty head;
The man is weak if he can't refrain
From the cup you say is fraught with pain.
It was something to her in after years,
When her eyes were drenched with burning tears
And she watched in lonely grief and dread,
And startled to hear a staggering tread.

It is nothing to me, the mother said;
I have no fear that my boy will tread
In the downward path of sin and shame,
And crush my heart and darken his name.
It was something to her when that only son
From the path of right was early won,
And madly cast in the flowing bowl
A ruined body and sin-wrecked soul.

It is nothing to me, the young man cried:
In his eyes was a flash of scorn and pride;
I heed not the dreadful things ye tell:
I can rule myself I know full well.
It was something to him when in prison he lay,
The victim of drink, life ebbing away;
The thought of his wretched child and wife
And the mournful wreck of his wasted life.

It is nothing to me, the merchant said,
As over his ledger he bent his head;
"I'm busy to-day with tare and tret,[1]
And I have no time to fume and fret."
It was something to him when over the wire
A message came from a funeral pyre—
A drunken conductor had wrecked a train,
And his wife and child were among the slain.

. . . . . .

Is it nothing for us to idly sleep
While the cohorts of death their vigils keep?
To gather the young and thoughtless in
And grind in our midst a grist of sin?
It is something, yes, all, for us to stand
Clasping by faith our Savior's hand:
To learn to labor, live and fight
On the side of God and changeless light.

* * * * * * * *

---

[1] "tare and tret." Outdated mercantile terms.

Vashti[2]

She leaned her head upon her hand
   And heard the King's decree—
"My lords are feasting in my halls;
   Bid Vashti come to me.

"I've shown the treasures of my house,
   My costly jewels rare,
But with the glory of her eyes
   No rubies can compare.

"Adorned and crowned, I'd have her come,
   With all her queenly grace,
And mid my lords and mighty men
   Unveil her lovely face.

"Each gem that sparkles in my crown,
   Or glitters on my throne,
Grows poor and pale when she appears,
   My beautiful, my own!"

All waiting stood the chamberlains
   To hear the Queen's reply.
They saw her cheek grow deathly pale,
   But light flashed to her eye:

"Go, tell the King," she proudly said,
   "That I am Persia's Queen,
And by his crowd of merry men
   I never will be seen.

"I'll take the crown from off my head,
   And tread it 'neath my feet,
Before their rude and careless gaze
   My shrinking eyes shall meet.

"A Queen unveiled before the crowd!
   Upon each lip my name!—
Why, Persia's women all would blush
   And weep for Vashti's shame.

---

[2] Vashti. See the Bible, Esther I.

"Go back!" she cried, and waved her hand,
 And grief was in her eye:
"Go tell the King," she sadly said,
 "That I would rather die."

They brought her message to the King;
 Dark flashed his angry eye;
'Twas as the lightning ere the storm
 Hath swept in fury by.

Then bitterly outspoke the King,
 Through purple lips of wrath—
"What shall be done to her who dares
 To cross your monarch's path?"

Then spake his wily counsellors—
 "O, King of this fair land,
From distant Ind to Ethiop,
 All bow to thy command.

But if, before they servants' eyes,
 This thing they plainly see,
That Vashti doth not heed thy will
 Nor yield herself to thee,

The women, restive 'neath our rule,
 Would learn to scorn our name,
And from her deed to us would come
 Reproach and burning shame.

Then, gracious King, sign with thy hand
 This stern but just decree,
That Vashti lay aside her crown,
 Thy Queen no more to be."

She heard again the King's command,
 And left her high estate;
Strong in her earnest womanhood,
 She calmly met her fate,

And left the palace of the King,
　　Proud of her spotless name—
A woman who could bend to grief
　　But would not bend to shame.

* * * * * * *

Bury Me in a Free Land

Make me a grave where'er you will,
In a lowly plain, or a lofty hill;
Make it among earth's humblest graves,
But not in a land where men are slaves.

I could not rest if around my grave
I heard the steps of a trembling slave;
His shadow above my silent tomb
Would make it a place of fearful gloom.

I could not rest if I heard the tread
Of a coffle gang to the shambles led,
And the mother's shriek of wild despair
Rise like a curse on the trembling air.

I could not sleep if I saw the lash
Drinking her blood at each fearful gash,
And I saw her babes torn from her breast,
Like trembling doves torn from their parent nest.

I'd shudder and start if I heard the bay
Of bloodhounds seizing their human prey,
And I heard the captive plead in vain
As they bound afresh his galling chain.

If I saw young girls from their mothers' arms
Bartered and sold for their youthful charms,
My eye would flash with a mournful flame,
My death-paled cheek grow red with shame.

I would sleep, dear friends, where bloated might
Can rob no man of his dearest right;
My rest shall be calm in any grave
Where none can call his brother a slave.

I ask no monument, proud and high,
To arrest the gaze of the passers-by;
All that my yearning spirit craves,
Is bury me not in a land of slaves.

* * * * * * *

Learning to Read
(Sketches of Southern Life, 1872)

Very soon the Yankee teachers
   Came down and set up school;
But, oh! how the Rebs did hate it, —
   It was agin' their rule.

Our masters always tried to hide
   Book learning from our eyes;
Knowledge didn't agree with slavery —
   'Twould make us all too wise.

But some of us would try to steal
   A little from the book,
And put the words together,
   And learn by hook or crook.

I remember Uncle Caldwell,
   Who took pot liquor fat
And greased the pages of his book,
   And hid it in his hat.

And had his master ever seen
   The leaves upon his head,
He'd have thought them greasy papers,
   But nothing to be read.

And there was Mrs. Turner's Ben,
   Who heard the children spell,
And picked the words right up by heart,
   And learned to read 'em well.

Well, the Northern folks kept sending
   The Yankee teachers down;
And they stood right up and helped us,
   Though the Rebs did sneer and frown.

And I longed to ready my Bible,
  For precious words it said;
But when I begun to learn it,
  Folks just shook their heads.

And said there is no use trying,
  Oh! Chloe, you're too late;
But I was rising sixty,
  I had no time to wait.

So I got a pair of glasses,
  And straight to work I went,
And never stopped till I could read
  The hymns and Testament.

Then I got a little cabin,
  A place to call my own—
And I felt as independent
  As the queen upon her throne.

* * * * * * * *

James M. Whitfield
(1823-1878)

Born in Exeter, New Hampshire, Whitfield moved, as a young man, to Buffalo, New York, where he probably spent much of his life as a barber and did what he could to promote current plans to colonize American Negroes in Central America. Toward this end he attended the National Emigration Convention of Colored Men that was called in 1854 by Martin Delany, who would later change his mind about such ambitions. Although otherwise friendly, Frederick Douglass, who admired Whitfield, attacked colonization urgings and when Whitfield replied vigorously in newspaper columns, there was a lively debate. Whitfield persisted, editing the pro-colonization *African-American Repository* in Buffalo, 1858, and is said to have died in California enroute to preliminary expeditions of Central America. His writings include *Poems* (1846), "How Long?" in Julia Griffith's *Autographs for Freedom* (Rochester, 1853); "Self-Reliance, Delusive Hope, and Ode for the Fourth of July," *The Liberator* of November 18, 1853; "Lines—Addressed to Mr. and Mrs. J.T. Holly, on the Death of Their Two Infant Daughters," *Frederick Douglass' Paper,* February 29, 1856; *Emancipation Oration* (San Francisco, 1867). He is best known for his volume, *America and Other Poems* (Buffalo, 1853), from which selections are taken. The melancholy, glowering and misanthropy and anger in Whitfield's verse is not to be mistaken for conventional romantic apparatus; he is genuinely angry, and the force of his verse indicates that, in more favorable circumstances, he might have become a more powerful poet. When he read his poems at Negro churches and public gatherings, it was mostly to propagandize his advocacy of emigration, and as such his poems sometimes suffer the usual lot of special urgings or "message" verse."

from America

America, it is to thee,
Thou boasted land of liberty,—
It is to thee I raise my song,
Thou land of blood, and crime, and wrong.
It is to thee, my native land,
From which has issued many a band
To tear the black man from his soil,
And force him here to delve and toil;
Chained on your blood-bemoistened sod,
Cringing beneath a tyrant's rod,
Stripped of those rights which Nature's God
Bequeathed to all the human race,
Bound to a petty tyrant's nod,
Because he wears a paler face.
Was it for this that freedom's fires
Were kindled by your patriot sires?
Was it for this they shed their blood,
On hill and plain, on field and flood?
Was it for this that wealth and life
Were staked upon that desperate strife,
Which drenched this land for seven long years
With blood of men, and women's tears?
When black and white fought side by side,
    Upon the well-contested field,—
Turned back the fierce opposing tide,
    And made the proud invader yield—
When, wounded, side by side they lay,
    And heard with joy the proud hurrah
From their victorious comrades say
    That they had waged successful war,
The thought ne'er entered in their brains
That they endured those toils and pains,
To forge fresh fetters, heavier chains
For their own children, in whose veins
Should flow that patriotic blood,
So freely shed on field and flood.
Oh, no; they fought, as they believed,
    For the inherent rights of man;

But mark, how they have been deceived
   By slavery's accursed plan.
They never thought, when thus they shed
   Their heart's best blood, in freedom's cause,
That their own sons would live in dread,
   Under unjust, oppressive laws:
That those who quietly enjoyed
   The rights for which they fought and fell,
Could be the framers of a code,
   That would disgrace the fiends of hell!

Could they have looked, with prophet's ken,
   Down to the present evil time,
Seen free-born men, uncharged with crime,
   Consigned unto a slaver's pen—
Or thrust into a prison cell,
With thieves and murderers to dwell—
While that same flag whose stripes and stars
Had been their guide through freedom's wars
As proudly waved above the pen
   Of dealers in the souls of men!
Or could the shades of all the dead,
   Who fell beneath that starry flag,
Visit the scenes where they once bled,
   On hill and plain, on vale and crag,
By peaceful brook, or ocean's strand,
   By inland lake, or dark green wood,
Where'er the soil of this wide land
   Was moistened by their patriot blood,—
And then survey the country o'er,
   From north to south, from east to west,
And hear the agonizing cry
Ascending up to God on high,
From western wilds to ocean's shore,
   The fervent prayer of the oppressed;

     . . . . . .

The shriek of virgin purity,
Doomed to some libertine's embrace,

Should rouse the strongest sympathy
    Of each one of the human race;
And weak old age, oppressed with care,
    As he reviews the scene of strife,
Puts up to God a fervent prayer,
    To close his dark and troubled life:
The cry of fathers, mothers, wives,
    Severed from all their hearts hold dear,
And doomed to spend their wretched lives
    In gloom, and doubt, and hate, and fear;
And manhood, too, with soul of fire,
And arm of strength, and smothered ire,
Stands pondering with brow of gloom,
Upon his dark unhappy doom,
Whether to plunge in battle's strife,
And buy his freedom with his life,
And with stout heart and weapon strong,
Pay back the tyrant wrong for wrong;

. . . . . .

Here Christian writhes in bondage still,
    Beneath his brother Christian's rod,
And pastors trample down at will,
    The image of the living God.

. . . . . .

Almighty God! 'tis this they call
    The land of liberty and law;
Part of its sons in baser thrall
    Than Babylon and Egypt saw—
Worse scenes of rapine, lust and shame,
    Than Babylonian ever knew,
Are perpetrated in the name
    Of God, the holy, just, and true;
And darker doom than Egypt felt,
    May yet repay this nation's guilt.
Almighty God! thy aid impart,
And fire anew each faltering heart,
And strengthen every patriot's hand,
Who aims to save our native land.

. . . . . .

Father! before thy throne we come,
  Not in the panoply of war,
With pealing trump, and rolling drum,
  And cannon booming loud and far;
Striving in blood to wash out blood,
  Through wrong to seek redress for wrong;
For while thou'rt holy, just and good,
  The battle is not to the strong;
But in the sacred name of peace,
  Of justice, virtue, love and truth,
We pray, and never mean to cease,
  Till weak old age and fiery youth
In freedom's cause their voices raise,
And burst the bonds of every slave;
Till, north and south, and east and west,
The wrongs we bear shall be redressed.

* * * * * * * *

The Misanthropist

In vain thou bid'st me strike the lyre,
  And sing a song of mirth and glee,
Or kindling with poetic fire,
  Attempt some higher minstrelsy;
In vain, in vain! for every thought
  That issues from this throbbing brain,
Is from its first conception fraught
  With gloom and darkness, woe and pain.
From earliest youth my path has been
  Cast in life's darkest, deepest shade,
Where no bright light did intervene,
  Nor e'er a passing sunbeam strayed;
But all was dark and cheerless night,
  Without one ray of hopeful light.
From childhood, then, through many a shock,
  I've battled with the ills of life,
Till, like a rude and rugged rock,
  My heart grew callous in the strife.

When other children passed the hours
   In mirth, and play, and childish glee,
Or gathering the summer flowers
   By gentle brook, or flowery lea,
I sought the wild and rugged glen
Where Nature, in her sternest mood,
Far from the busy haunts of men,
Frowned in the darksome solitude.
There have I mused till gloomy night,
Like the death-angel's brooding wing,
Would shut out everything from sight,
And o'er the scene her mantle fling;
And seeking then my lonely bed
To pass the night in sweet repose,
Around my fevered, burning head,
Dark visions of the night arose;
And the stern scenes which day had viewed
In sterner aspects rose before me,
And specters of still sterner mood
Waved their menacing fingers o'er me.
When the dark storm-fiend soared abroad,
And swept to earth the waving grain,
On whirlwind through the forest rode,
And stirred to foam the heaving main,
I loved to mark the lightning's flash,
And listen to the ocean's roar,
Or heal the pealing thunder crash,
And see the mountain torrents pour
Down precipices dark and steep,
Still bearing, in their headlong course
To meet th' embrace of ocean deep,
Mementoes of the tempest's force;
For fire and tempest, flood and storm,
Wakened deep echoes in my soul,
And made the quickening life-blood warm
With impulse that knew no control;
And the fierce lightning's lurid flash
   Rending the somber clouds asunder,

Followed by the terrific crash
  Which marks the hoarsely rattling thunder,
Seemed like the gleams of lurid light
  Which flashed across my seething brain,
Succeeded by a darker night,
  With wilder horrors in its train.

And I have stood on ocean's shore
  And viewed its dreary waters roll,
Till the dull music of its roar
  Called forth responses in my soul;
And I have felt that there was traced
  An image of my inmost soul,
In that dark, dreary, boundless waste,
  Whose sluggish waters aimless roll—
Save when aroused by storms' wild force
  It lifts on high its angry wave,
And thousands driven from their course
  Find in its depths a nameless grave.
Whene'er I turned in gentler mood
  To scan the old historic page,
It was not where the wise and good,
  The Bard, the Statesman, or the Sage,
Had drawn in lines of living light,
Lessons of virtue, truth and right;
But that which told of secret league,
  Where deep conspiracies were rife,
And where, through foul and dark intrigue,
  Were sowed the seeds of deadly strife;
Where hostile armies met to seal
  Their country's doom, for woe or weal;
Where the grim-visaged death-fiend drank
  His full supply of human gore,
And poured through every hostile rank
  The tide of battle's awful roar;
For then my spirits seemed to soar
  Away to where such scenes were rife,

And high above the battle's roar
    Sit as spectators of the strife—
And in those scenes of war and woe,
    A fierce and fitful pleasure know.

There was a time when I possessed
    High notions of Religion's claim,
Nor deemed its practice, at the best,
    Was but a false and empty name;
But when I saw the graceless deeds
    Which marked its strongest votaries' path,
How senseless bigots, o'er their creeds,
    Blazing with wild fanatic wrath,
Let loose the deadly tide of war,
    Spread devastation near and far,
Through scenes of rapine, blood and shame,
    Of cities sacked, and towns on flame,
Caused unbelievers' hearts to feel
    The arguments of fire and steel
By which they sought t' enforce the word,
    And make rebellious hearts approve
Those arguments of fire and sword
    As mandates of the God of love—
How could I think that such a faith,
    Whose path was marked by fire and blood,
That sowed the seeds of war and death,
    Had issued from a holy God?

There was a time that I did love,
    Such love as those alone can know,
Whose blood like burning lava moves,
    Whose passions like the lightning glow;
And when that ardent, truthful love
Was blighted in its opening bloom,
    And all around, below, above,
Seemed like the darkness of the tomb,
'Twas then my stern and callous heart,
Riven in its most vital part,
Seemed like some gnarled and knotted oak,
That, shivered by the lightning's stroke,

Stands in the lonely wanderer's path,
A ghastly monument of wrath.
Then how can I attune the lyre
    To strains of love or joyous glee?
Break forth in patriotic fire,
    Or soar on higher minstrelsy,
To sing the praise of virtue bright,
Condemn the wrong, and laud the right;
When neither vice nor guilt can fling
    A darker shadow o'er my breast,
Nor even Virtue's self can bring
    Unto my moody spirit, rest.
It may not be, it cannot be!
    Let others strike the sounding string,
And in rich strains of harmony,
    Songs of poetic beauty sing;
But mine must still the portion be,
    However dark and drear the doom,
To live estranged from sympathy,
    Buried in doubt, despair and gloom;
To bear my breast to every blow,
To know no friend, and fear no foe,
Each generous impulse trod to dust,
Each noble aspiration crushed,
Each feeling struck with withering blight,
With no regard for wrong or right,
No fear of hell, no hope of heaven,
Die all unwept and unforgiven,
Content to know and dare the worst,
Which mankind's hate, and heaven's curse,
Can heap upon my living head,
Or cast around my memory dead;
And let them on my tombstone trace,
"Here lies the Pariah of his race."

* * * * * * *

Stanzas for the First of August[1]

From bright West Indies' sunny seas
   Comes, borne upon the balmy breeze,
The joyous shout, the gladsome tone,
   Long in those bloody isles unknown;
Bearing across the heaving wave
The song of the unfettered slave.

No charging squadrons shook the ground,
   When freedom have her claims obtained;
No cannon, with tremendous sound
   The noble patriot's cause maintained;
No famous battle-charger neighed,
No brother fell by brother's blade.

None of these desperate scenes of strife,
   Which mark the woman's proud career,
The awful waste of human life
   Have ever been enacted here;
But truth and justice spoke from heaven,
And slavery's galling chain was riven.

'Twas moral force which broke the chain,
   That bound eight hundred thousand men;
And when we see it snapped in twain,
   Shall we not join in praise then? —
And prayers unto Almighty God,
Who smote to earth the tyrant's rod?

And from those islands of the sea,
   The scenes of blood and crime and wrong,
The glorious anthem of the free
   Now swells in mighty chorus strong;
Telling th' oppressed, where'er they roam,
Those islands now are freedom's home.

* * * * * * * *

---

[1] August 1, 1838. Slavery was abolished in the British West Indies.

To Cinque[2]

All hail! thou truly noble chief,
   Who scorned to live a cowering slave;
Thy name shall stand on history's leaf,
   Amid the mighty and the brave:
They name shall shine, a glorious light
   To other brave and fearless men,
Who, like thyself, in freedom's might,
   Shall beard the robber in his den;
Thy name shall stand on history's page,
   And brighter, brighter, brighter glow,
Throughout all time, through every age,
   Till bosoms cease to feel or know
"Created worthy, or human woe."
   They name shall nerve the patriot's hand
When, 'mid the battle's deadly strife,
   The glittering bayonet and brand
Are crimsoned with the stream of life:
When the dark clouds of battle roll,
And slaughter reigns without control,
Thy name shall then fresh life impart,
Are fire anew each freeman's heart.
Though wealth and power their force combine
   To crush thy noble spirit down,
There is above a power divine
   Shall bear thee up against their frown.

* * * * * * * *

---

[2]Joseph Cinque was one of fifty odd newly enslaved Negroes aboard the Spanish schooner *L'Amistad,* which sailed in June, 1839 from Havanna for Puerto Principe, Cuba; but, at sea, Cinque, a Mendi-speaking prince, led a revolt, killed the captain, set the white crew adrift, and commanded the Spanish owners to steer the ship to Africa. Instead of so doing, the two wily owners had the ship to sail North until, some sixty-three days later, it drifted to the shore off Long Island, where it was spotted and convoyed by the United States brig, *Washington,* to New London, Connecticut, the Africans being charged by the circuit court at New Haven for the murder of Captain Ferrer, and being claimed by the Spanish minister as reclaimable as property rescued from pirates. Gaining increasing admiration from ever mounting demonstrations by zealous abolitionists, the Africans eventually secured the services of seventy-three year old, ex-president John Quincy Adams, who argued for eight-and-a half hours for their freedom, in 1841, to return to Africa. The surviving Africans sailed for Sierra Leone in 1842.

Daniel A. Payne
(1811-1893)

His years spanning most of the nineteenth century, Daniel Payne is especially valuable to know for those interested in tracing the development of American Negro religious, educational and literary thought, for he had something to do with all such areas. He was remarkable in the amount of energy he expended on his endless travels throughout this country, from New Orleans to Canada, from Baltimore to the Midwest, and abroad, twice to England, expanding the bases of the African Methodist church, and encouraging Negro literary expression, such as that of A.A. Whitman and others, wherever he went. He was born in Charleston, South Carolina, of free parents, whom he lost before he was ten years old. He was apprenticed to a carpenter, then a tailor, but received some formal classical education at the local Minor's Moralist Society group's school. He began teaching free black students for $1.50 apiece, and slaves at night, and continued until 1834 when South Carolina passed a law, to be effective in 1835, forbidding blacks, slaves or freemen, to learn to read or write. Deeply hurt, he sat down and composed "The Mournful Lute, or The Preceptor's Farewell," (q.v.) and moved North to do what he could. With help he entered the Lutheran Seminary in Gettysburg, Pennsylvania, 1837, was ordained in 1839, but spent most of his preaching life as first a minister and then a Bishop in 1852 of the A.M.E. denomination. With Carl Schurz, he urged Lincoln on April 14, 1862, to sign the bill that would emancipate the slaves in the District of Columbia. In 1863 he led in the purchase of Wilberforce University in Ohio and was its president for sixteen years.

His writings are considerable in number, but the most important ones would include *The Semi-Centenary and the Retrospection of the African Methodist Episcopal Church* (Baltimore, 1866); and *The History of the A.M.E. Church* (Nashville, 1866). Also helpful is a biography, *Daniel Alexander Payne, Christian Educator* by Josephus R. Coam (Philadelphia, 1935). His *Recollections of Seventy Years* (Nashville, 1888) throws much light on the activities of many nineteenth century Negroes. There was a *Diary*, but his volume of verse, *Pleasures and Other Miscellaneous Poems* (Baltimore, 1850) reveals his own innermost sensibilities in a variety of quite ordinary poems. His poetry has the stridency of the fervent preacher and not enough attention is given to rhetorical or imagistic possibilities or other poetic considerations. Perhaps his worst fault is the repetition of end stopped lines, and his diction, a hybrid of classical and Biblical vocabularies, can prove distracting to many readers.

The Mournful Lute or the Preceptor's Farewell

Father and mother, authors of my birth,
Ye dwell in bliss; your son on sinful earth. . .

O, sainted parents, who my life have kept,
Preserved my sinful soul each night I slept;
Since God transported ye to realms of light,
And bade my youth in virtue take delight!
'Twas God. 'Tis he who still preserves my soul,
When foes unite, or waves of trouble roll,
Cared for my childhood, blessed my striving youth;
Me snatched from vice and led in paths of truth.

O, sainted mother, high in glory thou,
If God permits, behold thy Daniel now!
Good Lord, give strength; my feeble mind sustain,
Nor let my sighs ascend to thee in vain. . .

When Ignorance my mind in fetters bound,
He smote the fiend; then beams of light surround;
Broad beams of light described the way of truth,
And bade me lead therein benighted youth.

Oh, here's my bliss, that I the way have shown
To lovely youths which was before unknown;
From scientific shrines plucked golden fire,
And thrilled with notes divine the sacred lyre.

Did I conceive, five rolling years ago,
The luscious fruits which Science can bestow?
Oh, bend in praise devout before his throne!
'Twas God that gave the boon, and God alone.
My sire, when on the bed of death you lay,
Did thy blest soul in fervent accents pray
That I should be what now I feel I am—
Favored of God, preserved from every harm?

Thou didst, my sire; thrice blessed be thy name;
Come, Wisdom, clothe me in thy sacred flame;
Ye scientific truths, my mind control;
And thou, fair Virtue, guide my erring soul.
What's my ambition? What my great desire?
The youthful mind with knowledge to inspire.
Not worlds on worlds for this would I exchange,
Though cruel laws my noble scheme derange.

Soon from the land where first I drew my breath
I go a wanderer on the flying earth!
Where shall I go? O, Thou, my fortune guide,
Who led good Abram with his modest bride.
Him didst thou lead across the eastern wild,
Direct his steps and on his fortune smiled;
In foreign climes spread wide his fruitful boughs,
Made strong his bands and scattered all his foes.

Oh, I had thought the moral plants would grow,
From all the care my talents can bestow,
Like trees of virtue lift their blooming heads,
Where snowy clouds suspend their liquid beds!
Ye lads, whom I have taught with sacred zeal,
For your hard fate I pangs of sorrow feel;
Oh, who shall now your rising talents guide,
Where virtues reign and sacred truths preside?

Ye modest virgins, I have taught your minds
To fly from earth where sinful pleasure binds,
The rugged hill of science to ascend,
Where sacred flames with human fires blend.
Who now shall call your willing, joyful feet
In "wisdom's institute" to learn and meet
Sweet piety and science, gods of light,
Whose precepts lead your erring minds aright?

Who shall for you Minerva's field explore,
Spread open wide fair Nature's roseate door?
Oh, who shall help your op'ning wings to fly
Where virtue sits resplendent in the sky?
O, God of mercy! whither shall I go?
Where turn my steps—to weal, or else to woe?
Speak. I the sacred mandate wait to hear,
Nor shall I ocean dread nor tempest fear.

Eternal Goodness, from thy shining seat
Let Mercy fly to guide my wandering feet.
On distant lands I will thy servant be,
To turn from vice the youthful mind to thee.
Just two revolving moons shall light the shores
When Carolina's laws shall shut the doors
On this fine room, where Science holds his reign,
The humble tutor, hated Daniel Payne.

Oh, that my arms could reach yon burning sun,
And stop his motion till my work be done!
With these small fingers catch the flying moon—
Night should not triumph o'er the dazzling noon.
April should ne'er appear; but I would teach
Each yielding pupil till their minds could reach
The climax of proud science, and their plumes
Could soar where good John Locke or Newton blooms.

Each minute insect and each flying bird,
Each walking beast, whose tuneless notes are heard,
The scaly fish that lives not on the shore,
And man himself, the mighty being explore;

Aspiring mounts and hills, descending dales,
The floating air, when peace or storm prevails;
Oceans and seas, streams and expanding lakes,
When night leaps in, or sweet Aurora wakes.

    The flying rays of light, the spangled sky,
    On contemplation's wing mount ye on high.
    Bright cherubim and flaming seraphim,
    All things upon wide earth, th' eternal Him,
    Children, all, all are yours! Search, find them out.
    Knowledge, where are thy bounds? In depths without.
    The heavens, within the heavens, nor time,
    Nor vast eternity, the gods sublime,

Can in their sweeping compass e'er embrace!
He reigns o'er angels, guides the human race.
Seek not the joys which sinful earth can give;
They sparkle, perish, for a moment live.
Sweet innocents, behold each moving lip!
From cups of wisdom sacred sweet they sip.
What demon snatches from your hands those books,
And blasts your talents with his withering looks?

I weep. Flow, then, ye sympathetic tears!
Each bitter stream the stamp of sorrow bears.
Oh, who those smiling infants can see
Destined to night, and not lament with me?
Could tears of blood revoke the fierce decree,
The statesman touch and make my pupils free,
I at their feet the crimson tide would pour
Till potent justice swayed the senate floor.

As when a deer does in the pasture graze,
The lion roars—she's filled with wild amaze,
Knows strength unequal for the dreadful fight,
And seeks sweet safety in her rapid flight—
So Payne prepares to leave his native home,
With pigmy purse on distant shores to roam.
Lo! in the skies my boundless storehouse is!
I go reclining on God's promises.

Pupils, attend my last departing wounds;
Ye are my hopes, and ye my mental crowns,
My monuments of intellectual might,
My robes of honor and my armor bright.
Like Solomon, entreat the throne of God;
Light shall descend in lucid columns broad,
And all that man has learned for man can know
In streams prolific shall your minds o'erflow.

Hate sin; love God; religion be your prize;
Her laws obeyed will surely make you wise,
Secure you from the ruin of the vain,
And save your soul from everlasting pain.
Oh, fare you well, for whom my bosom glows
With ardent love, which Christ my savior knows!
'Twas for your good I labored night and day;
For you I wept, and now for you I pray. . .

Charleston, S.C., February 2, 1835.

from The Pleasures

Long hast thou slumber'd, O, my sounding lyre!
Now Muses wake thee, now thy song inspire;
Now will they tune each soft melodious string,
And in thy lay their sweetest numbers fling.
O lift thy voice on high and start the soul!
From sinful *Pleasure's* dark and foul control,
Point her to *those* whose holy breath imparts
The life of joy to men of virtuous hearts.
Paint thou the *One* in colors dark and dire,
Against her charms, the youthful mind inspire;
With holy hate, the *Other* then portray
In robes celestial, such as prophets say
The angels wore when from the courts above,
They came to men with messages of love.

. . . . . .

Pleasures of Vice are those which most pursue,
Regarding all their promis'd joys as true;

Nor will they heed the warning voice that cries,
The soul which sins, that soul in mis'ry lies.
But like the headlong horse or stubborn mule,
Despise all truth, condemn all righteous rule,
Delight in sin as swine delight in mire,
Till hell itself entomb their souls in fire!
Thus does the Drunkard, in the sparkling bowl,
Pursue the joys which charm his brutish soul;
But soon he feels the serpent's fang is there,
The gall of woe, the demon's awful star;
For in the visions of his crazied soul,
The Furies dance and horrid monsters roll.

Some find their pleasure in tobacco wads,
Delight in them as goats in chewing cuds;
Others believe they find it quite enough
In smoking cigars, or in taking snuff.
The glutton and the greasy epicure
Believe they have it—for they tell us sure—[1]
In eating venison, turtle-soup and clams,
Beef a la mode and lobsters, ducks and hams. . . .

But dandies find it in their curled hair,
Greas'd with pomatum or the oil of bear;
In fine mustaches, breast pins, golden chains;
In brass-capped boot-heels or in walking canes.
Some ladies find it on their boas and muffs,
In silks and satins, laces, muslin-stuffs
Made into dresses, pointed long and wide
With flounces deep, and bran-bustles beside;
All neat and flowing in Parisian grace;
With small sunshades to screen their smiling face;
Then up the streets, like pea-fowls bright and gay
They promenade on every sunny day.

Some seek for pleasure in the giddy dance,
Where Fashion smiles and Beauty's siren glance
The soul delights, and fills light bounding hearts
With dreams of love—such dreams as sin imparts;

---

[1] "sure" = "so" in original text.

Not the pure streams that flow, my God, from thee;
The streams of bliss—the love of purity.
In cock-fights others find it; some in dice;
Some in the chambers of lascivious vice.
The vile blasphemer seeks it in his shame,
Who sport like devils with the Holy Name.
O hapless wretches! fool'd and self-deceiv'd!
Angels weep o'er you! God himself is griev'd!

. . . . . .

I sing of Pleasure flowing from God,
Pleasure derived from all his works abroad;
'Tis felt whene'er the eyes survey the fields,
In verdant Spring, or when bright summer yields
Her fragrant flowers and her shady groves
Are vocal with the moans of turtle-doves. . . . . .

'Tis felt in scene where hills and mountains rise,
Like rugged columns to the bending skies,
While Murm'ring fountains gushing from their sides,
Roll toward the seas, in deep'ning, wid'ning tides,
Or rushing on o'er beds of jutting rocks,
Dash down the abyss in thund'ring cataracts—
With glitt'ring sprays impregn the humid air,
And paint the bow of smiling heaven there. . . . .

Go in the garden, where the roses bloom,
And fill the dancing breezes with perfume;. . . .

There, buzzing insects drink the sunny rays—
There, feeding, bask and terminate their days. . . . .

Men talk of Love! But few do ever feel
The speechless raptures which its joys reveal.
They mistake Love, that pure celestial thing,
Whose end is God, and in him has its spring,
For grovelling lust, that vile, that filthy dame,
Whose bosom ne'er ever felt the sacred flame,. . . . . .

But one I had, O rapturous thought![2]
The sweetest, dearest that was ever bought

[2]Mrs. Julia A. Farris Payne, his first wife, whom he married in 1847 and who died within
the year.

By Love's own treasure—brightest, best of all
The gems and diamonds of this jewel'd ball. . . .
Her form was graceful, and her eyes were bright,
Like morning stars, when rob'd in cloudless light!

May I Not Love?

May I not love the beauteous flow'rs
    That in the gardens grow?
Or those which deck wild Nature's bow'rs
    Upon the mountain's brow?

May I not love the brightest gem
    Upon a monarch's crown?
Or that still brighter diadem,
    Which Gabriel's head adorn? . . .

O, Science, may I not love thee,
    Thou giant son of heav'n;
In thee, what wond'rous charms I see!
    God's pow'r to mortals giv'n. . . . .

May I not love thee, art divine,
    Which makes the canvas breathe,
Whose mimic landscapes glow and shine
    With steams and flow'ry heath?

Sweet music! may I not love thee,
    Thou charmer of the soul,
Thy strains like drops of honey be,
    Thy notes like morning dews.

The charming Maid, may I not love—
    Whose pleasure is in books,
Whose heart is like the peaceful dove,
    With virtue's modest looks?. . . .

O, Poetry, thou child of love!
    Whose harp by God was giv'n;
Thy songs are echoes from above—
    Thy voice the breath of heav'n.

May not I love thee, thing of light
   For love is in thine eyes;
Thine is the eagle's sunny flight!
   Thy home is in the skies!

Lord, I *may* love them all for thee—
   Will love them for thy sake;
Will love, till in eternity,
   My loving soul shall wake!

       * * * * * * *

Elymas Payson Rogers
(1814?-1861)

Rogers was an abolitionist Presbyterian minister who used his verse-making abilities to score American political abuses of the antebellum Negro. He pastored in Newark, New Jersey, after teaching in the public schools in Rochester, New York, where he taught the gifted Jeremiah W. Loguen, whom he encouraged along his way toward becoming a Bishop of the A.M.E. Church. A fugitive slave, Loguen wrote his autobiography, *The Reverend J.W. Loguen, As a Slave and as a Freeman* (Syracuse, 1859), in which he included a poem, "Loguen's Position," by his mentor who helped him enroll at Oneida Institute, where Rogers later taught. Although he spoke too fast, Loguen did deliver his poems orally at various New England cities and towns, and seems to have designed both *The Fugitive Slave Law* (Newark, 1855) and *Repeal of Missouri Compromise Considered* (Newark, 1856) for platform rendition. Despairing of fair play for American Negroes, he went to Africa where, catching a fever a few days after landing, he died in 1861. Rogers has a wry, sardonic humor and he seems comfortable in satirizing political hypocrisies, although at times he is almost harsh to the point of cynicism.

from On the Fugitive Slave Law[1]

Law! What is law? The wise and sage,
Of every clime and every age,
In this most cordially unite,
That 'tis a rule for doing right.

---

[1] The Fugitive Slave Law (there was another Fugitive Slave law in 1793), was signed into law on September 18, 1850, by President Millard Fillmore.

Great Blackstone, that illustrious sire,
Whose commentaries all admire,
And Witherspoon, and Cicero,
And all distinguished jurists show
That law is but the power supreme
To shield, to nurture, or redeem
Those rights so sacred, which belong
To man; and to prohibit wrong.
But definitions more concise,
Than any framed by man's device,
The conscientious patriot draws
From the Eternal code of laws;
From which he clearly understands
That God's immutable commands
Are law throughout the universe,
Which human edicts can't reverse.

. . . . . .

In fifty, Congress passed a Bill,
Which proved a crude and bitter pill
At least in many a northern mouth,
Though sweet as honey at the South.

It was the object of this Act
(By priests and politicians backed)
That masters might with ease retake
The wretched slaves who chanced to break
Away from servitude thenceforth,
And sought a refuge at the North.

It was the purpose of this Act
To make the Northern States, in fact,
The brutal master's hunting grounds,
To be explored by human hounds
Who would, for shining gold, again
Bind on the bleeding captive's chain.

. . . . . .

From officers of baser sort,
The Bill sought sanction and support:
And lawyers bought of no repute
And bribed the dough-faced judge to boot.
It gave encouragement to knaves,
It mocked the suff'rings of the slaves
By giving, if the slave went free,
The judge five dollars as his fee.
But if the judge bound on his chains,
He won ten dollars for his pains.

. . . . . .

That Bill a law? some call it so,
But One above us answers, "No:
It conflicts with my firm decree;
A law therefore it cannot be.
I tell this nation, as I told
My servants in the days of old,
That none the wand'ring shall perplex,
Or e'er the honest stranger vex:
Deliver not the refugee
Who from his master flees to thee;
He who escapes his master's hand
Shall dwell among you in the land,
And to him ye shall not refuse
The dwelling place which he shall choose."

. . . . . .

Is this Bill law? hark! from below,
The voice of Lucifer cries, "No!
That bill is a complete gewgaw,
Unworthy of the name of law,
And certainly I ought to know,
'Twas manufactured here below,
And then to leading statesmen sent
Who urged it 'to the full extent.' "

. . . . . .

That Bill a law? the South says so,
But Northern freemen answer, No!

. . . . . .

That bill is law, doughfaces say;
But black men everywhere cry "Nay:
We'll never yield to its control
While life shall animate one soul

. . . . . .

No! let the monster be accursed
Who does not then attempt to burst
Their chains, and set the bondsman free,
And make the heartless tyrant flee."

E'en now I hear each freeman cry
That "human bloodhounds all shall die,

Whene'er the fugitive shall come,
My house shall ever be his home;
And let the worthless wretch beware
Who comes to seize his victim there.
If in his arrogance and pride
My threshold he shall e'er bestride,
I near to freedom's altar stand,
And lay thereon my solemn hand,
And on that sacred altar swear
His bleeding form shall welter there."

But whence that voice, so soft, so clear,
So musical within my ear?
It says, "We'll ever power defy
Beneath which helpless women sigh,
And seek to mitigate their grief,
And toil and pray for their relief.
We will for fugitives provide,
We will the trembling outcast hide:
This will we do while we have breath,
Fearless of prisons, chains, or death."

. . . . . .

Will faithful woman then betray
The fugitive, or turn away
From him her true and willing feet,
And thus contemptibly retreat?

To act so base, man may consent;
But woman is no recreant.

Will any then the Act obey?
Both male and female answer, Nay;
For he who heeds it must withdraw
His reverence for the Higher Law.
Whatever human laws may say
God's law we dare not disobey.

* * * * * * *

The Repeal of the Missouri Compromise Considered

'Tis done! the treach'rous deed is done;
Eternal infamy is won
By Legislators, who've decreed
The direful and unrighteous deed.

'Tis done! the fearful die is cast,
The dreadful rubicon is past;
Nor will the strife be o'er
Till Freedom bleeds at every pore.
The grave Nebraska leaders feel
That by their treacherous repeal
Of the Missouri Compromise,
They've plucked away from Freedom's skies
The glorious sun revolving there,
And buried hope in deep despair.

. . . . . .

"I want the land," was Freedom's cry;
And Slavery answered, "So do I!
By all that's sacred, I declare
I'll have my just and lawful share.
The Northern cheek should glow with shame
To think to rob me of my claim."
In twenty[2] tyranny prevailed,
And Northern men before it quailed

---

[2]The Missouri Compromise of 1820 said slavery was to be prohibited "forever" in any new United States Territories north of Missouri, which was admitted to the Union as a slave state.

And bowed to Slavery—sad mistake—
But all was for the Union's sake.
The glorious Union, they declared,
Must never, never be impaired!

. . . . . .

A few, of never-dying fame,
Would never yield to Slavery's claim,

. . . . . .

But these were a minority,
The others a majority;
And hence the "Compromise" was made,
And Slavery's claim was duly paid.

And, after gaining his desire,
He scarce was willing to retire
And, as he turned to take his leave,
He laughed immoderate in his sleeve,
And said he'd surely call for more
In eighteen hundred fifty-four.
"The rest," quoth he, "I cannot get,
I am not strong enough as yet;
But when I am maturely strong,
I'll seize the balance, right or wrong."

But Freedom cried, "Woe worth the day
When such a treacherous game you play."

"But hold!" said Slavery; "you're too fast;
I judge the future by the past.
I always have high heaven defied,
And man's authority denied;

. . . . . .

And I control the legislation
Of this great democratic nation,
And to my tried and cordial friends
My lib'ral patronage extends;
I raise them up to seats of power,

Although unworthy, base, and poor.
O'er each department I preside,
And all official actions guide:

I send ambassadors afar,
And, when I please, provoke a war
Ostensibly for public weal,
But 'tis in fact my burning zeal
To multiply my territory,
Instead of for the nation's glory.
And presidents I nominate
For confirmation by each State,
And no Chief-Magistrate is made
Without my all-sufficient aid.

. . . . . .

I know that Northern freemen might
Upon one platform all unite,
And freedom's banner there unfurl,
And through the ballot-boxes hurl
Me from my lofty station,
And send throughout this mighty nation
A grand and glorious jubilee
Which would the wretched captive free:
They might construe the Constitution
So as to crush my institution;

. . . . . .

The power of Congress regulates
Commercial acts between the States,
And, hence, can with the utmost ease
Confine me whereso'er they please.
Were I forbidden to migrate
From place to place, from State to State,
I soon should lack sufficient room,
Which would accelerate my doom.

. . . . . .

"And now," said Slavery, "I must go;
I've business down in Mexico;
But purpose to return this way
Upon the first auspicious day,
And with no acts preparatory
Enlarge my spacious territory."

Then Freedom gave a mournful sigh,
But made no audible reply.

. . . . . .

For thirty years the Compromise
Has met with favor in the eyes
Of Unionists throughout the nation,
Of every party, creed and station.

. . . . . .

But now the precious Compromise
In wild and reckless ruin lies.

And why this wild and daring deed,
For which our land must surely bleed?
Why is the landmark now removed,
The landmark which the sires approved?
Why is their wisdom cast aside,
Which thirty years have sanctified?

It is, indeed, O, sad to tell!
For 'tis a measure fresh from hell,
It is that Slavery may expand
O'er all our new and fertile land;
That tyrants may the helpless spoil,
And thrive on unrequited toil;

That they may there exert their sway
And more securely hold their prey,
And pass this scheme of degradation
To the succeeding generation;
The argument which some advance
Is still that Freedom hath a chance,
In Kansas and Nebraska now,
Equal to what the laws allow
To Slavery and its advocates
Inhabiting the Southern States;

But several obstacles intrude,
Which are of no small magnitude,
And lie directly in the way
Of Freedom's unrestricted sway:

The planters who the West encumber
Draw lands according to the number
Of the forlorn and wretched slaves,
Who will enrich the lordly knaves.
Beside what Government allots,
The master may, whene'er he votes,
Take of his human chattels ten
And make six Anglo-Saxon men.

But why did Congress pass this Bill,
When thousands loathed the bitter pill?
How dared they bring the measure forth,
While knowing well that at the North
Strong opposition would arise
From lovers of the Compromise?
While in the Senate it remained
And was there ably sustained,
A loud and earnest cry went forth
From every section of the North.
Upon the Compromise they stood
For Justice, Liberty and God,
And in his name protested strong
Against this monstrous public wrong.

But their remonstrance was attacked
By Mister Douglass,[3] who in fact
As father of the measure stands,
And soiled by his polluted hands.

We surely have no room to doubt
What Mister Douglass was about
Throughout this hocus-pocus measure
Pressed sore on Congress without leisure,
The secret of the whole affair
Lies near the Presidential Chair.
Said he, "I'll win it, if I can;
I'll trample on the rights of man;
I'll stride o'er Freedom's recent grave;
Or leap upon the prostrate slave;

---

[3]Stephen A. Douglass introduced the Kansas-Nebraska Bill, which became law in May, 1854; in effect the law repealed the Missouri Compromise of 1820, by now allowing new territories into the Union with or without slavery, whichever way the citizens decided.

Or even turn a somerset,
The Presidential Chair to get.
I grant, 'tis possible I may,
As abolition zealots say,
Be doing wrong religiously,
But I am right politically."

And was our champion all alone
When liberty was cloven down?
Was he the only Congressman
Who countenanced the treacherous plan?

No! Douglass only took the stand
As captain of the reckless band;
He undertook the vile crusade,
And others rallied to his aid;
Not all the Southern Enterprise
Could have repealed the Compromise,
Or ever brought the measure forth,
Without assistance from the North.

Why should not Northern members think
That they might innocently wink
At Slavery and its demands,
When such a law securely stands
As that, which hurries day by day
The panting fugitive away
From any section of the land,
To toil beneath the tyrant's hand!
Our noble Doctor Pennington,[4]
Distinguished as a clergyman,
And one of Freedom's advocates
Throughout Great Britain and the States,
By this vile law would be in danger,
The same as any obscure stranger,

---

[4]J.W.C. Pennington. Born a slave in Maryland, he made his way North and became quite learned through his own efforts and from a segregated education at Yale. A gifted Presbyterian minister in Hartford, Connecticut (where he pastored Ann Plato, the second American Negro woman, after Phillis Wheatley, to publish a volume of poems—1841—in the United States), Pennington was also a popular anti-slavery lecturer, speaking, by invitation, to distinguished European audiences. During one of his foreign lecture tours, he was awarded the degree of Doctor of Divinity by the University of Heidelberg. In his last years he succumbed to despair and drink.

Could he not show within a trice
That he has paid the market price
In some remote vicinity
Of Doctor of Divinity.

And Frederick Douglass (mighty man
Whose powerful eloquence can fan
The human passions to a flame
Whene'er he speaks in Freedom's name,)
Could not on Southern despots rail,
But for that precious bill of sale,
Which, like a keepsake in a locket,
He has secreted in his pocket;

This law has sought and seized its prey
And quickly hurried scores away
To cruel Slavery again,
To feel the lash and wear the chain.

And now when these are stubborn facts,
Let us not be surprised at acts
Like that of the Nebraska Bill,
Nor need our blood with horror chill.

'Tis clearly of the tyrant race,
We trace the features in its face;
'Tis of that same peculiar stock,
A chip from off the ancient block;
It is a sort of codicil,
Annexed to the old musty will;
And if the will be just and right,
The codicil no man should slight.
And so if Slavery's bloody code
And law for fugitives be good,
Then to repeal the Compromise
Was just, appropriate, and wise.

And when the framers of the law
Of eighteen hundred fifty saw
That they were lauded to the skies,
They sought to win a nobler prize.

But in the councils of the nation
Some lofty minds endured temptation,
No threats nor bribes which men could quote
Could gain the favor of their vote.
Though not unfrequently beset
By President and Cabinet,
They stood unterrified and free,
And would not basely bow the knee.

And during life it will be sweet
Their liberal speeches to repeat,
And it will be their heart's delight
That they contended for the right.
And when draws near their peaceful death,
And they shall yield their parting breath,
It cannot fail to cheer that night
To know that they stood by the right.

But all the blind Nebraskaites
Who have invaded human rights,
Will at the North in every case
Be overwhelmed in deep disgrace.
When their eventful life is o'er,
No one their loss will much deplore;
And when their kindred call their name,
Their cheeks will mantle o'er with shame;
But soon their names will be forgot,
The memory of them all shall rot.
And let their burying places be
Upon the coast beside the sea;
And let the ever-rolling surge
Perform a constant funeral dirge.
And when the stranger shall demand
Why these are buried in the sand,
Let him be told without disguise:
They trod upon the Compromise.

* * * * * * * *

Charles L. Reason
(1818-1898)

Reason was born of Haitian parents in New York City where he attended the New York African Free School, which had been established by the New York Manumission Society in 1787. Adept at mathematics especially, Reason proved able enough to be appointed, in 1832, as one of the newly hired all Negro faculty there. He used his salary largely to pay for tutorial lessons in mathematics, but, later, met rebuff, for racial reasons, by the Bishop of the New York Diocese, who forbade his full time entrance into the Theological Seminary of the Protestant Episcopal Church. Nevertheless, he was soon eligible for a professorship in Mathematics and Belle Lettres in 1849 at the New York Central College in McGrawville, Cortlandt County, where he taught until he accepted a principalship at the Institute for Colored Youth in Philadelphia. He left this position to return to New York and pursue a lengthy career as educational administrator of various New York City schools, being principal of grammar school No. 80, while H. Cordelia Ray (q.v.) was a teacher there. A cultured gentleman, given to the more reflective academic world, he was never ambitious for public office and only rarely composed for platform declamations, although he was active at various Negro conventions, urging against plans to colonize Negroes, encouraging them to make the most of American vocational careers instead. His personal qualities are attested to by several contemporaries, such as Bishop Payne in his *Recollections,* and William Simmons in *Men of Mark* (Cleveland, 1887), from which "The Spirit Voice," is taken. His verse only rarely lifted itself from the weight of his classical and historical allusions, but moved in a consciously stately plane of conventional address; yet it can be seen that, in different circumstances, he might have been able to have better utilized his bookish background.

The Spirit Voice
Or, Liberty Call to the Disfranchised
(State of New York)

Come! rouse ye brothers, rouse! a peal now breaks
From lowest island to our gallant lakes:
'Tis summoning you, who long in bonds have lain,
To stand up manful on the battle plain,
Each as a warrior, with his armor bright,
Prepared to battle in a bloodless fight.
Hark! How each breeze that blows o'er Hudson's tide
Is calling loudly on your birth-right pride
And each near cliff, whose peak fierce storms has stood,
Shouts back responsive to the calling flood.
List, from those heights that once with freedom rung,
And those broad fields, where Earth has oft-times sung,
A voice goes up, invoking men to prove
How dear is freedom, and how strong their love.
From every obscure vale and swelling hill
The spirit tones are mounting; louder still
From out the din where noble cities rise
On Mohawk's banks, the peal ascends the skies.
Responding sweet with morning's opening praise,
The sounds commingle, far, to where the rays
Of light departing, sink to partial sleep,
'Mid caverned gems in Erie's bosomed deep.
Nor yet less heard, from inland slope it swells,
In chiming music, with the village bells,
And mixes loud e'en with the ocean's waves,
Like shrill-voiced echo in the mountain caves.
'Tis calling you, who now too long have been
Sore victims suffering under legal sin,
To vow, no more to sleep, till raise and freed
From partial bondage, to a life indeed.
Behold ye now! here consecrate from toil
And love, your homes abide on holy soil.

To these, as sacred temples, fond you cling:
For, thence alone, life's narrow comforts spring,
'Tis here the twilight of existence broke,
The first warm throbbings of your heart awoke.
Here first o'er you, fond mothers watched and prayed,
Here friendship rose and holy vows were made.
On yon familiar height or gentle stream,
You first did mark the pleasant moonlight gleam.
Here, happy, laughed o'er life in cradled bloom
And here, first pensive, wept at age's tomb,
Yes; many a sire, with burnt and furrowed brow
Here died, in hope that you in freedom now
Would feel the boasted pledge your country gave,
That her defender should not be her slave.
And wherefore, round your homes has not been thrown
That guardian shield, which strangers call their own?
Why, now, do ye, as your poor fathers did,
Bow down in silence to what tyrants bid?
And sweat and bleed from early morn till eve,
To earn a dower less than beggars leave?
Why are ye pleased to delve at mammon's nod?
To buy that manhood which is yours from God,
Free choice to say who worthy is to lead
Your country's cause, to give your heart-felt need
Of praise to him that, barring custom's rule,
Would nobly dare attack the cringing tool
That with a selfish aim and ruthless hand,
Would tear in twain love's strong and holy band:
Why can ye not, as men who know and feel
What most is needed for your nation's weal,
Stand in her forums, and with burning words
Urge on the time, when to the bleeding herds,
Whose minds are buried now in polar night,
Hope shall descend; when freedom's mellow light
Shall break, and usher in the endless day,
That from Orleans to Pass'maquoddy Bay,
Despots no more may earthly homage claim,
Nor slaves exist, to soil Columbia's name.

Then, up! awake! nor let dull slumber waste
Your soul's devotion! life doth bid you haste;
The captive in his hut, with watchful ear,
Awaits the sweet triumphant songs to hear,
That shall proclaim the glorious jubilee
When crippled thousands shall in truth be free.
Come! rouse ye brothers, rouse! nor let the voice
That shouting, calls you onward to rejoice,
Be heard in vain! but with ennobled souls,
Let all whom now an unjust law controls
Press on in strength of mind, in purpose bent,
To live by right; to swell the free tones sent
On Southern airs, from this, your native State,
A glorious promise for the captive's fate.
Then up! and vow no more to sleep, till freed
From partial bondage to a life indeed.

New York, July 20, 1841.

* * * * * * * *

Francis A. Boyd

Known only by the publication of his volume, *Columbiana;/ or./ The North Star,/ Complete in one Volume* (Chicago, 1870), Boyd is, by his own needless admission, one more of those several nineteenth century Negro poets who prematurely displayed their literary wares to refute the white man's charges of black intellectual possibilities. Acknowledging the concern of the Reverend Henry Ward Beecher for his interest in "the injured and oppressed sons and daughters of Africa," the dedication reads, "I, a scion of that ancient race, take pleasure in dedicating the following lines to you." A paragraph long preface tells us that he was born in 1844, in Lexington, Kentucky, of free parents, Samuel and Nancy Boyd, and that he gained an education only through hardships. His slim, sixty-nine page volume is made up of five cantos, each of which is variously structured and rimed, although fatiguing iambic tetrameters predominate. *Columbiana* means to versify the rise and almost inexorable development of a personified Freedom as she drives her winged chariot from Egypt, over Israel, Greece and America, where she encounters an assortment of personified evils, chiefly Secessia (Southern forces for secession from the union); the struggles of Freedom makes up the narrative which, in discursive, obscure details about Civil War battles and anecdotes, culminates in the assassination of Lincoln, but despite such opposition and civil barbarism, the North Star still burns to light the inevitable path for Freedom. Boyd's verse is stilted, his rimes often forced, his bookish and apparently personal Civil War references leading him off on tangents that dissipate the story thrust. Pretentious in ambitious poetic design, sometimes tedious in his uneven, forced metrics, he nevertheless does manage to infuse, here and there, glimpses of honest feeling.

The Soliloquy
(From Canto IV)

Columbia on the battle-ground,
Amid the debris strewn around,
To fortune's awful change awoke,
And thus the mournful silence broke:
"On sanguine hope Secessia fed
E'er since the dawn of morning red,
'Twas then she swore, by northern Thor,
To be the heroine of the war.

"She defiance bade to Union laws,
Ignored the justice of the cause,
And boldly drew her glitt'ring glaive[1]
To hamper down the shudd'ring slave.
A mine of wealth was at her hand,
Proud mistress of the southern land,
Eviling in her heart's desire,
She dared to brave Jehovah's ire.

"Secessia, where now thy beauties fair,
The pride of rich planters, thy slaves, and where
That trade in cotton which had bought the world?
That fleecy king at last from power hurled.
Slave pens are desolate, and now the school
Revives where erst thou sat'st with leaden rule,
Where slave-songs pierced the much-offended skies,
The driver sits, half crazed, with sunken eyes;
Where by the pen of ever-living fame
Is traced in burning light immortal Lincoln's name.

"Secessia, on thy soil the Ethiop dwells
In glorious triumph o'er thy foul slave-cells;
No slavish chattels are discovered where
Thou chasedst erst the helot like a hare.

---

[1] "glaive." A broadsword.

Blacks, unaffrighted 'mid thy marble domes,
Among thy conquerors find enduring homes;
Spite of thy debris, vast and desolate,
They cleanse the fabric of this western state.

"These blacks are human proved, and freed from ban
By Abraham, that great and noble man,
Stern as the awful ruin he looked upon,
He finished when his work was but begun.
There in the regions of the sunny south
Secessia stormed and raved with wicked mouth,
And ere the axe of war her form had riven,
Her giant port looked up and laughed at heaven.

"Satanic form, both dark and sinister,
The very demons all avoiding her,
Though for an ensign she did fitly take
And wreath around her head the rattlesnake.
Her heart was stirred to slaughter when alone
She swayed the scepter on her cotton throne;
Hard was her heart, the adamatine flint
Could not more sternly brave the thunder's dint,
Than he dull ear the Ethiop's keen appeal—
Emancipation made her senses reel;
When the thunders of war began to mutter,
With thoughts of vengeance dark, too dread to utter.

"By her the southern Indians were chastised,
Who now sits stricken, stupid, paralyzed;
And yet her fierce eyes glare in frenzied mood
Over the southern wastes, as if she viewed
Her own state pictured in its solitude.
Dark! motionless as night she sits alone
In dust, since driven from her cotton throne,
And in her hypochondriac mind broods o'er
Of fancied wrongs and insults quite a store.
Secessia, die, and I'll forget thy schemes,
Disgrace the flag no more with bondmen's screams,
In death's embrace enjoy the Lethean hour,
Though conquered, you'll not feel the conqueror's power.

* * * * * * * *

The Dream
(from Canto V)

A ship is sailing, see! afar,
   The sign of change in war,
Firm as the ever-during rock,
   That State has stood aloof;
Aspiring high above each shock,
   Pure and rebellion proof.

Or Columbian virgin blushes
   In tinted roses sweet,
As through the great blue ocean rushes,
   Our noble steamers fleet;
And by the dingy pier, the firm
   Receptacle of stores,
E'en tons of silk, with stores of sperm,
   In plenty reach our shores.

The dream was fate, his time was out,
Amid the land's triumphant shout;
The honors of the thespic dome
   Was for the mighty North Star spread;
The grand saloon of freedom's home,
   A charm upon his triumph shed.

And beauty's brightest tribute paid
   By Laura Keene,[2] who knew her place;
Her genius under tax was laid,
   To shadow forth the play with grace.

Now, Ford's was spread with paintings rare,
But those great men expected there,
Were much engrossed throughout the day,
And business, too, called Grant away.

---

[2] Laura Keene (1826?-1873) English born actress, popular in light comedy on American stages from about 1852; She was acting in *Our American Cousin* at Ford's Theatre in Washington, D.C. on the night President Lincoln was assassinated by John Wilkes Booth there.

As Seward lingered deathly sick,
The fatal portents gathered thick;
The North Star bright to go was loth,
But all was dark without his cloth.
The bravest of the brave awaited,
To see the glorious ruler seated;
He gained his box, and sate him down
Beside his wife, the hall to crown,
And Major Wrathbone came to wait
Upon the honored head of state;
While Laura, clothed in diamond spray,
Did honor to the sparkling play.

But hark! a pistol shot was heard,
The ruler uttered not a word;
A dark form lept forth on the stage,
With bound of fate in hellish rage;
He waved a gleaming dagger high;
Sic Semper Tyrannis! his cry.

The wounded ruler did not speak,
The ladies gave a piercing shriek,
And Wrathbone soon was at his side,
To stem the flowing crimson tide.
All was disorder through the hall,
Then did Miss Keene for order call;
She hastened to the box of state,
Upon the suff'ring chief to wait;
On Laura's robe, his head laid now,
With rich perfume she laved his brow;
Next morn he gently closed his eyes,
And fled his spirit to the skies.

We laid his flesh among the dead;
George placed the laurel on his head;
And Europe joined the strain of praise,
That through Columbia ever strays.

Did not his proclamation raise
Up Charlotte Scott to sing his praise;
Though once a slave, the child of troubles,
She ranked with nature's gifted nobles.

Her voice was raised with touching cry,
She said his fame should reach the sky.
Her tongue the primal song displays,
To tell the glory of his days.
Sung be the song in prose or rhyme,
The freedmen sing the song sublime,
E'en from Maine to Louisiana,
Triumphant reign Columbiana.

Before we quench the hallowed fire,
Once more we strike the sacred lyre.
The North Star lingers in the sky,
Encircled by a snowy dove.
Sun, moon and stars confounded lie,
The North Star outshines all above,
'Tis shining here, and shining there,
Forever ruling everywhere.

* * * * * * *

James Madison Bell
(1826-1902)

Bell was born in Gallipolis, Ohio, which he left when he was sixteen for Cincinnati to become thereafter a plasterer by trade and an orating poet by avocation, holding, as his biographer says, "a trowel in one hand and his pen in the other." A restless man, anxious to help in the overthrow of slavery, he moved to Canada, where he strengthened his cherished friendship with John Brown, the martyr, for whom he solicited funds and helped recruit Negroes to assist in that aborted assault on Harper's Ferry in 1859. Leaving his large family in Canada temporarily, he moved to California, then back to Canada and on to Toledo, Ohio. All this while, Bell found time to appear at concert halls and public gatherings to read and declaim his verses to mark some major political event. Not to mitigate his obvious technical flaws, it is helpful to remember that Bell is best appreciated as something of an actor, his poems regarded as scripts. He proudly includes the locales of the places where he offered his orations; thus his *Triumph of Liberty* (Detroit, 1870) carries the full title of *A Poem,/ Entitled the/ Triumph of Liberty./ Delivered April 7, 1870,/ Detroit Opera House,/ On the Occasion of/ The Grand Celebration of the Final Ratification/ of the Fifteenth Amendment to the Con-/ stitution of the United States,* and goes headlong on for some 902 lines of verses that were accompanied by all the body flourishes and vocal modulations at his experienced command. Likewise, his *The Day and the War,* dedicated to his friend, John Brown, was delivered, we are told, at Platt's Hall, San Francisco, California, January 1, 1864, to celebrate the first anniversary of the Emancipation Proclamation.

His *Poetical Works of J.M. Bell* (Lansing, Michigan, 1901) contains more of his lengthy panegyrics, and a few of his clumsy lighter, shorter attempts, along with a biography by Bishop B.W. Arnett, who also assisted A.A. Whitman (q.v.). Bell's "Modern Moses" is a strong, sometimes unseemly satirical tirade against the one-term presidential career of Andrew Johnson (1865-1869), which saw a struggle between a progressive, Republican Congress and a Democratic, reactionary Chief Executive. Born a poor boy in Raleigh, North Carolina, Johnson (1805-1875) was an apprentice and then journeyman tailor who learned to write and figure from his wife, whom he married in 1825. He moved to Greenville, Tennessee, worked his way up through political ranks, and, a long-time critic of the rebellious South, he, a Democrat, was chosen by Republicans for the vice presidency. He succeeded the assassinated Lincoln in April, 1865. President Johnson promptly reversed his harsh condemnations of the South and became tolerant and conciliatory towards former rebels, vetoing progressive legislation such as The Freedmen's Bureau (designed to help dependent, penniless Negroes make the transition into free status), the Civil Rights Bill, declaring Negroes were not yet ready. He condemned the proposed 14th Amendment, attacked various liberal Northern figures like Charles Sumner, Wendell Phillips, but Congress usually overrode his vetoes. Angered, he took his reactionary Reconstruction Policy to the people, making an ill-fated tour, "the swing around the circle," but was so indiscreet on the trip that the angered country repudiated him by electing to Congress an overwhelming majority opposition. Johnson was barely acquitted from impeachment proceedings on May 26, 1868.

Bell lapses from strict satire in several places and argues *ad hominem,* and even raises unnecessary (and unfounded) references to Johnson's presidential motivations. The poem illustrates, as with E.P. Rogers, J.M. Whitfield, and others, that the early Negro took every opportunity in his writings to speak out against the wrongs of the country.

Modern Moses, or "My Policy" Man

There is a tide in men's affairs,
Leading to fame not wholly theirs—
Leading to high positions, won
Through noble deeds by others done.

And crowns there are, and not a few,
And royal robes and sceptres, too,
That have, in every age and land,
Been at the option and command
Of men as much unfit to rule,
As apes and monkeys are for school.

For seldom an assassin's blow
Has laid a benefactor low
Of any nation, age or clime,
In all the lengthened march of time,
That has not raised to power and might,
Some braggart knave or brainless wight,
Whose acts unseemly and unwise,
Have caused the people to despise
And curse the hours of his reign,
And brand him with the marks of Cain.
And yet to crown the mystery,
All these have had a *Policy*.

Though Cain was treach'rous and unjust,
And smote a brother to the dust—
'Tis not of him we wish to speak,
Nor of the wife he went to seek;
Nor of the blood his Nimrod spilt,
Or famous city which he built.

But choose we rather to discant,
On one whose swaggish boast and rant,
And vulgar jest, and pot-house slang,
Has grown the pest of every gang
Of debauchees wherever found,
From Baffin's Bay to Puget Sound.
And yet he occupies a sphere
And fills a more exalted chair,
(With arrogant unworthiness,
To his disgrace, I must confess),
Than any officer of State,
Or king, or princely magistrate
Of royal blood or noble birth,
Throughout the kingdoms of the earth.

But how he chance attain'd that hight,
Amid the splendor and the light,
The effulgent glory and the ray
Of this the nineteenth century,
May, to the superficial mind,
Seem much complexed and undefined;
But when the dark and shameless truth,
Is properly ascribed to Booth,[1]
The strangeness vanishes in haste,
And we through murder stand disgraced.
Disgraced! Perhaps some other word,
Or milder term should be preferred;
And if preferred, that term might be
Exposed to *My Policy.*

For you and I are well aware,
Just how he chanced obtain that chair;
For any *rustic lad* of skill,
Who knows the way to the nearest mill,
Would not regard the thing a task,
But say in substance, were he asked,
First and foully, through a stub and twist,
And then as the farmer claims his grist,
By being second on the list;
Why, 'tis just as plain to sanity,
As the logic of *My Policy.*

But as for *Mose,* he has been
And is to-day as free from sin
As that fond friend who kissed his Lord,
In presence of a Roman horde.
'Tis true he did somewhat disguise
His real intentions, and surprise
The loyal voters of the North,
By feigning hatred to the South;
Through which he gained their confidence,
And won that lofty eminence.

---

[1] Booth—John Wilkes Booth (1838-1865), American Shakespearean actor, assassinated President Abraham Lincoln at Ford's Theater in Washington, D.C. (April 14, 1865); escaped, but was shot or killed himself (April 26, 1865).

But to the physiognomy
Of him, my liege, My Policy,
Of rather more than medium size,
A blooming nose and hazel eyes,
And mien, that one might think him given
To beverage, morning, noon and even';
And judge that his proboscis wore
Its crimson from the overstore;

For there are some rare nectars known
And taken to impart a tone
To the stomach, which will produce,
By repetition and abuse,
The like results; hence, many think
His glow the sad effects of drink;
Others, more prone to charity,
Ascribe it to *My Policy.*

'Tis said he wonders why it is,
That all the land makes such a phiz,
And why they keep in strict reserve,
A shield for the olfactory nerve;
When e'er *My Policy* is brought
Within the radius of their thought.

They surely do not see the point,
But act as though some out-of-joint
Machine had gained the track,
And now was keeping progress back.
O, is it not a burning shame,
That any folks with such a name
For science and philosophy,
To thus regard *My Policy.*

Sumner[2] he claims is much at fault,
And Stevens[3] plotting a revolt

---

[2] Sumner—Charles Sumner (1811-1874), vigorous anti-slavery, United States Senator (1851-1874) and first prominent person to propose emancipation for slaves.

[3] Stevens—Thaddeus Stevens (1792-1868) another liberal, anti-slavery member of the House of Representatives (1849-1853; 1859-1868) who proposed impeachment of President Johnson and was chief manager of the trial that resulted in Johnson's acquittal.

Of Congress 'gainst the President,
And 'gainst his noble sentiment—
With which e'en Davis[4] doth agree,
And all his learned constituency;
Hence, Sumner must not there remain,
And Stevens' might we ought restrain,
And Phillips[5] should not be allowed
To exercise before the crowd,
His foul bombastic heresy,
In variance to *My Policy.*

His life he deems quite insecure,
And such a thought long to endure,
Is torturous in the extreme,
And breeds full many a fitful dream.
He fears some hireling knave may prove
Recreant to pretended love,
And give for *brandy,* water instead,
And thus consign him to the dead,
With all his virtue on his head.

'Tis said, that in the days agone;
He pledged himself to the forlorn;
He pledged himself the bondsman's friend,
And one on whom they might depend
For counsel, succor or redress,
In all their hours of wretchedness,
And swore that he would be their guide,
And lead them past the crimson tide,
And through the wilderness that lay
Between their night and that blest day
That shines forever on the rest
Of all the worthy, free and blest;
That he their *Moses* would become,
And lead them to a freeman's home

---

[4] Davis—Jefferson Davis (1808-1889), President of the Confederate States of America for a six year term beginning February 22, 1862, but terminating when he was captured by Union forces at Irwinville, Georgia, (May 10, 1865); although an ardent pro-slaver, he berated commercially ambitious Northern administration of Negro affairs.

[5] Phillips—Wendell Phillips (1811-1884), a Garrisonian abolitionist.

And swore that he would ne'er forsake
Them, nor his pledge or promise break,
Till every bondsman in the land
Should on the plains of freedom stand,

Pledged to the sacred cause of truth;
Pledged in the early days of youth;
Pledged by the summer, winter, spring,
And pledged by all the truth may bring;
With all these pledges on his soul,
And clothed with power to control
The future destiny of those,
His wards by all his recent oaths.

Mark well his action when for aid
Their suppliant prayer to him was made;
Witness an instance of his love,
And all your former doubts remove.
Mark when that bill[6] for the supply
Of starving millions met his eye;
A breadless, clotheless, houseless throng,
Thus rendered by his nation's wrong.
Does he the bill in haste receive
And sign, their suff'rings to relieve?

Yes, if withholding of the cup
From parched lips, whereof one sup
Would quite allay an inward pain,
And quite restore to health again
A prostrate mortal, doomed to die,
Unless his needs met swift supply,
Can be accounted as relief—
Then he in their deep hour of grief,
Did them relieve and kept his vow;
When with a dark and wrinkled brow,
He stamped his veto on their prayer,
And doomed the suppliants to despair.

---

[6]That bill. . . , i.e., the Freedmen's Bureau Bill. President Johnson successfully vetoed Congressional attempts to make the bill permanent.

School'd in his childhood to regard
Foul treason worthiest of reward,
And loyalty an empty name,
Meriting dark reproach and shame;
Therefore, he deems the rebels more
Worthy positions than before;
Before their nameless deeds of horror
Spread o'er our land the veil of sorrow;
And fain would from the very scurf,
E'en as from the rising surf
Of rebeldom, at once create
Grand officers of high estate,
And bring them to the nation's court,
His grave *My Policy* to support.

'Tis said the clergy everywhere,
Have held up holy hands in prayer
For his redemption from the thrall;
And pit of his apostate fall;
But recently by dream or word,
Have been most signally assured,
That there are no blest agencies
Of grace, outside the promises,
And in that almost boundless plan,
Salvation offered unto man,
Are no provisions that embrace
A proffered pardon in his case;
That it were madness to bewail,
Since all their efforts can but fail;
For he, to use a term uncivil,
Has long been mortgaged to the Devil;
But the fact which no one knows,
Is why the deuce he don't foreclose.
Perhaps he entertains a doubt,
And fears that Mose might turn him out;
Hence, *His Satanic* Majesty's
Endorsement of *My Policy.*

He claims that suffrage, if applied
To Negroes, should be qualified;
That they diplomacied, should hail
From Dartmouth, Harvard or from Yale,
Before entrusted for an hour
With manhood's great elective power.

But every rebel in the land,
From Maine to Georgia's distant strand;
Though dark their minds as rayless night,
Should exercise this manly right,
Though destitute of reason's force
As Balaam's ancient riding horse:
On these the boon he would confer,
Without a scruple or demur,
Because these gentlemen, quoth he,
Are members of *My Policy.*

His vetoes—gracious! what a list!
Never in time did there exist
Such an array of negative,
Bombastic and explanative;
'Tis said their reasons are profound,
Their logic almost passing sound;
And that such lucid rays they shed,
They're understood before they're read.

The Bureau Bill is deemed the first
Of numerous acts, by him reversed;
The power that bill sought to confer
On him, provoked his just demur,
And for this strange, unlikely fault,
His meekness rose in fierce revolt,
And flamed with wrath and power to kill,
He hurled his veto at the bill;
For actions of humanity,
Accord not with *My Policy.*

He next reversed the bill of rights,
Lest all the girls—that is the whites—
Should Desdemonias become,
And fly each one her cherished home,

And take to heart some sooty moor,
As Fathers did in days before.
If but the legal right were given,
He fears that six in every seven
Of all the maids in all the land,
Would give the matrimonial hand
Unto some swarthy son or other,
And some, perhaps, might wed a *brother.*

This horrid thought his wrath excites,
And swearing 'gainst all "woman's rights,"
He grasped the veto in his ire,
And doomed the *bill* to endless fire;
For all such reciprocity,
Was foreign to *My Policy.*
This ghost-like thought preyed on his soul,
And robbed him of all self control,
Till from his fears, lest they obtain,
He got the veto on the brain;
The inflated type, the very worst,
With which a mortal e'er was cursed.

And hence, when e'er an act is brought,
For which his signature is sought,
How plain soever the device,
He fancies that he "smells a mice,"
And forthwith runs the trap to bring
My Policy, and sets the spring,
And waits with pain-suspended cough,
To see the curious thing go off.

And when the fancied mouse is caught
Within his fancied trap of thought,
To hear him in that frenzied laugh,
And see that full three-fingered quaff
Pass down the lining of his throat,
And find a lodgment 'neath his coat,
Would crimson o'er the cheek with shame,
And send a tremor through the frame,

The which would cause the heart to yield
To poignant truth so oft revealed,
And in that act confess they see
The secrets of *My Policy.*

The little giant of the West—[7]
His labor done, was laid to rest,
And to eternalize his fame,
And thus immortalize his name,
Moses, with vassals of renown,
Comes swinging past from town to town;
And makes a quite imposing tour,
Save that he proves himself a boor
At divers times in divers ways,
All through his eagerness for praise,
For e'en despite the peerless Grant,
And monument he came to plant,
All those that were not wholly blind,
Could see he had an axe to grind;
The monument was but a ruse,
A subtle means to introduce
My liege of graceless dignity,
The author of *My Policy.*
'Tis said that he at times would come
To cities which were not "to home,"
From which long ere the pageant closed.
The peerless Grant grew indisposed,
And to the banks of Erie's Lake,
Repaired for reputation's sake.

But be this statement false or true,
It has the smallest part to do
With the matter of fact at hand,
Which is this, when through the land
He'd gone and played the *knave and clown,*
In every city, village, town,

---

[7]"The little giant of the West"—Stephen A. Douglass (1813-1861). See E.P. Rogers'
treatment of Douglass on pages 68-69.

And felt *My Policy* was sure
To win by virtue of the tour,
The people rise in mass and vote,
And thus most signally denote
By their vote and by their voice,
And by the subjects of their choice,
That they had blindly failed to see
The beauties of *My Policy*.

Hence, when the massive cavalcade
Swung round and round in grand parade,
With much chagrin, they're all dispensed,
Just where their fruitless tour commenced.

O, were I but a dramatist,
What stores of thought I would enlist,
What telling words I would indite,
And what a play my pen should write;
I'd hie me to the nation's dome;
Amid its splendors I would roam,
Discant on palace, hall and court,
And on the nation's grave support,
Until I placed upon the stage
The grandest burlesque of the age;

"Moses! Moses!" should be my theme;
Not He that through the crimson stream
Led out from Egypt Israel's host;
But "our Mose" of rant and boast,
Who from the nation's balcony,
Cajoled a drunken revelry,
In telling words of pothouse lore,
The which had ne'er been heard before,
Since Kidd,[8] the terror of the wave,
Placed men's life-chart within the grave.

Oh, Demosthenes! in silence rest,
Henceforth "our Mose" shall be the test
Of all oratorical display,
And for a sample, by the way,

---

[8]William Kidd, 1645?-1701, pirate, known as "Captain Kidd."

Witness his chaste and classic art,
In his description of sweetheart,
And Penny nibbling at his heels,
And then how graphic he reveals
His wond'rous buncombe, and his pluck,
In that grave story of the duck.
And when you have read, O think of the stage,
And the wonderful *star* of a wonderful age!

II

Formalist Poets

Phillis Wheatley
(1753?-1784)

A good deal has already been written about this precocious, African born Boston celebrity of the eighteenth century, whose poetic abilities made her an object of international curiosity and/or admiration since she began her life-long concern with letters. Kidnapped as a child, she was brought as a slave to Boston in 1761, when she was purchased by Mr. John Wheatley, a local merchant anxious to restock his supply of aging Negro servants. Her intellectual alertness was early noted and encouraged by the Wheatley family who exposed her to informal, tutorial sessions of the typical New England education which involved the classics and stressed the Bible, the most difficult parts of which she was able to read within sixteen months after being in the country. Never in the best of health—her letters to Obour (or Arbor) Tanner, an African domestic friend in Newport, Rhode Island, record her complaints—she was sent abroad for recommended recuperation in England, where she was feted by distinguished religionists and nobility, and was scheduled to see the King and Queen before word came from America that her mistress was failing.

Before she left London, she published there a collection of her poems, several of which had been already published in America, as *Poems on Various Subjects, Religious and Moral*, 1773. Upon her return to America, her fortunes declined: Mrs. Wheatley died in March, 1774, and in March, 1778, Mr. Wheatley died; in September of the same year, Mary Wheatley Lathrop, a daughter, tutor and friend, also died. Thrown on her own, she married John Peters, who has been described as too ambitious for the realities of his times. She mothered three children, all dying in infancy, the third with her as, reduced to common domestic work in a cheap boarding house in a run down section of Boston, she died in December, 1784. Peters, who was in and out of difficulties, obliged once, for instance, to sell one of her London gift books to pay a debt, is said to have taken the manuscript for a proposed second volume and gone South, dropping from notice thereafter. Other sources report that the manuscript was in the hands of a man in Philadelphia. That such a manuscript existed is certain, as her advertised proposal for its subscription publication lists thirty-three poems and thirteen letters by titles, and she fixed a selling price to subscribers, promising that, "Those who subscribe for six books will have a seventh gratis." As various of her unknown poems appear from time to time, it is not impossible that the manuscript will be found and published.

Phillis' literary career was a full one, beginning with her compositions as early as 1767, and with publication of an elegy on the death of the Reverend George Whitefield in 1770. It was the appearance of this poem in print that went far toward commending her to English audiences, and thereafter to eager American news-paper and magazine publishers. Numerous editions and several memoirs have appeared and continue to appear, the 1834 edition with memoir by Mrs. Margaretta Matilda Odell, a collateral descendant of Mrs. Wheatley, having special value. Julian D. Mason, Jr. in *The Poems of Phillis Wheatley* (Chapel Hill, 1966) offers the latest and most comprehensive survey of her life and most of her extant poems. Two hitherto uncollected poems by her are printed below.

While Thomas Jefferson in *Notes on Virginia*, 1784, dismissed her poetry as beneath criticism, General George Washington was more generous, responding to a poem from her ("To His Excellency General Washington," 1775) by writing her an invitation to visit his Cambridge, Massachusetts, headquarters, an invitation which she honored. Today, her reputation seems to be that of an unusually gifted but conventionally limited colonial American poet. She has been the target of criticism for ignoring the racial problems of her day, but her racial awareness in her poetry has been documented and her letters more pronouncedly reveal a solicitous concern for the favorable projection of the Negro. Her poetry is typical of her strong religious training and pioneering times, modelling itself after the currently acceptable English writers, John Milton, Alexander Pope,

but she can reach heights and express sentiments that are her own.
Her favorite vehicle is the popular pentameter couplet, but she uses
other forms with equally charming feminine ease.

To the University of Cambridge, in New England[1]

WHILE an intrinsic ardor prompts to write,
The muses promise to assist my pen;
'Twas not long since I left my native shore
The land of errors, and Egyptian gloom:
Father of mercy, 'twas thy gracious hand
Brought me in safety from those dark abodes.

    Students, to you 'tis giv'n to scan the heights
Above, to traverse the ethereal space,
And mark the systems of revolving worlds.
Still more, ye sons of science, ye receive
The blissful news by messengers from heav'n,
How *Jesus'* blood for your redemption flows.
See him with hands outstretched upon the cross;
Immense compassion in his bosom glows;
He hears revilers, nor resents their scorn:
What matchless mercy in the Son of God!
When the whole human race by sin had fall'n,
He deign'd to die that they might rise again,
And share with him in the sublimest skies,
Life without death, and glory without end.

    Improve your privileges while they stay,
Ye pupils, and each hour redeem, that bears
Or good or bad report of you to heav'n.
Let sin, that baneful evil to the soul,
By you be shunned, nor once remit your guard;
Suppress the deadly serpent in its egg.
Ye blooming plants of human race divine,
An *Ethiope* tells you 'tis your greatest foe;
Its transient sweetness turns to endless pain,
And in immense perdition sinks the soul.

---

[1] Published in her 1773 volume, this poem was composed, in slightly different form, as
early as 1767. She is speaking, of course, of Harvard University.

On Being Brought From Africa to America

'Twas mercy brought me from my *Pagan* land,
Taught my benighted soul to understand
That there's a God, that there's a *Saviour* too:
Once I redemption neither sought nor knew.
Some view our race with scornful eye,
"Their color is a diabolic die."
Remember, Christians, Negroes, black as Cain,
May be refined, and join th' angelic train.

* * * * * * * *

On the Death of the Rev. Mr. George Whitefield[2] 1770

HAIL, happy saint, on thine immortal throne,
Possessed of glory, life and bliss unknown;
We hear no more the music of thy tongue,
Thy wonted auditories cease to throng.
They sermons in unequalled accents flowed,
And ev'ry bosom with devotion glowed;
Thou didst in strains of eloquence refined
Inflame the heart, and captivate the mind.
Unhappy we the setting sun deplore,
So glorious once, but ah! it shines no more.

Behold the prophet in his towering flight!
He leaves the earth for heaven's unmeasured height,
And worlds unknown receive him from our sight.
There Whitefield wings with rapid course his way.
And sails to Zion through vast seas of day.
Thy prayers, great saint, and thine incessant cries,
Have pierced the bosom of thy native skies.
Thou, moon, hast seen, and all the stars of light,
How he has wrestled with his God by night.
He prayed that grace in ev'ry heart might dwell,
He longed to see America excel;

[2]Her first published work, this poem appeared in other versions and, reprinted many times, it established her as a poet. See Mason, pp. 66-71.

He charged its youth that ev'ry grace divine
Should with full lustre in their conduct shine;
That Savior, which his soul did first receive,
The greatest gift that ev'n a God can give,
He freely offered to the numerous throng,
That on his lips with list'ning pleasure hung.

"Take him, ye wretched, for your only good,
"Take him, ye starving sinners, for your food;
"Ye thirsty, come to this life-giving stream,
"Ye preachers, take him for your joyful theme;
"Take him, my dear Americans," he said,
"Be your complaints on his kind bosom laid:
"Take him, ye Africans, he longs for you;
"Impartial Savior is his title due:
"Washed in the fountain of redeeming blood,
"You shall be sons, and kings, and priests to God."

Great Countess,[3] we Americans revere
Thy name, and mingle in thy grief sincere;
New England deeply feels, the orphans mourn,
Their more than father will no more return.

But though arrested by the hand of death,
Whitefield no more exerts his lab'ring breath,
Yet let us view him in th' eternal skies,
Let ev'ry heart to this bright vision rise;
While the tomb, safe, retains its sacred trust,
Till life divine re-animates his dust.

* * * * * * * *

Thoughts on the Work of Providence

Arise, my soul; on wings enraptured rise,
To praise the monarch of the earth and skies,
Whose goodness and beneficence appear,
As round its center moves the rolling year;
Or when the morning glows with rosy charms,
Or the sun slumbers in the ocean's arms:

---

[3] Great Countess, i.e., Countess of Huntingdon (Selina Hastings, 1707-1791) wealthy, eccentric religionist, to whom Mr. Whitefield was chaplain.

Of light divine be a rich portion lent,
To guide my soul, and favor my intent.
Celestial muse, my arduous flight sustain,
And raise my mind to a seraphic strain!

Adored forever be the God unseen,
Which round the sun revolves this vast machine,
Though to his eye its mass a point appears:
Adored the God that whirls surrounding spheres,
Which first ordained that mighty Sol should reign,
The peerless monarch of th' ethereal train:
Of miles twice forty millions is his height,
And yet his radiance dazzles mortal sight
So far beneath—from him th' extended earth
Vigor derives, and ev'ry flow'ry birth:
Vast through her orb she moves with easy grace
Around her Phoebus in unbounded space;
True to her course, th' impetuous storm derides,
Triumphant o'er the winds, and surging tides.

Almighty, in these wond'rous works of thine,
What Power, what Wisdom, and what Goodness shine!
And are thy wonders, Lord, by men explored,
And yet creating glory unadored?

Creation smiles in various beauty gay,
While day to night, and night succeeds to day:
That wisdom which attends Jehovah's ways,
Shines most conspicuous in the solar rays:
Without them, destitute of heat and light,
This world would be the reign of endless night:
In their excess how would our race complain,
Abhoring life! how hate its lengthened chain!
From air or dust what num'rous ills would rise,
What dire contagion taint the burning skies,
What pestilential vapor, fraught with death,
Would rise, and overspread the lands beneath?

Hail, smiling morn, that from the orient main
Ascending dost adorn the heav'nly plain!

So rich, so various are thy beateous dies
That spread through all the circuit of the skies,
That, full of thee, my soul in rapture soars,
And thy great God, the cause of all adores.

O'er beings infinite his love extends,
His wisdom rules them, and his power defends.
When tasks diurnal tire the human frame,
The spirits faint, and dim the vital flame,
Then, too, that ever active bounty shines,
Which not infinity of space confines.
The sable veil, that night in silence draws,
Conceals effects, but shows th' Almighty cause;
Night seals in sleep the wide creation fair,
And all is peaceful but the brow of care.
Again, gay Phoebus, as the day before,
Wakes ev'ry eye, but what shall wake no more;
Again the face of nature is renewed,
Which still appears harmonious, fair and good.
May grateful strains salute the smiling morn,
Before its beams the eastern hills adorn.

Shall day to day, and night to night conspire
To show the goodness of th' Almighty sire?
This mental voice shall man regardless hear,
And never, never raise the filial pray'r?
To-day, oh, hearken, nor your folly mourn
For time misspent, that never will return.

But see the sons of vegetation rise,
And spread their leafy banners to the skies.
All-wise, Almighty providence, we trace
In trees and plants, and all the flow'ry race,
As clear as in the nobler frame of man,
All lovely copies of the Maker's plan:
The power the same that forms a ray of light,
That called creation from eternal night.
"Let there be light," he said: from his profound
Old Chaos heard, and trembled at the sound:

Swift as the word, inspired by power divine,
Behold the light around its Maker shine,
The first fair product of the omnific God
And now through all his works diffused abroad.

As reason's pow'rs by day our God disclose,
So may we trace him in the night's repose.
Say, what is sleep? and dreams how passing strange!
When action ceases, and ideas range
Licentious and unbounded o'er the plains,
Where Fancy's queen in giddy triumph reigns.
Hear in soft strains the dreaming lover sigh
To a kind fair, or rave in jealousy;
Or pleasure now, and now on vengeance bent,
The lab'ring passions struggle for a vent.
What pow'r, O, man! thy reason then restores,
So long suspended in nocturnal hours?

What secret hand returns the mental train,
And gives improved thine active pow'rs again?
From thee, O, man, what gratitude should rise!
And when, from balmy sleep the op'st thine eyes,
Let thy first thoughts be praises to the skies.
How merciful our God, who thus imparts
O'erflowing tides of joy to human hearts,
When wants and woes might be our righteous lot,
Our God forgetting, by our God forgot!

Among the mental pow'rs a question rose,
"What most the image of th' Eternal shows?"
When thus to Reason (so let her Fancy rove)
Her Great companion spoke, immortal Love:

"Say, mighty pow'r, how long shall strife prevail,
"And with its murmurs load the whisp'ring gale?
"Refer the cause to Recollection's shrine,
"Who loud proclaims my origin divine,
"The cause whence heav'n and earth began to be,
"And is not man immortalized by me?
"Reason, let this most causeless strife subside."
Thus Love pronounced, and Reason thus replied:

"Thy birth, celestial queen! 'tis mine to own,
"In thee resplendent is the Godhead shown;
"Thy words persuade, my soul enraptured feels
"Resistless beauty which thy soul reveals."
Ardent she spoke, and kindling at her charms,
She clasped the blooming goddess in her arms.

Infinite Love, wher'er we turn our eyes
Appears: this ev'ry creature's wants supplies;
This most is heard in Nature's constant voice;
This makes the morn, and this the eve rejoice;
This bids the fost'ring rains and dews descend
To nourish all, to serve one gen'ral end,
The good of man: yet man ungrateful pays
But little homage, and but little praise.
To him, whose works arrayed with mercy shine,
What songs should rise, how constant, how divine!

* * * * * * * *

On Recollection

Mneme[4] begin. Inspire, ye sacred Nine,
Your vent'rous Afric, in her great design.
Mneme, immortal pow'r, I trace thy spring:
Assist my strains while I thy glories sing:
The acts of long departed years, by thee
Recovered, in due order ranged we see:
Thy pow'r the long-forgotten calls from night,
That sweetly plays before the fancy's sight.

Mneme in our nocturnal visions pours
The ample treasures of her secret stores;
Swift from above, she wings her silent flight
Through Phoebe's realms, fair regent of the night;
And, in her pomp of images displayed,
To the high-raptured poet gives her aid,
Through the unbounded regions of the mind
Diffusing light, celestial and refined.
The heav'nly phantom paints the actions done
By ev'ry tribe beneath the rolling sun.

---

[4]Mneme, i.e., Mnemosyne—in Greek mythology, the goddess of memory and mother of the Muses.

Mneme, enthroned within the human breast,
Has vice condemned, and every virtue blessed.
How sweet the sound when we her plaudit hear!
Sweeter than music to the ravished ear,
Sweeter than Maro's entertaining strains,
Resounding through the groves, and hills, and plains.
But how is Mneme dreaded by the race
Who scorn her warnings and despise her grace!
By her unveiled each horrid crime appears,
Her awful hand a cup of wormwood bears.
Days, years misspent, oh, what a hell of woe!
Hers the worst tortures that the soul can know.

Now eighteen years their destined course have run
In fast succession round the central sun.
How did the follies of that period pass
Unnoticed, but behold them writ in brass.
In Recollection see them fresh return,
And sure 'tis mine to be ashamed and mourn.

Oh, Virtue! smiling in immortal green,
Do thou exert thy pow'r, and change the scene;
Be thine employ to guide my future days,
And mine to pay the tribute of my praise.

Of Recollection such the pow'r enthroned
In ev'ry breast, and thus her pow'r is owned.
The wretch who dared the vengeance of the skies,
At last awakes in horror and surprise,
By her alarmed, he sees impending fate,
He howls in anguish, and repents too late.

But Oh! what peace, what joys are hers t'impart
To ev'ry holy, ev'ry upright heart!
Thrice blessed the man, who, in her sacred shrine,
Feels himself sheltered from the wrath divine!

* * * * * * *

On Imagination

Thy various works, imperial queen, we see.
How bright their forms! how decked with pomp by thee!
Thy wondr'ous acts in beauteous order stand,
And all attest how potent is thine hand.

From Helicon's refulgent heights attend,
Ye sacred choir, and my attempts befriend:
To tell her glories with a faithful tongue,
Ye blooming graces, triumph in my song.

Now here, now there, the roving Fancy flies,
Till some loved object strikes her wand'ring eyes,
Whose silken fetters all the senses bind,
And soft captivity involves the mind.

Imagination! who can sing thy force?
Or who describe the swiftness of thy course?
Soaring through air to find the bright abode,
Th' empyreal palace of the thundering God,
We on thy pinions can surpass the wind,
And leave the rolling universe behind:
From star to star the mental optics rove,
Measure the skies, and range the realms above.
There in one view we grasp the mighty whole,
Or with new worlds amaze th' unbounded soul,

Though Winter's frowns to Fancy's raptured eyes
The fields may flourish, and gay scenes arise;
The frozen deeps may break their iron bands,
And bid their waters murmur o'er the sands.
Fair Flora may resume her fragrant reign,
And with her flow'ry riches deck the plain;
Sylvanus may diffuse his honors round,
And all the forest may with leaves be crowned;
Show'rs may descend, and dews their gems disclose,
And nectar sparkle on the blooming rose.

Such is thy pow'r, nor are thine orders vain,
Oh, thou, the leader of the mental train;
In full perfection all thy works are wrought,
And thine the sceptre o'er the realms of thought.
Before thy throne the subject-passions bow,
Of subject-passions sov'reign ruler Thou;
At thy command joy rushes on the heart,
And through the glowing veins the spirits dart.

Fancy might now her silken pinions try
To rise from earth, and sweep th' expanse on high;
From Tithon's bed now might Aurora rise,
Her cheeks all glowing with celestial dies,
While a pure stream of light o'erflows the skies.

The monarch of the day I might behold,
And all the mountains tipped with radiant gold,
But I reluctant leave the pleasing views,
Which Fancy dresses to delight the Muse;
Winter austere forbids me to aspire,
And northern tempests damp the rising fire;
They chill the tides of Fancy's flowing sea,
Cease then, my song, cease th' unequal lay.

* * * * * * *

To His Excellency General Washington

Celestial choir! enthroned in realms of light,
　　Columbia's scenes of glorious toil I write.
While freedom's cause her anxious breast alarms,
She flashes dreadful in refulgent arms.
See mother earth her offspring's fate bemoan,
And nations gaze at scenes before unknown!
See the bright beams of heaven's revolving light
Involved in sorrows and the veil of night!
The goddess comes, she moves divinely fair,
Olive and laurel binds her golden hair:

Wherever shines this native of the skies,
Unnumbered charms and recent graces rise.
Muse! bow propitious while my ben relates
How pour her armies through a thousand gates,
As when Eolus heaven's fair face deforms,
Enwrapped in tempest and a night of storms;
Astonished ocean feels the wild uproar,
The refluent surges beat the sounding shore;
Or thick as leaves in Autumn's golden reign,
Such, and so many, moves the warrior's train.
In bright array they seek the work of war,
Where high unfurled the ensign waves in air.
Shall I to Washington their praise recite?
Enough thou know'st them in the fields of fight.
Thee, first in peace and honors,—we demand
The grace and glory of thy martial band.
Famed for thy valor, for thy virtues more,
Hear every tongue thy guardian aid implore!
One century scarce performed its destined round,
When Gallic powers Columbia's fury found;
    And so may you, whoever dares disgrace
The land of freedom's heav'n—defended race!
Fixed are the eyes of nations on the scales,
For in their hopes Columbia's arm prevails.
Anon Britannia droops the pensive head,
While round increase the rising hills of dead.
Ah! cruel blindness to Columbia's state!
Lament thy thirst of boundless power too late.
Proceed, great chief, with virtue on thy side,
Thy every action let the goddess guide.
A crown, a mansion, and a throne that shine,
With gold unfading, Washington! be thine.

(April,   1776)

* * * * * * *

To S(cipio) M(oorhead)[5] A Young African Painter,
On Seeing His Work

To show the lab'ring bosom's deep intent,
And thought in living characters to paint,
When first thy pencil did those beauties give,
And breathing figures learned from thee to live,
How did those prospects give my soul delight,
A new creation rushing on my sight?
Still, wond'rous youth, each noble path pursue,
On deathless glories fix thine ardent view:
Still may the painter's and the poet's fire
To aid thy pencil, and thy verse conspire!
And may the charms of each seraphic theme
Conduct thy footsteps to immortal fame!
High to the blissful wonders of the skies
Elate thy soul, and raise thy wishful eyes.
Thrice happy, when exalted to survey
That splendid city, crowned with endless day,
Whose twice six gates on radiant hinges ring:
Celestial Salem blooms in endless spring.
Calm and serene thy moments glide along,
And may the muse inspire each future song!
Still, with the sweets of contemplation blessed,
May peace with balmy wings your soul invest.
But when these shades of time are chased away,
And darkness ends in everlasting day,
On what seraphic pinions shall we move,
And view the landscapes in the realm above?
There shall thy tongue in heav'nly murmurs flow,
And there my muse with heav'nly transport glow:
No more to tell of Damon's tender sighs,
Or rising radiance of Aurora's eyes,
For nobler themes demand a nobler strain,
And purer language on th' ethereal plain.
Cease, gentle muse! the solemn gloom of night
Now seals the fair creation from my sight.

* * * * * * * *

[5] S.M. is identified as Scipio Moorhead, a Negro artist, servant to Rev. John Moorhead of Boston, by Mr. S.F. Haven of Worcester, Mass. See E.A. Duyckinck and A.L. Duyckinck, *Cyclopedia of American Literature* (New York, Charles Scribner, 1855), p. 368.

An Ode
On The Birthday of Pompey Stockbridge[6]

While hireling scribblers prostitute their pen,
Creating virtues for abandoned men,
Ascribing merit to the vicious great,
And basely flatter whom they ought to hate—
Be mine the just, the grateful task to scan
Th' effulgent virtues of a *sable* man;
Trace the good action to its source sublime
And mark its progress to the death of time.
Alternate seasons quickly pass away,
And the *sixth* lustre crowns this natal day
Since first my Pompey, humble, modest, wise,
Shot the bright dawn of reason from his eyes:
Nor was his morn o'ercast by folly's cloud;
Ne'er pressed his footsteps 'mong the giddy crowd:
Even the gay season of luxuriant youth
Was wisely spent to ascertain the truth.
Religious precepts formed his darling plan,
And virtue's dictates stamped him *real* man,—
Long may Pompey live, long live to prove
The sweets of virtue, and the joys of love;
And when these happy annual feasts are past,
That day be happiest which will be his last;
Then may his soul triumphantly ascend,
Where *perfect bliss* shall never know an end.

On Friendship[7]

Let Amicitia[8] in her ample reign
Extend her notes to a celestial strain,

---

[6] Unsigned by Miss Wheatley (or Mrs. Peters), this broadside has neither publisher nor date affixed, but is thought to have been written by her on the basis of general characteristics of style.

[7] A hitherto unpublished poem by Miss Wheatley, this piece is one of several which she wrote in her teens, this one written when she was fifteen years old; in this same year she composed "On Atheism" also: See Lorenzo J. Greene, *The Negro in Colonial New England* (New York, 1942), p. 245. In the Moorland Collection at Howard University, there is a facsimile of the original manuscript as it is reproduced here, with by line and date, but with no punctuation at all. Thanks are due Mrs. Dorothy Porter for the use of the copy. See note to Miss Wheatley's "To the University in Cambridge," page 99. See also appendix A for other instances of early Negro teenage verse efforts.

[8] Amicitia is Latin for friendship.

Benevolent, far more divinely bright;
Amor, like me, doth triumph at the sight
When to my thoughts in gratitude employ;[9]
Mental imaginations give me joy;
Now let my thoughts in contemplation steer
The footsteps of the superlative fair.

Boston   Phillis Wheatley
July 15, 1769

---

[9]"Imploy" in the handwritten manuscript.

Ann Plato

There is factually nothing known of Miss Plato except that she was a Negro member of the Colored Congregational Church in Hartford, Connecticut in 1841, so identified in the preface by her pastor, the Reverend J.W.C. Pennington, about whom much is known. Certainly Hartford of the 1840's was one of New England's busiest centers for anti-slavery agitation and sentiment. Frederick Douglass spoke there during this time, as did other abolitionist lecturers. Pennington, himself an escaped slave, and long active as convention official and uncompromising opponent of segregation and slavery, must have touched on racial injustices that faced his congregation daily. Yet Miss Plato in her volume says practically nothing about such matters. Her book, entitled *Essays;/ Including/ Biographies and Miscellaneous Pieces,/ in/ Prose and Poetry* (Hartford, 1841) is overly ambitious in its intended scope, and pretentious, clumsy in treatment. 122 pages long, it is made up of two kinds of prose, essays and biographies, and a more interesting third section given to poems.

There are sixteen, self-righteous, routine essays on such topics as "Education," "Religion," "Benevelence," "Employment of Time," "Life is Short," etc., which, mercifully brief, have most value as species of essay composition of the times. In "Education," she praises Christian missionary educators who "carried a message of love to the burning clime of Africa," and other remote parts of the world. As in her poetry, so in her capsule biographies of obscure persons, evidently Negro female domestics friends of the author, Miss Plato refers only obliquely to things racial. In the third of her four biographies, she notes that Miss Eliza Loomis Sherman was quite ill, but had she "wished for shelter beneath a Georgia clime, that

privilege would not have been granted her, on account of the laws."
Only one of her twenty poems. "To the First of August,"
acknowledges a pertinent major event, here celebrating the August 1,
1838 abolition of slavery in the British West Indies. On the evidence
of several poems that describe the preparation and duties of school
teaching, she may have been so engaged, but in none of her poems is
there any reference to the color of her pupils. Her immature gropings
might well be due to the likelihood of her actual youth—Pennington,
for instance, refers more than a dozen times to her youth in his three
and a half page preface; all of the four subjects of her biographies,
departed friends, were also quite young, one dying at age seventeen.
Assuming that she is being autobiographical, she may have been as
young as fifteen years old, for in one piece, "Lines/ written upon
being examined in the school studies for the preparation of a
teacher," she writes:

> Oh, may each youthful bosom catch the sacred fire,
> And youthful mind to virtue's throne aspire—
> *Now fifteen years their destined course have run,*
> *In fast succession round the central sun;*[1]
>
> (italics mine)

Her verse rarely gets aloft and never sustains a steady poetic flight,
but she may never have intended as much, the upper regions of
poetic fancy being anathema for one of her apparent puritanical
piety. Her topics are eulogistic, domestic and moralistic matters, but
when she is romantic, as in "Forget Me Not," she is more generally
appealing. Often sentimental and melodramatic to excess, she does
struggle, now and again, for originality in her variety of rime, but
settles too often for assonantal rime (e.g., "Her tongue in silence now
does sleep,/ And she no more time's call can greet," from
"Reflections"); at other times she will leave a line unrimed
altogether, and her spelling and punctuation need attention. Important historically as the author of the second volume of poetry by
an American Negro woman[2] published in the United States, Miss
Plato can engender a few rewarding passages.

---

[1] See lines 13-14 of Phillis Wheatley's "On Recollection," p. 106.

[2] There is said to have been an earlier volume by unidentified "Rosa and Maria," *Poems* (South Carolina, 1834). See William D. Snow, "Extract From an Unpublished Poem on Freedom, *"Autographs for Freedom,* (Rochester, 1854) edited by Julia Griffiths, p. 269n.

Reflections, Written on Visiting
the Grave of a Venerated Friend

Deep in this grave her bones remain,
She's sleeping on, bereft of pain;
Her tongue in silence now does sleep,
And she no more time's call can greet.

She lived as all God's saints should do,
Resigned to death and suffering too;
She feels not pain or sin oppress,
Nor does of worldly cares possess.

White were the locks that thinly shed
Their snows around her honored head,
And furrows not to be effaced
Had age amid her features traced.

I said, "My sister, do tread light,
Faint as the stars that gleam at night,
Nor pluck the tender leaves that wave
In sweetness over this sainted grave."

The rose I've planted by her side,
It tells me of that fate decried;
And bids us all prepare to die,
For that our doom is hast'ning nigh.

Oh, that the gale that sweeps the heath
Too roughly o'er your leaves should breathe,
Then sigh for her—and when you bloom,
Scatter your fragrance o'er her tomb.

Alone I've wandered through the gloom,
To pour my lays upon her tomb;
And I have mourned to see her bed
With brambles and with thorns o'erspread.

O, surely, round her place of rest
I will not let the weed be blest;
It is not meet that she should be
Forgotten or unblest by me.

My sister said, "Tell of this grave!"
Go ask, said I, the thoughtless wave;
And spend one hour in anxious care —
In duty, penitence, and prayer.

Farewell! let memory bestow,
That all may soon be laid as low,
For out of dust, God did compose:
We turn to dust, to sleep, repose.

* * * * * * * *

Forget Me Not

When in the morning's misty hour,
When the sun beems (sic) gently o'er each flower;
When thou dost cease to smile benign,
And think each heart responds with thine,
When seeking rest among divine,
        Forget Me Not.

When the last rays of twilight fall,
And thou art pacing yonder hall;
When mists are gathering on the hill,
Nor sound is heard save mountain rill,
When all around bids peace be still,
        Forget Me Not.

When the first star with brilliance bright,
Gleams lonely o'er the arch of night;
When the bright moon dispels the gloom,
And various are the stars that bloom,
And brighten as the sun at noon,
        Forget Me Not.

When solemn sighs the hollow wind,
And deepen'd thought enraps (sic) the mind;
If e'er thou doest in mournful tone,
E'er sigh because thou feel alone,
Or wrapt in melancholy prone,
        Forget Me Not.

When bird does wait thy absence long,
Nor tend unto its morning song;
While thou art searching stoic page,
Or listening to an ancient sage,
Whose spirit curbs a mournful rage,
        Forget Me Not.

Then when in silence thou doest walk,
Nor being round with whom to talk;
When thou art on the mighty deep,
And do in quiet action sleep;
If we no more on earth do meet,
        Forget Me Not.

When brightness round thee long shall bloom,
And knelt remembering those in gloom;
And when in deep oblivion's shade,
This breathless, mouldering form is laid,
And thy terrestrial body staid,
        Forget Me Not.

"Should sorrow cloud thy coming years,
And bathe thy happiness in tears,
Remember, though we're doom'd to part,
There lives one fond and faithful heart
        That will forget thee not."

To the First of August

Britannia's isles proclaim
    That freedom is their theme;
And we do view those honored lands
    With soul-delighting mien.

And unto those they held in gloom,
    Gave ev'ry one their right;
They did disdain fell slavery's shade,
    And trust in freedom's light.

Then unto ev'ry British blood,
    Their noble worth revere,
And think them ever noble men,
    And like them hence appear.

And when on Britain's isles remote
   We're then in freedom's bounds,
And while we stand on British ground,
   "You're free—you're free!" resounds.

Lift ye that country's banner high,
   And may it nobly wave,
Until beneath the azure sky,
   Man shall be no more a slave.

And, oh, when youth's ecstatic hour,
   When winds and torrents foam,
And passion's glowing noon are past
   To bless that free born home;

Then let us celebrate the day
   And lay the thought to heart,
And teach the rising race the way
   That they may not depart.

* * * * * * *

The Natives of America

"Tell me a story, father, please,"
And then I sat upon his knees.
Then answered he, "What speech make known,
Or tell the words of native tone,
Of how my Indian fathers dwelt,
And of sore oppression felt;
And how they mourned a land serene—
It was an ever mournful theme."

"Yes," I replied,—"I like to hear,
And bring my father's spirit near;
Of every pain they did forego,
Oh, please to tell me all you know.
In history often do I read
Of pain which none but they did heed."

He thus began. "We were a happy race,
When we no tongue but ours did trace;
We were in ever peace,
We sold, we did release—
Our brethren, far remote and far unknown,
And spoke to them in silent, tender tone.
We all were then as in one band;
We joined and took each other's hand.
Our dress was suited to the clime;
Our food was such as roamed that time,
Our houses were of sticks composed—
No matter, for they us enclosed.

But then discovered was this land indeed
By European men, who then had need
Of this far country. Columbus came afar,
And this before we could say, 'Ah,
What meaneth this?'—We fell in cruel hands.
Though some were kind, yet others then held bands
Of cruel oppression. Then, too, foretold our chief—
'Beggars you will become—is my belief.'
We sold, then brought some lands,
We altogether moved in foreign lands.

War ensued. They knew the handling of firearms.
Mothers spoke—no fear this breast alarms,
'They will not cruelly us oppress,
Or this our lands possess.'
Alas, it was a cruel day. We were crushed.
Into the dark, dark woods we rushed
To seek refuge.
My daughter, we are now diminished, unknown,
Unfelt. Alas, no tender tone
To cheer us when the hunt is done;
Fathers asleep—were silent, every one.

Oh, silent the honor, and fierce the fight,
When my brothers were shrouded in night;
Strangers did us invade—strangers destroyed
The fields, which were by us enjoyed.

Our country is cultured, and looks all sublime,
Our fathers are sleeping who lived in the time
That I tell. Oh, could I tell them my grief
In its flow, that in roaming we find no relief.

I love my country, and shall until death
Shall cease my breath.
Now, daughter dear, I've done.
Seal this upon thy memory; until the morrow's sun
Shall sink, to rise no more;
And if my years should score,
Remember this, though I tell no more."

* * * * * * *

George Marion McLlelan
(1860-1934)

Born in Belfast, Tennessee in 1860 into some means, G.M. McLlelan lead a busy, productive life, largely in the name of race improvement. He was extensively educated at Fisk, B.A., 1885, and M.A., 1890, and a B.D. at the Hartford (Connecticut) Theological Seminary in 1886. Although, or perhaps because, he was well educated, he was kept on the go, serving as financial agent for Fisk University seeking funds up and down the eastern seaboard, but especially in New England. He married in 1888, was a teacher and chaplain at State Normal School, Normal, Alabama, pastor at a Congregational Church in Memphis, 1897-1899; a teacher of English and Latin at Central High school in Louisville, 1911-1917. He moved to Los Angeles in 1924, devoting his last years to soliciting funds for the establishment of an anti-tubercular sanitorium for colored people.

As busy as he was, he seemed always concerned, self consciously if dutifully, that his fellow blacks be more favorably regarded by his fellow whites. Towards this end, as he admits, he wrote to counter the ignorant charges that the Negro had not contributed or could not contribute anything to American literature. His own anxiety, the extent and pace of his fund-raising travels sometimes are reflected in the hurried poems, some of which are dated Hartford, Connecticut; Longmeadow, Massachusetts; Columbus, Mississippi. Nevertheless, he published several volumes: *Poems* (Nashville, 1895); *Book of Poems and Short Stories* (Nashville, 1895); *Old Greenbottom Inn* (1896); *Songs of a Southerner* (Boston, 1896); *Path of Dreams* (Louisville, 1916). McLlelan shows genuine promise, especially in lyricism. When he does not fall into the sticky mires of sentimentalism, he is consciously subdued and controlled, as in his romantically ambitious "Legend of Tannhauser," which he here adapts for his own purposes.

If the formalism of his precise meters and restrained imagery seem sometimes dry of life, there is mitigation in the brevity of his short pieces. If his subject matter only rarely concerns racial matters, as in "A Color Bane," from *Poems,* and "A Decoration Day," from *Path of Dreams,*" he has the virtue of speaking in his own voice.

A January Dandelion

All Nashville is a chill, and everywhere
Like desert sand, when the winds blow,
There is each moment sifted through the air,
A powdered blast of January snow.
O, thoughtless dandelion, to be misled
By a few warm days to leave thy natural bed,
Was folly growth and blooming oversoon;
And yet, thou blasted yellow-coated gem,
Full many a heart has but a common boon
With thee, now freezing on thy slender stem.
When the heart has bloomed by the touch of love's warm breath
Then left and chilling snow is sifted in,
It still may beat but there is blast and death
To all that blooming life that might have been.

* * * * * * * *

The Color Bane

There was profusion in the gift
    Of beauty in her face,
And in her very form and air
    An inexpressible grace.

Her rustling silk, moire antique,
The daintless taste would please;
Her life in all appearances
Was opulence and ease.

It could be seen from head to foot,
And in her piercing eye,
That she had had advantage of
All that hard cash could buy.

But oh! it was so sad to see
That in her heart was pain,
That caste should force this Negro queen
To cold and proud disdain.

That one so beautiful as she
Could any sphere adorn,
Should so be made to hate a heart
And give back scorn for scorn.

For *all* her wealth and gifts of grace
Could not appease the sham
Of justice that discriminates
Against the blood of Ham.

* * * * * * * *

Eternity

Rock me to sleep, ye waves, and drift my boat
With undulations soft far out to sea;
Perchance where sky and wave wear one blue coat,
My heart shall find some hidden rest remote.
My spirit swoons, and all my senses cry
For Ocean's breast and covering of the sky.
Rock me to sleep, ye waves, and outward bound,
Just let me drift far out from toil and care,
Where lapping of the waves shall be the sound,
Which mingled with the winds that gently bear
Me on between a peaceful sea and sky,
To make my soothing slumberous lullaby;
Thus drifting on and on upon thy breast,
My heart shall go to sleep and rest and rest.

* * * * * * * *

Love is a Flame

Love is a flame that burns with sacred fire
  And fills the being up with sweet desire;
Yet, once the altar feels love's fiery breath,
  The heart must be a crucible till death.

Say love is life; and say it not amiss,
  That love is but a synonym for bliss.
Say what you will of love—in what refrain,
  But knows the heart 'tis but a word for pain.

* * * * * * * *

In the Heart of a Rose

I will hide my soul and its mighty love
  In the bosom of this rose,
And its dispensing breath will take
  My love where'er it goes.

And perhaps she'll pluck this rose,
  And quick as blushes start,
Will breathe my hidden secret in
  Her unsuspecting heart.

And there I will live in her embrace
  And the realm of sweetness there,
Enamored with an ecstasy
  Of bliss beyond compare.

* * * * * * * *

A September Night

The full September moon sheds floods of light,
And all the bayou's face is gemmed with stars
Save where are dropped fantastic shadows down
From sycamores and moss-hung cypress trees.
With slumberous sound the waters half asleep
Creep on and on their way, 'twixt rankish reeds,
Through marsh and lowlands stretching to the gulf.
Begirt with cotton-fields Anguilla sits

Half bird-like dreaming on his summer nest
Amid her spreading figs and roses still
In bloom with all their spring and summer hues.
Pomegranates hang with dapple cheeks full ripe,
And over all the town a dreamy haze
Drops down. The great plantations stretching far
Away are plains of cotton downy white.
Oh, glorious is this night of joyous sounds
Too full for sleep. Aromas wild and sweet,
From muscadine, late-blooming jessamine,
And roses, all the heavy air suffuse.
Faint bellows from the alligators come
From swamps afar, where sluggish lagoons give
To them a peaceful home. The katydids
Make ceaseless cries. Ten thousand insects' wings
Stir in the moonlight haze, and joyous shouts
Of Negro songs and mirth awake hard by
The cabin dance. Oh, glorious is this night.
The summer sweetness fills my heart with songs
I cannot sing, with loves I cannot speak.

(Anguilla, Mississippi, September, 1852)

* * * * * * * *

The April of Alabama

Fair Alabama, "Here we rest," thy name —
And in this stretch of oak and spotted ash,
Well said that long past swarthy tribe who came
Here, "Alabama," in these glamour wilds.
To-day thy April woods have had for me
A thousand charms, elusive loveliness,
That melt in shimmering views which flash
From leaves and buds in half-grown daintiness
From every tree and living thing there smiles
A touch of summer's glory yet to be.
Already overhead the sky resumes
Its summer softness, and a hand of light
All through the woods has beckoned with its blooms

Oh honey suckle wild and dogwood white
As bridal robes—
                  With bashful azure eyes
All full of dew-born laughing falling tears
The violets more blue than summer skies
Are rioting in vagrancy around
Beneath old oaks, old pines and sending out
Like prodigals their sweets to spicy airs.
And as to-day this loveliness for years
Unknown has come and gone. To-day it wears
Its pageantry of youth with sylvan sound
Of many forest tribes which fairly shout
Their ecstacies. But soon with summer smiles
Will such a gorgeousness of flaming hues
Bedeck those Alabama glamour wilds
As ever burst to life by rain and dews.

* * * * * * *

Day Break
from Path of Dreams, 1916

Awake! arise oh, men of my race,
    I see our morning star,
And feel the dawn-breeze on my face
    Creep inward, from afar.

I feel the dawn, with soft-like tread,
    Steal through our lingering night,
Aglow with flame our sky to spread
    In floods of morning light.

Arise! my men, be wide awake
    To hear the bugle call,
For Negroes everywhere to break
    The band that binds us all.

Great Lincoln, now with glory graced,
    All God-like with the pen,
Our chattel fetters broke, and placed
    Us in the ranks of men.

But even he could not awake
    The dead, nor make alive,
Nor change stern Nature's laws which make
    The fittest to survive.

Let every man his soul inure,
    In noblest sacrifice,
And with a heart of oak endure
    Ignoble, arrant prejudice.

Endurance, love, will yet prevail
    Against all laws of hate;
Such armaments can never fail
    Our race its best estate.

Let none make common cause with sin,
    Be that in honor bound,
For they who fight with God must win
    On every battle ground.

Though wrongs there are, and wrongs have been,
    And wrongs we still must face,
We have more friends than foes within
    The Anglo-Saxon race.

In spite of all the babel cries,
    Of those who rage and shout,
God's silent forces daily rise
    To bring his will about.

Our portion is, and yet will be,
    To drink a bitter cup
In many things, yet all must see
    The race is moving up.

Oh! men of my race, awake! arise!
    Our morning's in the air,
There's scarlet all along the skies,
    Our day breaks everywhere.

* * * * * * * *

The Sun Went Down in Beauty

The sun went down in beauty
  Beyond the Mississippi side,
As I stood on the banks of the river
  And watched its waters glide;
Its swelling currents resembling
  The longing, restless soul,
Surging, swelling, and pursuing
  Its ever receding goal.

The sun went down in beauty,
  But the restless tide flowed on,
And the phantom of absent loved ones
  Danced on the waves and were gone;
Fleeting phantoms of loved ones,
  Their faces jubilant with glee,
In the spray seemed to rise and beckon,
  And then rush on to the sea.

The sun went down in beauty,
  While I stood musing alone,
Stood watching the rushing river
  And heard its restless moan;
Longings, vague, untenable,
  So far from speech apart,
Like the endless rush of the river,
  Went surging through my heart.

The sun went down in beauty,
  Peacefully sank to rest,
Leaving its golden reflection
  On the great Mississippi's breast;
Gleaming on the turbulent river,
  In the coming gray twilight,
Soothing its restless singing,
  And kisses its waters goodnight.

(Five additional stanzas complete this poem in McLlelan's *Poems,*
1895)

A Decoration Day

The reign of death was there,
Where swept the winter winds with
    pipes and moans,
And, stretched in silence bare,
A colonnade of gray sepulchral stones.

But then it was May
And all the fields were bright and gay
    With tune
That Decoration Day,
And blossoms wore their hues and breath
    Of June.

A motley crowd that came,
But who more fit than they that once
    were slaves,
Despised, unknown to fame,
With love should decorate the
    soldiers' graves?

Black feet trod cheerily
From out the town in crowds or
    straggling bands,
And flowers waved and flaunted merrily
    From little Negro hands.

And far, far away
From home and love, deep in a silent bed,
Beneath the sky of May,
Was sleeping there, in solitude, the dead.

But for the hearts that day
Who in the distant North was sore and sighed,
Black hands, with sweets of May,
Made green the graves of those who for them died.

* * * * * * * *

from The Legend of Tannhauser and
Elizabeth

I

The Venusburg

In Germany the fabled Venusburg
A broad and fertile valley overlooked,
In fair Thuringia. . . . The minstrel knights
And nobles, skilled in voice and on the harp,
Were wont to gather in the Landgrave's hall
And there contest in song. In this fine art
The sweetest singer of Thuringia
Was young Tannahuser, who, by his fair face
And wondrous melodies in song, had won
The heart of proud Elizabeth. And yet
This noble knight was dreamy in his mood
And restless in his life, dissatisfied,
And longed for change and new experiences.

And in this dreamy mood, with harp in hand,
He passed, one day, the grotto of the Venusburg.
The great enchantress of this fateful place
Put forth her magic spells and drew him on.
And when Tannhauser raised his eyes he saw
A country beautiful and strangely new. . . .

For one long year, with ever changing scenes,
Tannhauser stayed within the Venusburg
And thought that he was happy there. The change
In shifting scenes, the wild bacchantes, and
The nymphs in mimic war, in graceful dance,
Afforded for his ever restless soul
The wild excitement which he craved. . . .

Tannhauser, now enthralled by magic spells,
Had long forgotten all his former life—
His friends, his love for fair Elizabeth,
His love for God, for Christ and righteousness,
And all the good and true which come to man
By sacrifice and overcoming sin

Were banished from his mind, so lost was he
To all the life within the Venusburg.

And yet, the restless nature of his soul
That led him into sin was destined to
Arouse him to his lost estate. One day
Tannhauser felt himself awake once more.
He fancied that he heard the clanging peals
Of church bells far away, and through his mind
There struggled back the long forgotten life; . . .
In wild appeal to Venus now he cried:
"Are these things lost to me?" And, rising from
Her couch, with quick though mild rebuke she bade
Him call to mind for her a scene less sad,
For she remembered well the world from which
She was dethroned and basely relegated to
This under-realm. Tannhauser, now aroused,
Felt all his restlessness, and would not be
Denied. In vain she wove about him now
Her magic spells. Tannhauser pleaded for
Releasement from her power, to live again
His former life, to know the natural joys,
The sorrows and the common things of earth.
In wrath she charged him with ingratitude
To her for all the lavished joys which she
Had given him. But when she saw in vain
Her wrath affected him, in softer tones
She promised him more perfect joys, and things
More beautiful. . . . With stormy passion moved,
Tannhauser seized his harp and smote the strings,
And sang in mighty voice. He pledged to sing
When in the upper world, of Venus and
Her praise alone, but to that upper world
He now must go. The great enchantress saw
Her power on him now was gone, and bade him go.
Then in a moment flashed away from him
The Venusburg and all its wondrous spells;
And, stretched full length upon the mountain side,
Tannhauser found himself too weak to rise

Up from the grassy slope at first. Confused
In mind, up to the wide blue sky he gazed,
While slowly came to him the memory
Of all his former life, the bitter truth
Of sin in going to the Venusburg. . . .
And soon the Landgrave and five minstrel knights
Drew near and recognized Tannhauser, and
With words of welcome and much kindness asked
Where he had been. "I wandered in strange lands,"
Tannhauser said. "I pray you question not,
But let me pass." The Landgrave saw his mood
And courteously forbore to further press
And question him, but pointed out how sad
Had been the princess, fair Elizabeth,
In his long absence from the hall, and asked
That he should join the coming revels of
The minstrelsy of song in Wartburg Hall. . . .

II

The Contest of Song and Love

The Landgrave's gilded hall was all bedecked
In preparation for the minstrel knights
Who would contest in skill upon the harp.
Though named were all contestants long before,
Tannhauser's name was added to the list
In recognition of his marvelous skill
And, too, in honor of his coming home. . . .

At last the hour arrived, and to the hall
The princess came. Her white, soft draperies,
Embroidered in rich colors, fell around
Her graceful form in many folds, and on
Her brow a crown of fretted gold proclaimed
Thuringia's princess, fair Elizabeth. . . .

Into the minstrel hall the noble knights
Came, bearing each his harp. Elizabeth

In queenly beauty stood with welcome smiles,
But yet with searching eyes for one above
All other knights. . . .

The Landgrave, smiling, came into the hall,
And in her joy Elizabeth herself
Threw in his arms, so great her happiness.
Together mounted they the royal seat
To wait the coming of the knights and guests,
All bidden to the feast of love and song.
When the guests had all arrived,
The Landgrave stood and said the contest was
Of love in song, and he who won should have
The hand of fair Elizabeth, he pledged;

Then came deep silence as the pages passed
The golden cup in which each minstrel dropped
A folded slip of paper with his name.
Then from the golden cup Elizabeth
Drew out a name and gave it to the page
Who raised his voice and cried,
"Herr Wolfram Eschenback in song begin."
Upon his feet Von Eschenbach arose
And to his harp's soft rippling cadences
Began to sing: first of brave knights and to
Fair ladies present in the hall. Then to
Elizabeth his pent-up soul in song
Poured out the mighty passion of his love.
He sang in noble fervor to the star
Of love embodied in the princess fair.
Applause from all the guests and minstrels rang
Save from Tannhauser, seeming lost in dreams,
From which he did not rouse until the page
Announced his name as next upon the slip
Drawn by the princess from the golden cup.

He took his harp, but hardly knowing what
He did, for wild excitement seized his mind.
Once more rose-colored mists before his eyes
Arose, and voices whispered in his ears.

He stood as blind, with throbbing heart, and swayed
As sways an oak with storm and tempest tossed.
"I, too, have seen the fount of love," he cried,
And then his vow, back in the Venusburg:
That Venus, when he sang, should be his theme,
Enchained his memory. He smote his harp
And sang with stormy music till the roof
With praise of Venus rang. Still higher rose
His voice in eulogy of fairest, then,
Of all enchantresses. At last he flung
Away his harp and cried, "I fly, I fly
Back to the Venusburg." Entranced, transfixed,
He stood, his harp unnoticed at his feet.

In horror-stricken tones the nobles cried,
"Hear him! Hear him! So to the Venusburg
This wandering knight has been. Press forward, all,
And in his blood bathe every sword." With cries
The ladies hastened from the hall, save fair
Elizabeth, who stood there shuddering
Betwixt her horror and her mighty love.
Increased the clamor and the great tumult
From every side as came the cry, "Kill him!"
And, pressing on, the nobles drew their swords
To do their deadly work. "Brave knights, stop" cried
Elizabeth; "Or else kill me. Stand back!" . . .

The nobles cried, "This fallen and false knight
You should be first indeed to scorn." She said,
"Why do you speak of me? Of this poor knight,
Of him and his salvation, you should speak.
This knight, by dreadful magic bound, can yet,
Through sorrow and repentance, break his chains,
And win forgiveness from the pitying Lord.
I plead for him, for his dear life I plead."

Tannhauser, softened by her pleading words
And his own deep remorse, bowed low his head
And wept. The knights, now softened by his grief,
More gently spoke, but still in deep reproach.

At last the Landgrave spoke with kindness and
Command, the course Tannhauser must pursue,
Because around him clung the magic spells
And dark enchantment lingered in his heart.
He must go forth and not return again
To fair Thuringia till his soul was free
From all the spells of Venus. He advised
Tannhauser to unite himself with pilgrims,
Then setting out for Rome to seek the Pope
And pray for pardon for their sins. . . .

III

The Pilgrimage and Staff

Now full of hope and deep repentance too,
Tannhauser hastened on his pilgrimage
To Rome. The road was long and rough and full
Of weariness, with none to aid him save
His staff. But his own deep remorse, also
His reborn faith in God, his reverent love
Now for Elizabeth made easy all the way. . . .

At last when many days were passed he came
To Rome. The bells were pealing forth in joy,
And anthems filled the air in promise of
The pardons for the weary pilgrim band,
As one by one they sought the presence of the Pope
And from him found the full assurance of
Forgiveness for their sins. Then came at last
Tannhauser's turn. In deep repentance now
He humbly knelt and told of all his sin:
The Venusburg, its dark and evil spells,
His wasted year, his fearful seizure in
The minstrel hall. For mercy now he begged
The Pope, and from enchantment to be freed.
But sternly spoke his papal lord, "If you
Have been into the Venusburg, and there
Enchanted by its magic powers and spells,
You will succumb again, and you may hope
For God's forgiveness when my staff puts forth

Green leaves." Struck dumb with grief and deep
   despair
Tannhauser staggered forth. In hopelessness
He fell upon the ground and wished for death. . . .

And far, far away in secret prayed
Elizabeth in agonizing love
To God that He might save Tannhauser's soul,
And bring him back to her from magic powers
Redeemed. The year passed on and bringing near
The time the pilgrims must return from Rome. . . .
Thus, day by day, down to the Virgin's shrine,
Where passed the pilgrims on their road from Rome,
She came to pray, until one day there came
Upon the wind the echo of a song
Which she well knew. "It is their song," she cried. . . .
Still onward came the pilgrims as they sang
Triumphantly of God—His mighty love,
And His forgiveness of their sins. And they,
Unseeing, passed her by while she saw them,
But saw not with them that dear pilgrim face
She sought. "No more will he return," she said,
And, with the wound of death upon her face,
She sought the palace hall to wait and die. . . .

A few more days were passed so quietly
None in the palace thought Elizabeth
Was near the end of life, or that her grief
And love were yet so great that she must die.
They thought her youth would yet assert itself
And time would bring a solace to her love,
And heal her broken heart. But scarcely was
The sun up from the glowing East when she
One morning called the Landgrave to her bed,
And all the household dear, and bade them all,
A last farewell. And while they wept for her
She closed her eyes and died. So gently did
She pass she seemed as one who slept. . . .

Wolfram von Eschenbach stood on a hill
One day above the shrine more sacred now
To him because in prayer Elizabeth
Had knelt so often there. The twilight hour
Came on and brightly shone the evening star, . . .
And, while he sang, he saw in ragged garb
A pilgrim leaning hard upon his staff
As he approached, and on his haggard face
The marks of deep despair and hopelessness.
And when the pilgrim spoke he recognized
Tannhauser, whom he kindly welcomed home.
"Tell me the story of your pilgrimage,"
He said. Briefly Tannhauser told him all,
And said, "When I have seen Elizabeth
Once more, I leave this valley never to
Return again." "Alas," Von Wolfram said,
"Elizabeth is dead. She died for you." . . .
Tannhauser fell upon the earth
With grief too much to bear. And while he lay,
Behold, swift messengers came from the Pope
And bore aloft the papal staff and sang
Of a great marvel wrought by God, for now
The staff put forth green leaves in token of
Tannhauser's full redemption from his sins.
The evening star in gentle radiance
Shone down upon the pilgrim's face at last
Reposing in the calm and peace of death.

Henrietta Cordelia Ray
(1850-1916)

A descendant of an old Cape Cod, New England family, Henrietta Ray was one of two daughters to the distinguished minister and eloquent abolitionist, Reverend Charles B. Ray of Falmouth, Massachusetts. She was carefully reared in New York, receiving an excellent traditional education which helped her to graduate from both New York University in Pedagogy and from the Sauveueur School of Languages, where she became proficient in Greek, Latin, French and German in addition to developing into an English scholar. A lifelong companion to her next older sister, Florence, she became a schoolteacher with her, serving at grammar school No. 80 while Charles L. Reason (q.v.) was principal. Teaching bored her and she preferred tending her invalided Florence, vacationing throughout New England and encouraging the antislavery work of her father. Her published works include *Commemoration Ode* or *Lincoln/ written for the occasion of the/ unveiling of the Freedman's monument/ in Memory of Abraham Lincoln/* April 14, 1876 (New York, 1893); *Sonnets* (New York, 1893); *Poems* (New York, 1887), and with her sister, *Sketch of the Life of the Rev. Charles B. Ray* (New York, 1887). Selections are from *Poems,* which reprints many of the pieces from her *Sonnets.* Miss Ray's verse shows much, perhaps too much, of her intellectualized learning in both subject matter and in routine, conventionally academic rendition. Her personal feelings are not always spontaneously evident, and when they appear, as in the sonnet to her father, parts of the translation, "Antigone and Oedipus," and some lyrics, she is by turns bookishly mannered and charmingly feminine and strongly passionate.

To My Father

A leaf from Freedom's golden chaplet fair,
We bring to thee, dear father. Near her shrine
None came with holier purpose, nor was thine
Alone the soul's mute sanction; every prayer
Thy captive brother uttered found a share
In thy wide sympathy; to every sigh
That told the bondman's need thou didst incline.
No thought of guerdon hadst thou but to bear
A long part in Freedom's strife. To see
Sad lives illumined, fetters rent in twain,
Tears dried in eyes that wept for length of days—
Ah! was not that a recompense for thee?
And now where all life's mystery is plain,
Divine approval is thy sweetest praise.

* * * * * * * *

Milton

O, poet gifted with the sight divine!
To thee 'twas given Eden's groves to pace
With that first pair in whom the human race
Their kinship claim: and angels did incline—
Great Michael, holy Gabriel—to twine
Their heavenly logic, through which thou couldst trace
The rich outpourings of celestial grace
Mingled with argument, around the shrine
Where thou didst linger, vision-rapt, intent
To catch the sacred mystery of Heaven.
Nor was thy longing vain; a soul resolved
To ponder truth supreme to thee was lent;
For thy not *sightless* eyes the veil was riv'n,
Redemption's problem unto thee well solved.

* * * * * * * *

Shakespeare

We wonder what the horoscope did show
When Shakespeare came to earth. Were planets there,
Grouped in unique arrangement? Unaware
His age of aught so marvellous, when lo!
He speaks! men listen! what of joy or woe
Is not revealed! love, hatred, carking care,
All quiv'ring 'neath his magic touch. The air
Is thick with beauteous elves, a dainty row,
Anon, with droning witches, and e'en now
Stalks gloomy Hamlet, bent on vengeance dread.
One after one they come, smiling or scarred,
Wrought by that mind prismatic to which bow
All lesser minds. They by thee would be fed,
Poet incomparable! Avon's Bard!

* * * * * * * *

Robert G. Shaw[1]

When War's red banner trailed along the sky,
And many a manly heart grew all aflame
With patriotic love and purest aim,
There rose a noble soul who dared to die,
If only Right could win. He heard the cry
Of struggling bondmen and he quickly came,
Leaving the haunts where Learning tenders fame
Unto her honored sons; for it was ay
A loftier cause that lured him on to death.
Brave men who saw their brothers held in chains,
Beneath his standard battled ardently.
O friend! O hero! thou who yielded breath
That others might share Freedom's priceless gains,
In rev'rent love we guard thy memory.

---

[1]Robert Gould Shaw (1837-1863) was the Boston born colonel of the 54th Massachusetts volunteers, the first regiment of Negro troops from a free state mustered into United States service. He was killed leading his troops on an assault on Fort Wagner, South Carolina.

Antigone and Oedipus

Slow wand'ring came the sightless sire and she,
Great-souled Antigone, the Grecian maid,
Leading with pace majestic his sad steps,
On whose bowed head grim Destiny had laid
A hand relentless; oft the summer breeze
Raised the gold tresses from her veined cheek,
As with a dainty touch, so much she seemed
A being marvelous, regal, yet meek.

Thus spake sad Oedipus: "Ah! whither now,
O daughter of an aged sire blind,
Afar from Thebes' pure, crested colonnades,
Shall we, sad exiles, rest and welcome find?
Who will look on us with a pitying eye?
But unto me sweet resignation's balm
Suff'ring and courage bring; yet moments come
When naught restored my spirit's wounded calm.

"O rare dim vales and glitt'ring sunlit caves!
O vine-clad hills soft with the flush of dawn!
O silver cataract dancing off the sea,
And shad'wy pines and silent dewy lawn!
I ne'er can see you more. Alas, alas.
But whither go we? Speak! O daughter fair;
Thou must indeed be sight unto thy sire.
Does here a temple consecrate the air?"

"My father! grieve not for our distant land."
Thus made Antigone reply: "I see
Amid the forest's music-echoing aisles,
A spot of peace and blessed repose for thee.
In solemn loftiness the towers rear
Their stately pinnacles; my eyes behold
The holy laurel decked in festive robes,
The olive pale, waving in sunset gold.

"In the green leafage, tender nightingales
Are chanting dulcet harmonies meanwhile,
In the clear river's liquid radiance
The early stars, of sheen resplendent smile.

It is a sacred spot; here we may shun
Dangers that threaten, and in sweet content
Ere we need wander more, a few short days
May in these hallowed shades be calmly spent.

"My father! sorrow not because of Fate!
Perchance the gods may kindly deign to look
With glance benignant on our mournful doom.
Together thou and I, can we not brook
Th' assaults of stern-browed Destiny? May not
The fatal mesh contain some golden thread,
Ere it be spun complete with all thy woe?
Father! my father, raise thy drooping head."

"Immortal asphodels ne'er crowned a brow
More greenlike than is thine, my peerless child,
Calm-browed Antigone. Ah, woe, sad fate!"
Then spake Antigone with aspect mild:
"My father, cease thy sadness. Wherefore grieve?
Oh, let us dream that from the azure sky,
The Gods gaze on us with a pitying glance.
O, let us hope a little ere we die."

* * * * * * *

The Dawn of Love

Within my casement came one night
The fairy Moon, so pure and white.
   Around my brow a coronet
   Of shining silver quaintly set
With rainbow gems, she there did place;
But where I turned my wistful face,
Lo! she had vanished, and my gaze
Saw naught save shadows 'mid the haze.

I felt a throb within my heart,
In which sad sorrow had no part;
   Within my soul a yearning grew;
So sweet, it thrilled me through and through.

A flute's soft warble echoed nigh,
As if an angel fluttered by;
And on my lips there fell a kiss;—
Speak! fairy Moon, interpret this!

* * * * * * *

IDYL

Sunrise

Down in the dell,
A rose-gleam fell
From azure aisles of space;
There with light tread
A maiden sped,
Sweet yearning in her face.

Amid the sheen,
The lark, I ween,
Thrilled love-lays to his mate;
The maiden sang,
Her joy notes rang;
"He cometh, so I wait."

Noontide

Upon the grass,
Soft! let her pass!
Bend back, ye purple flowers.
With fawn-like grace,
Hope in her face,
She nears those sylvan bowers—

Where sunbeams glide
This fair noontide,
And tint each bending bough,
And many a fold
Of purest gold,
Enwreathes her marble brow.

Yes! he is there!
The amber air
Grew soft with love-notes while
Such perfect peace
It ne'er should cease
Illumines her eyes and smile.

Sunset

In western skies
Rare radiance lies
Aslant from jeweled seas.
The nightingale
Tells not a tale
More tender to the breeze

Than he to her;
No thought could stir
The calm within her soul:
When life's a dream,
Does it not seem
That love can all control?

Midnight

The gem-like stars
Through fleecy bars
Send down their ambient light;
'Tis splendor's reign,
Before her fane[2]
Each suppliant kneels to-night.

The tryst is o'er,
Yet what a store
Of love the maid doth hold.
The gift is fair
As moon-kissed air,
And bright as burnished gold.

* * * * * * * *

---

[2]"fane." An archaism meaning temple or church.

III

Romantic Poets

John Boyd

இஇஇ

What little is known of the life of John Boyd is provided by C.R. Nesbitt, Esq., Deputy Secretary and Registrar of the Government of the Bahamas, a sympathetic official who saw the manuscript of Boyd's poems through a London publication in 1834. Born and reared on New Providence island, where he received a sparse education, he was largely self taught, there being no library system on the island. While he is said to have never left New Providence, one of his poems, "Vanity of Life," found its way to the February 16, 1833, pages of the Boston based *Liberator*, thereby establishing a link, however tenuous, with American blacks of the time. Anxious that Boyd's own untouched writing style, punctuation and grammar be put before the public, Nesbitt did not edit the manuscript, to the embarrassment of all concerned. *The Vision/ and other/ Poems,/ in Blank Verse/* by John Boyd/ a man of colour/ is a publishing scramble. As it is, it contains parts of a lengthy title poem, and three other shorter pieces, but pages 5-8 and 13-16 are missing; one poem, "Sketch of a Varying Evening Sky," is printed twice, and a note of errata on page 23 helps no one. Wherever and however he learned, Boyd shows genuine promise, and is often controlled throughout his conventionalized apostrophes and reflections on nature, subjects that have led other poets off into endless flights of tiresome rhapsodizing. The influence of Milton's grand sweeping view and Biblical narrative source are seen, as is neo-classical diction, but Boyd's voice is his own, and is heard clearly in "Ocean," although his habit of extravagant use of adjectives persists.

The Vision/ a Poem in Blank Verse

Argument

Description of the Celestial Regions, as they appeared in a vision to the author—allusion to the scriptural doctrine of the Saviour; description of Sin and Death in a chained and guarded state. Justice. Mercy supplicating the Deity. The happy state of Saints, and infantine innocents in Heaven. Sentinels of Heaven. Planets—the beauties of a clear starlight night. Apostrophe. A star, the harbinger of salvation in pointing out the birth place of our Saviour—led wise men of the East to Bethlehem. Reflections. The powerful intercession of Mercy in various conditions of life. Allusion to the Fall of Man. The effective intercession of Mercy in preventing, until the fulness of time, the Destruction of the World. Address to the Deity. Conclusion.

Methought the Moon, pale regent of the sky,
Crested, and filled with lucid radiance,
Flung her bright gleams across my lowly couch;
And all of Heaven's fair starry firmament
Delightful shone in hues of glittering light,
Reflecting, like to fleecy gold, the dewy air.
In this my vision was a space ethereal,
Thickly inlaid with beams of massive gold:
And gems of varied shapes and lustre,
Irradiating from a central halo,
Illumining the measureless expanse;
Precincting where the Sire invisible
His ancient seat holds of Omnipotence:
In sacred inaccessible realms of light,
Imperviously screen'd from human sight;
And even from Angel's superior ken.
There, at the base of a stupendous dome,
Myriads of the empyreal host,
Cherubs and Angels, with Archangels joined,
Raised the loud strain of harmony divine,
And hymned afar the almighty power!
Fervent hosannas struck the astonish'd ear,
As when in the midhour of calmest night,

Stillness pervadeth the awakened wave,
Roused by the secret power that moves the deep,
It heaves its loud surge on the sounding shore;
And distant 'wakes the slumbering Mariner
With its reverberating awful tones!
Thus repercussive rung th' harmonic strain,
And died away amidst th' ethereal choir!
Far on the right, pre-eminent and meek,
On the throne of heaven's imperial Sire,
Sat the all-righteous, immaculate,
Once bleeding, suffering Christ Saviour of Man—
Encircled with glory's resplendent beams,
Which, dazzling sheen played around his crown;—
In rich effulgence and majestic state,
There all collected shone the vast splendor
Of unnumbered orbs of light celestial,
Beaming, and forming his grand tiara;
While at his feet, the broken crimsoned cross
Of crucifixion lay, whereon he bled
For Man—a great memorial of his love!
In dark and dreary realms, below the belt
Of heaven's immense and thronged highway,
Far, far exiled, grim Death and ghastly Sin
Lay coiled, like snakes in one huge scaly fold,
Shorn of their direful envenomed stings;
'Waiting the sentence of the Judge Supreme,—
Pondering on their inexpiable doom,—
Racked with despair, and fell internal rage,
Potent no more to delude and torment
The frail offspring of Eden's hapless pair,
Both chained and guarded, there they helpless lay!
Then stern-eyed Justice with her golden scales,
Conspicuous in equal balance hung,
Poises the fixed fate of Men and Spirits;
In her potent right hand she brandishes
A flaming, sharp, two-edged sword of fire
The good to separate from the bad profane.
There, too, sat dove-eyed Mercy! Soft-smiling
Through tears—with blandest purity of tone,

On suppliant knees at the empyreal throne!
The dew-drops of mild compassion pouring—
Now serene, and breathing hope and love divine,
As the Sire of heaven her ceaseless plea approves.
These are th' eternal attributes of God,
The moral agents of his sacred will,
Of his fiat on the final doom of Man:
There holy Saints chaunt celestial strains,
And swell the grand chorus of heaven's choir!
Saints, once like us, frail mortal men on earth,
The penal curse on Adam doomed to suffer,
During their toilsome pilgrimage below;

     . . . . . .

E'en here let us pause, and deeply ponder
On the wondrous, mystic combination,
That mitigates grim death's envenom'd sting,
And redeems from the angry penal curse,
On Adam past, by th' Eternal's decree.
In the wide vista of life's chequer'd scene,
Mercy preserves the component accordance
Of this sphere, and sets the grace of heaven
Vivid in the moral excellence of man;
Far as creation's ample space extends.
When pestilence shakes her dark raven wing,
And points her desolating, devouring beak;
When stern war spreads his sanguiferous arms
Far o'er the earth, then mercy hovers near,
And sheds balm from her renovating wings;
Thence hope, and heartfelt joy, life's vital springs,
Lift the weak mourner from his couch of gloom,
And bear his uplifted heart to heaven's realms!
What, but mercy, the universe preserves?
When the black cup of turpitude o'erflows,
And man, Cain-like, thirsts for his brother's blood;
When fraught with lust, and fell remorseless ire,
Oppression, insatiate of despoil,
Broods ill, then mercy stops the arm of fate,
And inverts the hideous, woe-engend'ring scene.

When grief's sharp anguish, and care's rankling dart,
Struck deep their poison in my suffering breast,
Death's cold grasp had quenched the vital flame,
But mercy, triumphant, spread her light wings,
And fann'd again to life the expiring spark!
Oh mercy! ethereal maid! thee I invoke!
Inspire my strain, and let me sing thy charms;
Sing how thou sooth'st the agonies of man,
And fill'st the empyrean realms above
With the fount-streams of charity and love.
Fair shines the God-born maid! a beam of grace
In golden radiance crowns her hallow'd brows;
Suppliant, watching with inquiring gaze,
Ev'ry movement of unceasing active fate;
And soft'ning the rigours of stern-ey'd justice,
With soft pity's gentlest embalming tear.
At that memorable, eventful hour,
Pregnant with impending woe, when the first pair
Drew down, and seal'd the angry curse of heav'n
On the frail and sinful issue of their loins;
When grim-featur'd Satan smil'd in ghastly mood,
And roused the choir of hell to frantic joy;
When each imp skipt widly o'er the dire precincts,
With hellish glee exulting at the thought
Of final triumph o'er the race of Man—
'Twas then, when all nature, shuddering, shrank
At the foul and terrific infanticide,
That mercy her covering arms outspread,
And arrested vengeance's consuming course!
Else had planet o'er planet clustering,
Fled from their orbits, and burst in ruin—
Each star had fled from its sphere, flinging fierce fires
In conflict rude o'er the astonish'd globe!
The sun, moon, and all the host of heaven,
Had else shut up their lights, or pour'd effluent
Floods of combustion, and destruction dire,
Prone through the expansive air, o'er earth and sea.
The sharp light'ning's flash—the comet's glare—
Had rack'd creation's basis to its centre,

And chaos spread again his viewless void!
But Mercy, beauteous attribute of God—
Mercy! seraph-daughter of the highest heav'n,
Soften'd stern justice, and pardon pled for man.
Lo! the immortal soul stain'd and polluted,
Lab'ring under the afflicting curse of sin,
Is with the mystic hyssop purged and cleans'd—
Is spiritualiz'd, and meet for heav'n.
To thee, oh Mercy, then be the meed of praise,
That blooms in time and in eternity!
For man draws nearer to his eternal source
When he th' influence of thy spirit breathes.
Great source of being! whose stupendous power
Rolls like thy thunder through the plural worlds,
Let me raise a grateful votive hymn to thee,
And with thy praise immortalize my song!
Ethereal harpers, who the empyrean throng,
Aid me to swell the sweet hosanna-lay
And glorify the unborn Spirit of Being!
Angels of light, unfold your radiant wings!
Ye gales of symphony, join the vocal choir!
Cerulean waves! and you, ye starry host
Of heaven! join in unison with me,
And loudly chaunt the superb hymn of praise,
To him who tracks your path, and bids you flow!
All that breathe the vital air, raise the strain
To him who call'd you into being, feeds you
With his care, and cheers the tenor of your days
With joy, and ev'ry attribute of love!

Sketch of a Varying Evening Sky

The lucid night effulgent glows,
    Amid the cerulean sky!
O'er the expanse her radiance flows,
    From the flame-filled founts on high!
White clouds float in the atmosphere,
    And curtain the light realms of air.

What varying forms the clouds assume,
   As they hover o'er the fields of space!
Like craggy mountains wrapt in gloom,
   And now like steeds in any race—
Now in fantastic forms they throng,
   Borne by the airy breeze along!

Yon star is wrapt in a dark cloud,
   Enveloped in a hazy gloom,
That hangs over her, like a shroud
   On those who've ripened for the tomb—
And now its passeth far away,
   Again she shines with splendid ray!

So the bright star of virtue beams,
   Serene in the clear sky of life,
Till adverse clouds obscure her gleams,
   And mists o'erspread her, dense and rife—
But soon the clouds disperse and fly,
   Still she shines in her native sky!

Ocean

When the fiat of the most High,
Thy fountains burst, and copiously
Thy secret springs, with ample store,
Pour'd forth their waves from shore to shore
Wide as the waters roll, oh, wave.
And in their sweep great empires lave,
Beneath the blue outstretched sky,
Whose measureless space doth fill the eye;
Fast as the winged breeze expands,
O'er thee to far-distant lands,
Resistless did thy currents flow,
On the unfathom'd depths below;
Circling with the horizon round,
Thou flowedest with murmuring sound:
Thy dark-blue wave still onward goes,
And scorns to rest in dull repose;

Glittering in the sunbeam of day,
And urging on thy wonted way
At night thy billows running high,
Foam to the stars that light the sky.
Beneath the concave firmament,
Flow ceaseless on, swift element;
As in nature's primeval hour,
Thy all-ruling mighty power
From the ethereal fount pour'd down
Thy waves, the deep abyss to crown!
Great highway of nations scattered round!
Thou vast elemental profound!
Mankind dispers'd in various lands
By thee are drawn in social bands;
Heart communes with heart, knowledge speeds
From clime to clime, and noble deeds
Of aged past, are borne afar
From the east to the western star.
Varied tribes of the scaly brood
People thy realm in infinitude.
The flying fish, by instinct hurled,
Winged vistant to either world,
(Amphibious of sea and air
And unconfin'd to either sphere.)
Darts its fast-fleeting form along,
The wonder of the finny throng;
The huge leviathan of the deep
That ploughs the wave with ample sweep;
The dolphin's variegated dye
Pictures hues of sea, light, and sky.
Lo! the extended ocean vales
Are studded thick with floating sails,
Bounding over the dark azure course
And passing on with wafted force.
Now the billowy mountains rise
Curling to the dark-palled skies!
Now the dense sleet begins to pour,
Lightnings flash, and sea-waves roar,

Thunders peal, and loud commotion
Spreads dismay o'er the dreary ocean!
At length the Storm has spent its powers,
The cloudless sun now gilds the hour;
The heavens smile—the gale subsides:
The sea impels her temperate tides—
Wave mounts on waves in milder bound
And the clear horizon around
Joins with the waves that greet the sky,
In concert of renewed joy!
Nor less in thoughts of grateful love,
Human hearts enraptur'd move,
Extolling him while high decree
Controls the winds, and rules the sea!
The spheres of water and of air,
Most mysteriously cohere,
As if worlds of sea and sky were join'd,
The earthly to the unearthly kind.
O! 'tis romantic to view the scene,
When the smooth ocean-wave rolls serene,
And links the firmament's kind kindred hue
With its own ethereal mass of blue!
When the mind's eye looks and drinks its fill,
From the brown-peak of some lofty hill,
Angels might rejoice the sight to scan,
And yet 'tis given to thankless man.

The Creole Poets

The late Dr. E. Maceo Coleman of Morgan State College has brought several of the early 19th century Creole poets of New Orleans to the attention of readers in his *Creole Voices* (Washington, D.C., 1945). There have been other notices of the group, but these poets and prose writers deserve even more consideration, for, fully examined, they constitute something of a genuine minor literary movement that, studied, would help illuminate the general development of American Negro literature. It has its literary, psychological and sociological interests, for instance, to chart their recorded feelings that were designed to accommodate the moods, sensibilities and tastes of a group of people who were classified as neither Negroes nor white.

Their poetry does not seem at all typically American, but mostly Continental, specifically and understandably French. Their work is strikingly melodious, highly sophisticated, even pretentious expressions of romantic love or carnival gaiety or of airy intimacies. Not so much, if at all, do they write of the fact, clear to most, that despite their mixture of Spanish and French blood, their classical training and writings in French and Spanish, Latin and Greek, and despite their wealth, derived in some instances from the number of slaves they owned, they were still subject to the indignities from a prejudiced dominant society. When racial realities became unbearably obvious and intractable, some of them, affluent and creatively inspired enough, left New Orleans and America for their spiritual motherland, France. Others, of different temperaments, remained, adapted, and made commercially inventive and/or cultural contributions; one of them, Joanni Questy, besides extensive journalism and teaching languages, wrote *Paul,* an unpublished novel.

Their poetry, represented by four of their poets here, first appeared in a volume, *Les Cenelles* (New Orleans, 1845), "the first published anthology of Negro verse in America," as Charles Rousseve in his *The Negro and Louisiana* (Xavier University Press, New Orleans, 1937) recognized. Armand Lanusse (1812-1867) was born and died in New Orleans, having contributed to local Creole newspapers, *L'Union* and *La Tribune* and, after serving as a conscripted Confederate soldier, he divided his time between his duties as principal of the Catholic School for Indigent Orphans of Color until 1866, and urging his fellows to contribute their poetry for the publication of *Les Cenelles.* Victor Séjour was born 1817 in New Orleans, but having a wealthy father he was able to escape local racial frustrations and go to France, where except for brief visits to his mother in New Orleans, he lived for the rest of his life, which was cut short by tuberculosis in 1874. In France he was a very popular dramatist, twenty-one of his best plays being staged there, the first in 1844. In the 1850's, at least three of his plays were produced in New Orleans. A companion to several major French literary figures, praised for his literary merit by Napoleon III, he speaks from a broader, more politically oriented viewpoint than do his fellow Creoles. Vital statistics concerning Nelson Debrosses are not available, which seems in keeping with his Haitian gained experience in Voodoo, aspects of which he practised in New Orleans. There is not much known either of Nicol Riquet, who is said to have spent his entire life in New Orleans, where he was a cigarmaker by trade and a genial, prolific writer of light poetic pieces by avocation.

Un Frère
Au Tombeau de Son Frère
(25 Deptembre 1836)
(Armand Lanusse)

Bien loin de tes parens, sur la rive étrangère,
La Mort a sur ton front fait tournoyer sa faux;
Et moi, je suis venu, dans ma douleur amère,
Demander à ces croix, ces saules, ces tombeaux:
    "Où repose mon frère?—

"C'est donc ici—pleurons—qu'une larme sincère
Arrose le gazon qui couvre ton cercueil!
Loin de moi, d'autres mains ont fermé ta paupière
Quand de la vie, hélas! tu franchissais le seuil,
    Mon infortuné frère!—

"A vingt-six ans, Numa, tu finis ta carrière!
Mais tes nombreaux amis toujours te pleureront.
Au seul ressouvenir de ton franc caractère
Crois-moi, longtemps encour leurs coeurs palpiteront—
    Dors en paix, mon bon frère!

"Non, je ne doute point de ce divin mystère:
Nous devons tous au ciel, un jour, nous réunir.
Tranquilles et contens auprès de notre mère,
D'un bonheur éternel là nous pourrons jouir.—
    Au revoir, mon cher frère!"

Translation of Arman Lanusse's
Un Frère/Au Tombeau de Son Frère

(Far from your people and on some foreign place, unfeeling Death
has cut you down; and in my biting grief I come seeking among these
crosses, these willows, these tombs—"Where is my brother's resting
place?" And this is it. Then let my tears take my feelings into the
ground that covers you. O, hapless brother, you were far from me
when, some other hand shutting your eyelids, you crossed the
threshold blind. O, Numa, at only twenty six your life has ended, but
a greater number of friends will always weep for you. Remembering
but once your free soul, and, Numa, believe me, their hearts will beat
often enough for you—then sleep in peace, good brother. Also, I do
not doubt divine concern at all: we shall, brother, friends and all, be
together in heaven one day, where, in calm content, beside our
mother, we shall know eternal joy. Until then, my beloved brother.
Translated by Richard Allsop and William H. Robinson.)

Le Retour de Napoléon
Victor Séjour
I

Comme la vaste mer grondant sous le tropique,
Le peuple se rua sur la place publique,
    En criant le voilà!
Un cercueil!–O douleur!–Un cercueil pour cet homme,
Qui fit de sa patrie une seconde Rome!–
    O douleur! Tout est là.

Quand naguère il rentrait vainqueur dans nos murailles,
Le front ceint des lauriers de deux mille batailles,
    Simple dans sa grandeur;
Ce même peuple, hélas! pressé sur son passage,
Saluait sa venue, exaltait son courage,
    Et rayonnait de sa splendeur.

Oh! c'est alors, alors que la France était belle!–
Elle passait: les rois s'inclinaient devant elle,
Comme les épis mûrs sous le souffle du vent.
Elle allait, elle allait semblable à la tempête,
Et le monde ébranlé, devenant sa conquête,
    Etait derrière, elle devant.

Plus rien.–Tout est fini.–Salut, ô capitaine;
Salut, ô mon consul à la mine hautaine.
Tu fus auguste et grand, tu fus superbe et beau;
Tu dépassas du front Annibal et Pompée,
L'Europe obéissait au poids de ton épée–
Comment peux-tu tenir dans cet étroit tombeau?

Pleurez, peuple, pleurez;–il est là, triste et pâle,
Comme le froid linceul de sa couche fatale;
Pleurez votre Cesar, l'intrépide guerrier;
Pleurez.–Le soldat meurt sur le champ de bataille,
Emporté, l'arme au bras, par l'ardente mitraille;
    Il est mort prisonnier.

Ah! quand, seul et pensif, debout sur Sainte-Hélène,
Ses regards se tournaient vers la France lointaine,
    Comme vers une étoile d'or;
Son front s'illuminait d'un souvenir de flamme;
Il s'écriait: "mon Dieu, je donnerais mon âme,
    Pour le revoir encor.

"Non, non, ce n'est pas moi que l'indignée Angleterre,
"Comme un lion captif, retient sur cette terre:
    "Noble France, c'est toi.
"C'est toi, ton avenir, ta puissance, tes gloires,
"Tes vingt ans de combat, tes vingt ans de victoires;
    "Ce n'est pas moi, ce n'est pas moi!"

II

    Oh! ne le laisse point, ô France,
    Attendre en vain sa délivrance—
    Couvre-toi de ton bouclier
    Tiens, voici ton cheval de guerre;
    Rapide comme le tonnerre,
    Va délivrer le prisonnier.

Peuple, réveillons-nous,—poussons le cri d'alarmes—
Soldats, vieux vétérans, couvrex-vous de vos armes.
    Au nom de votre honneur,
Ne laissons point, Français, s'endormir notre haine;
Nous avons deux proscrits au roc de Sainte-Hélène,
    La gloire et l'empereur.

III

Mais non, il est trop tard;—sur le nouveau calvaire,
La mort a foudroyé le géant populaire;
    Il est mort, il est mort!
Accablé, délaissé, trahi par sa patrie;
En murmurant: "Je meurs, ô ma France chérie,
    Et, malgré moi, je pleure sur ton sort."

IV

On nous rend son cercueil! Flétrissante ironie!—
Ah! notre honneur, Français, touche à son agonie!
Nous devrions rougir, car son propre bourreau,
Après avoir creusé sous ses pieds un abîme,
Apres s'être repu du sang de la victime,
        Nous fait l'aumône du tombeau.

Nous devrions rougir, nous, peuple qu'on renomme,
D'oser nous approcher des restes du grand homme,
        L'insulte sur le front;
D'oser lever les yeux, quand, d'une main punique,
On nous rend, d'un part, sa dépouille héroïque;
        De l'autre, on nous jette un affront.

Honte à nous! Ill fallait le laisser dans son île;
Loin de nos lâchetés il reposait tranquille—
Ou bien, pour le ravoir, lui couvert de lauriers,
Lui vainqueur d'Austerlitz, lui le fils de la gloire,
Ill fallait, l'arme au bras, conduit par la victoire,
        Le ramener dans nos foyers,

C'eût été digne et beau!—le tambour, la mitraille,
Nos soldats chauds encor d'une grande bataille,
        Le poudre et le canon,
La France relevée, et l'infâme Angleterre,
Expiant ses forfaits les deux genoux en terre—
C'est ainsi qu'il fallait fêter Napoleon.

N'importe, il est ici! Courage, noble France,
On ne peut prolonger ta honte, ta souffrance,
        Car sur le marbre du tombeau,
Ravivant dans nos coeurs notre haine trompée,
Nous irons, jeunes, vieux, aiguiser notre épée,
        Ebréchée à Waterloo!!

The End

Translation of Victor Séjour's Le Retour de Napoléon
The Return of Napoleon

(As the sea groans under the burning sun, the people wail and writhe about the public place, moaning, "There it is. A coffin for the man who made his country a second Rome. All our glory's there." Not long ago, he rode round inside our walls, victorious, his brow green with laurels of two thousand battles won, yet simple in his grandeur, these same crowds swarming about his every pathway, hailing his arrival, exalting his valor, thrilling from his splendour. Oh, it was then that France was magnificent! Inexorably she rose, kings bowed before her like so many rows of unripened corn beneath a swift oncoming breeze. And on and on she swept, an unleashed tempest wild, and the whole world shaken, adding to her conquests, was left behind, and France moved on ahead. No more. All is over. All that glory's gone. Yet, hail, O, captain! Hail, my consul of proud bearing. You were august, you were grand, you were superb and glorious too. You surpassed even Hannibal and Pompey, all of Europe bowed down beneath the weight of your sword—how then can you be held down within this narrow tomb? Weep, France, weep; he *is* there, drear as the cold shrouds of his stone resting place. Weep for your Caesar, dashing warrior; weep—. The soldier, sword in hand, in the middle of the cannon roar, the Soldier dies on the field of battle; he died a prisoner. Ah, when, alone and pensive, brooding on Saint Helena, his thoughts turned toward distant France as if he were looking for a golden star, his brow burned with the flame of memory; he cried, "My God, I would give my soul to see France once more. No, it is not I whom the vexed English hold on this island like some captive lion; Noble France, it is you, your destiny, your powers, your glories, your twenty red years of struggle, your twenty bright years of victories. It is not I, it is not I." II. Then do not, O France, do not let him await his deliverance in vain. Now, up with your shields, into your saddles of war horses, like struck lightning go now and deliver up the prisoner. Up, Frenchmen! Up! Blast forth the battle cries. Soldiers, hardened veterans, to arms in the name of our French honor, no time now to let righteous anger sleep—we have two in shameful exile there on the rock of Saint Helena: Glory! The Emperor!

III. But no, no, it is too late now. Like a modern crucifixion, death has lightning struck the people's giant. He is head. He is dead.

Overwhelmed, deserted, betrayed by his own country, sighing, "I die, beloved France, but, fight my tears as I may, I weep for your now darkened destiny." IV. We are left with his coffin. Disgraceful. Ah, France, our injured honor writhes in its own agony. She should redden in shame that his very executioner, having dug an abyss beneath his feet, and having glutted himself with his victim's blood, tosses us the charity, the alms of a corpse. We should redden with due shame, we, the people once renowned around the world, if we dare approach these still remains of that great man, with such insults still on our brows; if we should dare to raise our bowed heads, when, from one treacherous hand, we are given—and we accept—these heroic spoils, and, from another, we are tossed—and we accept— insults. Shame to us and ours. It might have been better to have left him on his island, far from such cowardice—he might have rested there in a better peace than this. Or else, to reclaim him, once covered with victory laurels, him, conqueror of Austerlitz, him, child of glory, we should have—sword in hand—made victory accompany his return to our households. That would have been proper!—the drum, the cannon's roar, our soldiers still flushed from the heat of battle, powder and grapeshot, and France again supreme, while wretched England expiated her sins, grovelling on her knees—that, and only that, is the way we should have hailed Napoleon. No matter, he is here. Courage, noble France, such shame and suffering will not last forever for, our wrath once spent out on the marble of his tomb, and our hearts will burn again for action, and we shall arise, young and old, to sharpen and hone our greatest swords that were blunted at Waterloo. Translated by William H. Robinson.)

Le Retour au Village aux Perles
Nelson Debrosses

Elle folâtre en ces lieux pleins de charmes,
Tout me le dit, oui, mon coeur le sent bien.
Séjour joyeux, tu bannis mes alarmes,
Dieu des armours, quel bonnheur est le mien!

Bosquet fleuri, témoin de notre flamme,
Je te revois, ce n'est point une erreur,
Ruisseau chéri, c'est à toi que mon âme
Veut en ce jour confier son bonheur.

Mais la voila! comme elle est embellie;
Ah! que d'attraits, que d'aimables appas!
Elle sourit,—combien elle est jolie!
Charmante Emma, je vole sur tes pas.

Mars 1828

The End

Translation of Nelson Desbrosses' Le Retour au Village aux Perles

Return to the Village of Pearls

    (Her spirit dances here and there in these enchanting places. Yes, everything reflects a memory of her whom I feel so deeply within me. How it delights me here! O, God of love, who sweeps away my fears, such joy is mine! And see!—O, I am sure of it—that flower-bosomed grove again, the witness of our secret passion, and, too, the cherished brook to which my soul would on this day confide its happy memory. But look! There she is! And how enriched is her beauty. Ah, what enchantment, what disarming grace! She smiles—how beautiful she is. Darling Emma, I leap to your embrace. Translated by Richard Allsop.)

Rondeau Redoublé
Aux Franc Amis
Nicol Riquet

De francs amis demandent un rondeau.
Allons, ma muse, il faut faire merveille!
N'écrivons plus désormais pour de l'eau,
De bon vin vieux on nous paiera bouteille.

Pour t'obtenir, ô doux jus de la treille!—
Il faut rimer dans un genre nouveau,
Il ne faut pas ici que je sommeille,
De francs amis demandent un rondeau.

De vin Bacchus nous promet un tonneau,
De fleurs l'Amour nous offre une corbeille;
Du dieu du vin j'aime mieux le cadeau,
Allons, ma muse, il faut faire merveille!

La nuit souvent pour écrire je veille,
Au jour, mes vers tombent dans l'eau; c'est beau!
Dès à présent, muse, je te conseille,
N'écrivons plus désormais pour de l'eau.

Je sens sortir du fond de mon cerveau
Un nouveau vers à rime sans pareille;
Allons toujours, nous ferons un tableau:
De bon vin vieux on nous paiera bouteille.

A la censure, hélas! qui nous surveille,
Vite en passant ôtons notre chapeau,
A ses discours ouvrons bien notre oreille
Pour n'être pas nommé poètereau—
    De francs amis.

Translation of Nicol Riquet's
Rondeau Redoublé

Double Rondeau
To Candid Friends

(My candid friends are calling for a rondeau! Come, Muse, we must work a wonder! No more shall what we write be cast into the wash, rather we shall reap reward in rich ready wine. And for that prize, the sweet juice of the vine, we must now rime in an uncommon way. This poet must not nod—his candid friends are calling for a rondeau! Bacchus promises a great cask of wine, and Venus too makes offer of a gift of flowers, but I would rather have the favor of the God of wine. So come, Muse, we must work a wonder. I often sit up late into the night to write, and yet by light of day my lines are cast into the wash! Muse, let us resolve from this point forward never more to write lines for the wash. I can feel, struggling up from the depths of my mind, a new word-music with a matchless rime. Let us press on and we will produce a pretty picture: and reap reward in rich and ready wine. Let us acknowledge with our bow that censure, alas, that still hangs over us, and pass it quickly by, but let us keep an ear open to those opinions, lest we earn the name of poetaster—from our candid friends. Translated by Richard Allsop.)

George B. Vashon
(1822-1878)

A prominent teacher, lecturer, lawyer and writer, George B. Vashon finished Oberlin college with an A.B. in 1844 and an M.A. in 1849. For a while he taught, as one of three Negro professors, at New York Central College, an Abolitionist supported institution (the other two Negro professors were Charles L. Reason, and William G. Allen), then at College Faustin, Port-au-Prince, Haiti. Having been admitted to the New York bar in 1847, he settled down to practice in Syracuse, interrupting that career to become principal of a Negro school in Pittsburgh, Pennsylvania, where he met and married Susan Paul Smith, Boston trained daughter of a prominent musician who once played a command performance for Queen Victoria. Returning to his legal training, he was dean of the Howard University Law school until he left for Mississippi, where in Rodney, he succumbed to an epidemic of yellow fever on October 5, 1878.

Vashon contributed to various publications, including the distinguished *Anglo-African Magazine* which led an on-again, off-again career from 1859 through the Civil War. The impact of the French Revolution, 1789-1799, reverberated to its colonies in the Caribbean, where the mulattoes, free men of color, of whom Vincent Ogé was one, felt compelled to resort to armed revolution against white colonialists to secure the freedom which they believed was theirs as put forth in a decree passed by the National Assembly, March 27, 1790. Affluent, well educated in France, Ogé refused the advice of Thomas Clarkson and Abbé Gregoire, English and French anti-slavery agents, and rashly returned to Santo Domingo to help lead a short-lived armed uprising. When the revolution failed, and he was refused refuge in Spanish Santo Domingo, whose authorities handed him over to island French authorities, Ogé was broken on the wheel, drawn and quartered, the four parts of his body hung up in four leading cities of the island. Twenty-one followers were condemned to the gallows, seventeen others were sent to the galleys, their considerable property holdings confiscated. Vashon has undoubted strength and, in places, considerable skill, but he seems especially effective in his general control of sentiment.

from Vincent Ogé

(Fragments of a poem hitherto unpublished, upon a revolt of the free persons of color, in the island of Santo Domingo (now Haiti), in the years 1790-1791.)

There is, at times, an evening sky—
  The twilight's gift—of sombre hue,
All checkered wild and gorgeously
  With streaks of crimson, gold and blue; . . .

So glorious that, when night hath come
  And shrouded it in deepest gloom,
We turn aside with inward pain
And pray to see that sky again.
Such sight is like the struggle made
When freedom bids unbare the blade,
And calls from every mountain glen—
  From every hill—from every plain,
Her chosen ones to stand like men,
And cleanse their souls from every stain
Which wretches, steeped in crime and blood,
Have cast upon the form of God.
Though peace like morning's golden hue,
  With blooming groves and waving fields,
Is mildly pleasing to the view,
  And all the blessings that it yields
Are fondly welcomed by the breast
  Which find delight in passion's rest,
That breast with joy forgoes them all,
While listening to Freedom's call.
Though red the carnage,—though the strife
Be filled with groans of parting life,—

Though battle's dark, ensanguined skies
Give echo but to agonies—
    To shrieks of wild despairing,—
We willingly repress a sigh—
Nay, gaze with rapture in our eye,
Whilst "Freedom!" is the rally-cry
    That calls to deeds of daring.

                    . . .

The waves dash brightly on thy shore,
    Fair island of the southern seas!
As bright in joy as when of yore
    They gladly hailed the Genoese,—
That daring soul who gave to Spain
    A world—last trophy of her reign!

Basking in beauty, thou dost seem
A vision in a poet's dream!
Thou look'st as though thou claim'st not birth
With sea and sky and other earth,
That smile around thee but to show
Thy beauty in a brighter glow,—

                    . . .

If Eden claimed a favored haunt,
    Most hallowed of that blessed ground,
Where tempting fiend with guileful taunt
    A resting-place would ne'er have found,—
As shadowing it well might seek
    The loveliest home in that fair isle,
Which in its radiance seemed to speak
    As to the charmed doth Beauty's smile,
That whispers of a thousand things
    For which words find no picturings. . .

A home where balmy airs might float
    Through spicy bower and orange grove;
Where bright-winged birds might turn the note
    Which tells of pure and constant love;
Where earthquake stay its demon force,
    And hurricane its wrathful course;

Where numph and fairy find a home,
And foot of spoiler never come.

. . .

And Ogé stands mid this array
Of matchless beauty, but his brow
Is brightened not by pleasure's play;
He stands unmoved—nay, saddened now,
As doth the lorn and mateless bird
That constant mourns, whilst all unheard,
The breezes freightened with the strains
Of other songsters sweep the plain,—
That never breathes forth a joyous note,
Though odors on the sephyrs float—
The tribute of a thousand bowers,
Rich in their store of fragrant flowers.
Yet Ogé's was a mind that joyed
With nature in her every mood,
Whether in sunshine unalloyed
With darkness, or in tempest rude.
And, by the dashing waterfall,
Or by the gently flowing river,
Or listening to the thunder's call,
He'd joy away his life forever.
But ah, life is a changeful thing,
And pleasures swiftly pass away,
And we may turn, with shuddering,
From what we sighed for yesterday.

The guest, at banquet-table spread
With choicest viands, shakes with dread,
Nor heeds the goblet bright and fair,
Nor tastes the dainties rich and rare,
Nor bids his eye with pleasure trace
The wreathed flowers that deck the place,
If he but knows there is a draught
Among the cordials, that, if quaffed,
Will send swift poison through his veins.
So Ogé seems; nor does his eye

With pleasure view the flowery plains,
The bounding sea, the spangled sky. . .

The loud shouts from the distant town,
Joined in with nature's gladsome lay;
The lights went glancing up and down,
Rivalling the stars—nay, seemed as they
Could stoop to claim, in their high home,
   A sympathy with things of earth,
And had from their bright mansions come,
   To join them in their festal mirth.
For the land of the Gaul had arose in its might,
And swept by as the wind of a wild, wintry night;
And the dreamings of greatness—the phantoms of power,
Had passed in its breath like the things of an hour.
Like the violet vapors that brilliantly play
Round the glass of the chemist, then vanish away,
The visions of grandeur which dazzlingly shone,
Had gleamed for a time, and all suddenly gone.
And the fabric of ages—the glory of kings,
Accounted most sacred mid sanctified things,
Reared up by the hero, preserved by the sage,
And drawn out in rich hues on the chronicler's page,
Had sunk in the blast, and in ruins lay spread,
While the altar of freedom was reared in its stead.
And a spark from that shrine in the free-roving breeze,
Had crossed from Fair France to that isle of the seas;
And a flame was there kindled which fitfully shone
Mid the shout of the free, and the dark captive's groan;
As, mid contrary breezes, a torch-light will play,
Now streaming up brightly—now dying away.
     . . .

The reptile slumbers in the stone,
Nor dream we of his pent abode;
The heart conceals the anguished groan,
   With all the poignant griefs that goad

The brain to madness;
Within the hushed volcano's breast,
    The molten fires of ruin lie;—
Thus human passions seem at rest,
    And on the brow serene and high
        Appears no sadness.

But still the fires are raging there,
Of vengeance, hatred, and despair;
And when they burst, they wildly pour
Their lava flood of woe and fear,
And in one short—one little hour,
Avenge the wrongs of many a year.

        . . .

And Ogé standeth in his hall;
    But now he standeth not alone;—
A brother's there, and friends; and all
    Are kindred spirits with his own;
For mind will join with kindred mind,
As matter's with its like combined.
They speak of wrongs they had received—
Of freemen, of their rights bereaved;
And as they pondered over the thought
Which in their minds so madly wrought,
Their eyes gleamed as the lightning's flash,
Their words seemed as the torrent's dash
That falleth, with a low deep sound,
Into some dark abyss profound,—
A sullen sound that threatens more
Than other torrents' louder roar.
Ah! they had borne well as they might,
    Such wrongs as freemen ill can bear;
And they had urged both day and night,
    In fitting words, a freeman's prayer;
And when the heart is filled with grief,
    For wrongs of all true souls accursed,
In action it must seek relief,
    Or else, o'ercharged, it can but burst.

Why blame we them, if oft they spake
Words that were fitted to awake
The soul's high hopes—its noblest parts—
The slumbering passions of brave hearts,
And send them as the simoom's[1] breath,
    Upon a work of woe and death?

And woman's voice is heard amid
    The accents of that warrior train;
And when has woman's voice ever bid,
    And man could from its hest refrain?
Hers is the power over his soul
    That's never wielded by another,
And she doth claim this soft control
    As sister, mistress, wife, or mother.
So sweetly doth her soft voice float
    O'er hearts by guilt or anguish riven,
Its seemeth as a magic note
    Struck from earth's harps by hands of heaven.
And there's the mother of Ogé,
    Who with firm voice, and steady heart,
And look unaltered, well can play
    The Spartan mother's hardy part;
And send her sons to battlefields
    And bid them come in triumph home,
Or stretched upon their bloody shields,
    Rather than bear the bondman's doom.
"Go forth," she said, "to victory;
Or else, go bravely forth to die! . . . .

But if your hearts should craven prove,
Forgetful of your zeal—your love
For rights and franchises of men,
My heart will break; but even then,
Whilst bidding life and earth adieu,
This be the prayer I'll breathe for you:
'Passing from guilt to misery,
May this for aye your portion be,—

---

[1]Simoom—hot, violent, sand-laden wind of African deserts.

A life, dragged out beneath the rod—
An end, abhorred of man and God—
As monument, the chains you nurse—
As epitaph, your mother's curse!' "

. . .

A thousand hearts are breathing high,
And voices shouting "Victory!"
     Which soon will hush in death;
The trumpet clang of joy that speaks,
Will soon be drowned in the shrieks
     Of the wounded's stifling breath,
The tyrant's plume in dust lies low—
Th' oppressed has triumphed o'er his foe.
But ah! the lull in the furious blast
May whisper not of ruin past;
It may tell of the tempest hurrying on,
To complete the work the blast begun.
With the voice of a Siren, it may whisp'ringly tell
Of a moment of hope in the deluge of rain;
And the shout of the free heart may rapturously swell,
While the tyrant is gathering his power again. . . .

Though the hearts of those heroes all well could accord
With freedom's most noble and loftiest word;
Their virtuous strength availeth them nought
With the power and skill that the tyrant brought.
Gray veterans trained in many a field
Where the fate of nations with blood was sealed,
In Italia's vales—on the shores of the Rhine—
Where the plains of fair France give birth to the vine—
Where the Tagus, the Ebro, go dancing along,
Made glad in their course by the Muleteers' song—
All these were poured down in the pride of their might,
On the land of Ogé, in that terrible fight.
Ah! dire was the conflict, and many the slain,
Who slept the last sleep on that red battle-plain!
The flash of the cannon o'er valley and height
Danced like the swift fires of a northern night,
Or the quivering glare which leaps forth as a token
That the King of the Storm from his cloud-throne has spoken.

Their lives to their country—the backs to the sod—
Their heart's blood to the sword, and their soul to God!
But alas, although many lie silent and slain,
More blessed are they far than those clanking the chain,
In the hold of the tyrant, debarred from the day;—
And among these sad captives is Vincent Ogé!

. . .

Another day's bright sun has risen,
And shines upon the insurgent's prison;
Another night has slowly passed,
And Ogé smiles, for 'tis the last.
He'll droop beneath the tyrant's power—
The galling chains! Another hour,
And answering to the jailor's call,
He stands within the Judgment Hall.
They've gathered there—they who have pressed
Their fangs into the soul distressed,
To pain its passage to the tomb
With mockery of a legal doom. . . .

They've gathered there, in that dark hour—
The latest of the tyrant's power,—
An hour that speaketh of the day
Which never more shall pass away,—
The glorious day beyond the grave,
Which knows no master—owns no slave.
And there, too, are the rack—the wheel—
The torturing screw—the piercing steel,—
Grim powers of death all crusted o'er
With other victims' clotted gore.
Frowning they stand, and in their cold,
Silent solemnity, unfold
The strong one's triumph o'er the weak—
The awful groan—the anguished shriek—
The unconscious mutterings of despair—
The strained eyeball's idiot stare—
The hopeless clench—the quivering frame—
The martyr's death—the despot's shame.

The rack—the tyrant—victim,—all
Are gathered in that Judgment Hall.
Draw we a veil, for 'tis a sight
But fiends can gaze on with delight. . .

Sad was your fate, heroic band!
Yet mourn we not, for yours' the stand
Which will secure to you a fame
That never dieth, and a name
That will, in coming ages, be
A signal word for Liberty.
Upon the slave's o'erclouded sky,
     Your gallant actions traced the bow,
Which whispered of deliverance night—
     The meed of one decisive blow.
Thy coming fame, Ogé! is sure;
Thy name with that of L'Ouverture,
And all the noble souls that stood
With both of you, in times of blood,
Will live to be the tyrant's fear—
Will live, the sinking soul to cheer!
Syracuse, New York
August 31, 1853

Benjamin Clark

Little is known of Clark, and, a fugitive slave, such obscurity may well have been designed. He was born in a slave state, which he refuses to identify, had "but one year's tuition at school," removed to York, Pennsylvania, where he married and reared a large family, writing poetry in his spare moments. He was a delegate from his adopted hometown to the 1835 Annual Convention of Free People of Color, that was held in Philadelphia. "The Past, The Present and The Future," the prose part of his volume of the same title, (1867) shows his acquaintance with readings in history and literature in an account of the cruelties of the white man against the black man down through history, an evaluation of the American Post Bellum black, and a prognosis of his future in the country. He is decidedly against colonization—"individuals emigrate, not nations." A short prose narrative documentary piece, "The Fugitive," recounts what might well have been his own adventures, as two fugitives fight and kick their way to freedom after being lured into deceptive refuge by white men anxious for ransom. Clark's verse topics in sixty-five poems are fairly confined to matters of domesticity and, of course, racial injustices; he is often competent in skill, but barely avoids banality and cloying sentimentality. His parody, "Do They Miss Me?" is contrived for propagandistic ends, but his "No Enemies" shows a mind that is capable of searching meditation.

The Emigrant

Adieu to the land of my birth—
    Proud land of the slave and free!
What charms has thy bosom on earth
    For men of complexion like me?

In this boasted land of the free,
    I've suffered contumely and scorn;
And cannot relate what I see
    Is resumed for millions unborn.

If places on earth can be found
    Untainted by slavery's breath,
I'll find them, or search the world round
    Till my sorrows are ended in death.

Thy liberty is but a name—
    A byword—a jargon, in fine!
They freedmen of color—oh, shame!
    Are glad to escape from thy clime.

Adieu to thy stripes and stars,
    That vauntingly flaunt over the main!
Adieu to thy Lynch-laws and jars,
    Thy fetters, thy charter, and chain!

I go to the Isles of the Sea,[1]
    Where men are not judged by their hue,
Where all are protected and free—
    My native land, therefore, adieu!

* * * * * * * *

The Seminole

Bold champion of a noble race,
Who never feared the pale man's face,
Or nation tried'st thou to disgrace,
            Or name of Seminole;

---

[1] Isles of the Sea, i.e., The British West Indies.

Who, for the rescue of thy wife,
Upraised the tomahawk and knife,
And led thy brethren to the strife;—
                    'Twas the brave Oceola![2]

Roused by the war-whoop's distant sound,
Scattered thou death and carnage round
Thine everglade, or sacred mound,
                    And lands of Seminole.

But, ah! the fatal moment, when
Thou placed reliance on the men,
Who, under flag of truce, did then
                    Deceive thee, Oceola!

Fame will record it to the shame
Of those who planned, and those who came
To desecrate fair Freedom's name
                    By robbing Seminole;

But thou, Floridian, art the boast
Through thy wild romantic coast,
While all thy bare unconquered host
                    Remember Oceola!

                    * * * * * * *

What Is a Slave?

A slave is—what?
    A thing that's got
Nothing, and that alone!
    His time—his wife—
    And e'en his life,
He dare not call his own.

---

[2]Oceolo, Seminole chieftan hero of Seminole wars in Florida during the early nineteenth century—featured in A.A. Whitman's *Twasinto's Seminoles,* Oceola, who married the daughter of a fugitive Negro slave, was ambushed under a flag of truce. See A.A. Whitman, pp. 194-195.

A slave is—what?
　Ah! dreadful lot
Is his that's doomed to toil,
　Without regard,
　Or just reward,
Upon another's soil.

A slave is—what?
　Ah! cruel thought,
That I should have to be
　In constant strife,
　Throughout my life,
Deprived of Liberty.

A slave is—what?
　A perfect naught,
Shorn of his legal right;
　And then compelled
　To work, he's held
The remnant of his life.

A slave is—what?
　A being bought,
Or stolen from himself,
　By Christians, who
　This trade pursue
For sordid, paltry pelf.

A slave is—what?
　A being sought
Throughout this wide domain;
　Through bog and glen,
　By dogs and men,
For lucre—cursed gain!

A slave is—what?
　I pray do not
Insist; I cannot know,
　No words impart,
　Or, painter's art,
Describe a slave—ah, no!

A slave is—what?
Tell I can not,—
The task I would not crave;
If you would know,
Then straightway go,
And be yourself a slave!

* * * * * * * *

The Pauper's Grave

No friend to wipe the sweat of death
From off his face,
Or kindred, when he drew his breath
In this deserted place.

So, here he lies beneath the soil,
Where wild weeds grow;
The poor, the pauper, freed from toil,
In rough-hewn boxes low.

No marble monument to tell
In doubtful truth,
That he had acted ill or well
In hoary age or youth.

A simple board is all that's seen,
Or points to where
In silence sleeps the poor plebeian,
Released from earthly care.

* * * * * * * *

Requiescat in Pace
(On the Death of Caroline Millen Clark,
Who Died, 1st December, 1857)

Just like a rose in early spring,
That blooms and withers in a day;
So thou, poor, fragile sickly thing,
Was early called away.

'Tis hard indeed to bid farewell
  To one beloved, so young and mild;
None but a parent's heart can tell
  The love he bears his child.

We stood around thy dying bed,
  We heard thee offer up a prayer
Unto thy Father God, who said,—
  "Come, and my kingdom share."

We know that thou art called away,
  But, ah! 'tis hard with thee to part;
It breaks the tender ties that lay
  Entwined around the heart.

'Twas in the budding time of life,
  Ere crime had made its deadly stain,
Thou left a world of sin and strife,
  In heaven above to reign.

A little while, then, Caroline,
  In that bright world we'll meet again,
Where, like the sun, thou shalt outshine,
  Among the holy train.

* * * * * * *

Do They Miss Me?
A Parody

"Do they miss me at home—do they miss me?"
  'Twould be an assurance to me
To know that I'm really forgotten,
  My face they could never more see.

"Do they miss me at home—do they miss me?"
  By light, as the horn echoes loud,
And the slaves are marched off to the corn field,
  I'm missed from that half-naked crowd.

"Do they miss me at home—do they miss me?"
  The hut, with its bare floor of dirt,
Where the ash-cake is waiting to greet me,
  When done with my thankless day's work.

"Do they miss me at home—do they miss me?"
  The driver his lash used to ply,
As the blood trickled down from my shoulders,
  The flesh from my body would fly.

"Do they miss me at home—do they miss me?"
  The blood hounds are scenting my track,
And for long weary days they have hunted
  In order to hurry me back.

"Do they miss me at home—do they miss me?"
  The pockets are empty of cash,
While the auction-block's waiting to meet me,
  The trader stands by with his lash.

"Do they miss me at home—do they miss me?"
  In the fields of rice, sugar and grain;
If they do, I am glad, I assure you,
  They never shall see me again.

                    * * * * * * *

Love

  Oh! gentle sir, calm and secure,
    Lone on your pillow wake,
  A lady, knocking at your door,
    Has brought her heart to break.

  That heart is offered to you now;
    Will you accept the prize,
  Or disregard love's open vow,
    And hide it from your eyes?

  Ah! gentle sir, love's not a dream
    Of fancied visions bright;
  But rather like a limpid storm
    That's running day and night.

  'Tis like a precious gem that lay
    Within the earth concealed,
  Until the mighty orb of day
    Its beauties hath revealed.

                    * * * * * * *

No Enemies

"He has no enemies!" you say.
    I pity his condition;
His manhood he has thrown away,
    His candour and position.

"He has no enemies!" Well, then,
    The reason is,—he never
Has heart enough to act but when
    He sees "which way's the weather."

His principles are very light,
    If he is not contented
To be traduced for doing right,
    When once he has assented.

"He has no enemies!" Indeed!
    Then what has he been doing?
Or, what on earth can be his creed?
    What hath he been proving?

A truckling—vacillating course,—
    Unmanly, undecided;—
His little puny soul is worse
    Than sixpence twice divided!

Then give me one of upright heart,
    Who dares the truth to utter,
And acts a nobler, manlier part,
    Though enemies do mutter.

A man of earnest, iron will,
    Whose enemies are many;
And yet, whose virtue, strength, and skill,
    Are undeterred by any:

Aye! like the sturdy forest oak,
    Through which the winds do rattle,
Stands firmer from the heavy stroke,
    Prepared for Truth to battle.

Such is the man, whose noble soul,
   When roused to proper action,
Disdains a sordid, base control,
   Or enemies' detraction.

Who knows, when virtue's lost or fled,
   That time is really trying;
For if the man is not then dead,
   He truly must be dying.

                    * * * * * * * *

Joseph Seaman Cotter
(1861-1949)

Cotter was born of mixed parentage in Nelson County, Kentucky, where circumstances interrupted his elementary education and obliged him to work, as a teamster, in a distillery, as a brick-yard worker, until he was twenty-four years old, when he re-entered night school and studied to become a teacher and educational administrator, his career for the rest of his life, becoming principal of the Colored Ward School in Louisville, where he also taught English literature and composition. He published many poems in local newspapers, including the *Courier-Journal,* whose editor, Thomas Watkins, supplied a preface for his *Links of Friendship* (Louisville, 1898), from which the selections, below, are taken. Among his other publications are *A Rhyming* (1895), *Negro Tales* (1902), a four act play in blank verse, *Caleb, The Degenerate* (1903), and *A White Song and a Black One* (1909). There is a professionalism to most of Cotter's writings, which, however reflective of his obvious bookishness, tries to find expression in the precision of his meters, the ambitions of his riming, and in the intellectualized attempts at probings of human nature. No bombastic orator or discursive narrator, he means to explore the complexity of human matters beyond the too often over simplified black-white confrontations.

Frederick Douglass

O, eloquent and caustic sage!
Thy long and rugged pilgrimage
To glory's shrine has ended;

And thou has passed the inner door,
And proved thy fitness o'er and o'er,
   And to the dome ascended.

In speaking of thy noble life,
One needs must think upon the strife
   That long and sternly faced it;
But since those times have flitted by,
Just let the useless relic die
   With passions that embraced it.

There is no evil known to man
But what, if wise enough, he can
   Grow stronger in the bearing;
And so the ills we often scorn
May be of heavenly wisdom born
   To aid our onward faring.

Howe'er this be, just fame has set
Her jewels in thy coronet
   So firmly that the ages
To come will ever honor thee,
And place thy name in company
   With patriots and sages.

Now thou art gone, the little men
Of fluent tongue and trashy pen
   Will strive to imitate thee;
And when thy find they haven't sense
Enough to make a fair pretense,
   They'll turn and underrate thee.

* * * * * * *

Contradiction

He was a man who lived a peaceful life,
   Yet died from a continual round with strife.
His being born without a single fear
   Made him of course an abject coward here;
He grew so fast his limbs were duly stunted,
   And breathed so smoothly that he always grunted;

The more he learned, the more he saw he needed
   To keep his empty mental-garden weeded;
When men were killed outright and resurrected,
   He held such little things should be expected;
And to become, thought he, extremely wise,
   One simply has to misapply his eyes;
And seeing things as they will never be,
   Leads ever on to true philosophy.
By placing twilight at the early dawn,
He stopped his motions while he still went on;
Humility in him was two-edged pride;
And, likewise, sin was pure and glorified.
He made an everlasting truce with death,
Then straightway turned and drew his latest breath.

* * * * * * *

The Poet

What boots it, Poet, that from realms above
   Come messages for thee to tersely state,
If, after scattering the seeds of love,
   Thou straightway choked them with the weeds of hate?

* * * * * * *

Prologue to a Supposed Play

My worthy hearers, have you come tonight
To feast on comedy that's brisk and light,
And gladly spend an idle hour or two
In viewing pictures that are just like you?
If this is what you want, just let me say
You couldn't turn your heads a better way;
And for each cent you gave to enter here
You should take back a modicum of cheer,
And weigh yourselves so well that you will be
Arrayed against your insufficiency.

But this is preaching? Well, the comic stage
Has preached through ridicule to every age.
Man scorns his shallow deed and sordid pelf
When he's employed in laughing at himself.
So let us preach in every way that can
Lift man up to the dignity of man.
Now, don't be too exact, but let good sense
Decide the point of honest eminence;
And bear in mind that what is trite and true,
If well managed, is worthy through and through.

But to the play. It comes in five long acts,
In which the weapons used are naked facts.
There is no effort made to polish darts
That find a lodgement in deceitful hearts,
Nor to put on the rouge an honest mask,
For that would be, indeed, a fruitless task.
The characters are plain, as you will see,
And richly freighted with humanity;
And, by the way, their actions prove in making
A man of noble parts; the undertaking
Is such that nature seldom deigns to run
The same material on from sire to son.

The actors are a queer and jolly set,
Whose fun increases as you fume and fret;
So, should they hurl at you eccentric airs,
Just dodge as though they struck you unawares,
Or jesting strive to make a pointed hit,
Just hold your peace and let it pass for wit.
Now, my good hearers, hint what I shall say next.
You want to hear no more? Bring on the play next?
Well, here it is, and if you don't grow wiser,
Censure yourselves as well as the advisor.

* * * * * * * *

Answer to Dunbar's "After a Visit"

(The following is an answer to a poem written by Paul L. Dunbar after his visit to Kentucky.)

So, you be'n to ole Kentucky,
    An' you want to go ag'in?
Well, Kentucky'll doff her kerchief
    An' politely ask you in.
An' she'll loosen from her girdle
    What perhaps you didn't see—
Keys that fit the other cupboards
    Of her hospitality.

Not that she's inclined to hold back
    With the good, and give the worst;
But, you know, in all fair dealin',
    What's first must be the first.
So, when she takes key the second
    An' gives it a twist er two,
(Maybe I ought not say it)
    It'll most nigh startle you.

An' then keys the third and fourth, sir,
    (Not to speak of all the rest)
Wouldn't stop at crackin' buttons,
    They'd jest smash that Sunday vest.
And your happiness would find, sir,
    A momentum then and there,
That would carry it a-sweepin'
    Through the stronghold of despair.

Now, the grippin' o' the hand, sir,
    An' the welcome that you say
Was so firm and true an' all that
    Has a kind o' curious way.
At the first it's sorter slow like,
    Till it forms a league with you,
Then it makes a kind of circuit
    That jest thrills you thro' and thro'.

But maybe I had better
     Not discuss this aftermath,
For it might stir up your feelings
     To the righteous point of wrath,
As you brood o'er what you lost, sir,
     By not stayin' with us longer.
Ah, well, come to see us often,
     Ole Kentucky'll make you stronger.

So, you be'n to ole Kentucky,
     An' you want to go ag'in?
Well, Kentucky's standin' waitin'
     Jest to take you wholly in,
An' she'll loosen her vast girdle
     So that you can fully see
All the roots, fruits, leaves an' branches
     Of her hospitality.

* * * * * * * *

On Hearing James W. Riley Read
(From a Kentucky Standpoint)

To tell the truth, each piece he read
Set up a jingle in my head
That bumped and thumped and roared about,
Then on a sudden just crept out,
Gently and slowly at the start,
Then made a bee-line for my heart.

And more than once I thought maybe
His charming Hoosier poetry
Would be a guide to lead me over
To the Elysian fields of clover.

To find faults with his worst or best
Would be like finding fault with the rest
After a fellow has been in
The dirt and dust up to his chin,
And bathed and stretched beneath the trees,
Whose branches fairly hug the breeze.

In these hackneyed and sordid days,
When censure thorns the bud of praise,
And many think they ought not to
Give genius half its honest due,
And never fail to bombard it
With silly quips and shallow wit,
I like to just go hunt it up
And sup and sip and sip and sup;
And then I like to speak my praise
In honest thought and simple phrase,
And let the giver know that I
Delight in him and tell him why,
And not go wavering to and fro,
But just come out and tell him so.

* * * * * * * *

Emerson

He tilled the old deserted fields with zeal,
    And honored every common thing he saw
By making it a part of the great seal
    That holds secure the universal law.

* * * * * * * *

Oliver Wendell Holmes

Who can hold up the intellect and say:
"From here to there scampers a vein of wit
With laughing humor by the side of it,
Assisting cold philosophy to play
The game of thinking"? Not a single ray
That boldly shines therefrom will ever admit
Of close analysis. So, bit by bit,
We fall to guessing out the mind's true way
Of forming wholes. An astute analyst!
And royal merchant in the mart of song!
Because of this we see as through a mist
Thy charming whole. Yet know to thee belong,

Howe'er they be arranged, the God-like three—
Wit, humor, and sublime philosophy.

* * * * * * * *

Let None Ignobly Halt
"the paths of glory lead but to the grave"—Gray

Let none ignobly halt because
They tell us glory's fickle wave
Rolls on in keeping with set laws
And bears but to the old, dark grave;
For whatsoever course we take
Heads straight to this unwelcome goal,
So, spur the will and grandly make
The voyage with elated soul.

* * * * * * * *

Answer to Dunbar's "A Choice"

They please me so—these solemn lays
That tell what God to man decrees.
The world so seldom mends its ways
That poets should by swift degrees
Put back the frail, bring forth the strong,
And wed stern facts to sober song
With a ring so clear that our barks must steer
To the haven where the God-kissed air
Makes the soul-wine sweet through earth-brewed lees.

* * * * * * * *

My Poverty and Wealth

This life of mine is poor indeed,
    If it be measured by
The little mankind, in their need,
    Reap from my charity.

But rich it is beyond the power
    Of my dull eyes to see,
When measured by the gracious dower,
    Which they bequeath to me.

* * * * * * * *

Albery Allson Whitman
(1851-1902)

Praised by several leading literary figures, including William Cullen Bryant, as a genuine poet, A.A. Whitman was a widely popular romantic poet of his time among black and white readers, and not without reasons. He was born, as he never tired of saying in his prose prefaces and in digressive flights of verse, in Green River country, near Munfordsville, Hart County, Kentucky on May 30, 1851, into a technical slavery he never acknowledged in the ordinary sense. "I was in bondage,—*I was never a slave*,—the infamous laws of a savage despotism took my substance—what of that? Many a man has lost all he had, except his manhood." (My italics) Orphaned as a young boy, he became free by proclamation of the Emancipation notice, wandered across the country and abroad, pausing every now and again to attend various schools at Troy, Ohio, and under Bishop Daniel A. Payne at Wilberforce University, always recording his romantic reactions to the varieties of nature in a prolific output of poetry. His first volume was *Essay on the Ten Plagues and Other Miscellaneous Poems* (before 1873), followed by *Leelah Misled* (Elizabethtown, Kentucky, 1873); *Not a Man and Yet a Man, with Miscellaneous Poems* (Elizabethtown, Kentucky, 1877); *Twasinta's Seminoles, or Rape of Florida* (St. Louis, 1885; a slightly revised edition of *Rape of Florida*, published the year before); a reprinting of both *Not a Man* and *Twasinta's Seminoles*, both "carefully revised," appeared in newer editions in 1890 along with *Drifted Leaves* (St. Louis). *The World's Fair Poem: The Freedman's Triumphant Song*, with "The Veteran" (Atlanta, 1893) was followed by his last work, *An Idyl of the South, An Epic Poem in Two Parts*

(New York, 1901). "The Veteran," which was recited by Mrs. Caddie Whitman, the poet's wife, at the Chicago World's Fair, appeared in *Drifted Leaves*. There are sermons also.

As has been said, Whitman was prolific, but he was also prolix. His platform readings of some of his poems helped to establish his wide speaking popularity, for, an elder in the A.M.E. Church, and although he became addicted to the bottle, he was warmly regarded as the poet-evangelist throughout the A.M.E. circuit, especially in Ohio and Kansas. His "Stonewall Jackson," which was composed in 1886, and appeared in *Drifted Leaves*,[1] was dedicated to the Confederate veterans and "received wide circulation in the press throughout the country." Mrs. Whitman recited the piece in many opera houses, North and South, and before the joint legislatures of Mississippi, "to warm applause." But it is in his lengthier poems that Whitman displays his prolixity. *Leelah Misled* (39 pages in small print), *Not a Man* (213 pages),[2] *Twasinta's Seminoles* (97 pages), and "The Octoroon," the first of his two part epic, *An Idyl of the South* (126 pages), are really romantic novels in verse. The feeble, undeveloped plots of these pieces are repeatedly interrupted as he freely reminisces about his beloved homeland, his childhood delights at nature, or he will, just as freely, take time out to chide America's slow pace in fulfilling its spiritual destiny. He has a full supply of romantic stereotype characters and conventions. His heroes and heroines, for instance, are never dark-skinned Negroes, but are mixed, handsome, rugged, daring, righteous and beautiful. The slave hero of *Not a Man* is one Rodney, who has "eighty-five per cent of Saxon in his veins," is twenty years old, six-foot three inches tall, broad of shoulder and brawny of arm. For his heroic efforts in rescuing his master's daughter, Rodney is sold into slavery where he meets, falls in love with, and, after hairbreadth adventures, take to Canada one Leeona, a "fair Creole," with "raven locks of hair."

Twasinta's Seminoles recounts the intermittent wars of 1816-1818 and 1835-1842 (Whitman is concerned with the years 1825-1833) between the United States Dragoons and Seminole Indians with their

---

[1] And again in *The Afro-American Encyclopedia* (Nashville, 1895).

[2] Lengthy as Whitman's *Not a Man* is, over 5000 lines, there are other longer poems by other early Negro poets, e.g., Rev. Robert E. Ford's *Brown Chapel, a Story in Verse* (n.d., n.p., Preface dated Baltimore, 1903), 307 pages in twenty-one cantos of ten-lined stanzas riming aaabcdcdee, for some 8600 lines; Maurice Corbett's *Harp of Ethiopia* (Nashville, 1914), 273 pages of 8-lined stanzas riming aabbccdd, well over 7500 lines.

fugitive slaves allies in Florida, resulting in the relocation of most of
the Indians who, ambushed under a flag of truce, were obliged to
start life anew in Santa Rosa, Texas. "The Octoroon" tells the story
of an octoroon, Leena, "a blue-eyed slave," who is loved by her
young master Maury: "There was the Norman iron in his blood./
There was the Saxon in his sunny hair/ That waved and tossed in an
abandoned flood;/ But Norman strength rose in his shoulders
square." To frustrate his son's unsouthern notions about loving a
slave, however blue-eyed, old man Maury sells the girl to a lecherous
army officer from whose drunken advances she escapes, but so exerts
herself that she dies—in the arms of Maury who had set out to rescue
her. Although Whitman, in his *World's Fair Poem,* urges white
Americans to acknowledge the Negro's role in the country's history,
he seems more characteristic in his metrical romances. "The
Southland's Charms and Freedom's Magnitude," which is part 2 of
his *Idyl of the South,* is a rhapsodic plea for manifold conciliation
between the North and the South, the former slave and his white
master. For all of his emoting, his lengthy digressions from simple
plots that use Currier and Ives like stock heroes and heroines,
contented, banjo-plunking, dancing plantation Negroes, Whitman
does exhibit, throughout his work, an uncommon facility in a wide
range of metrics and stanzas. For instance, there are two plots to *Not
a Man,* and to narrate the major story that treats the adventures of
Rodney's escape from slavery and eventual marital refuge in
Canadian domesticity, he uses, mostly, the couplet form; but, aware
of the narrative distance he must travel, he varies (and sometimes
wrenches) this form, from iambic trimeters to tetrameters to the
predominance of pentameters. He also uses five stress unrimed
anapest lines. Thus from "Chapter 13":

> Here hope our lovers found,
> And love about them wound
> Her silver cords the tighter;
> As fears vanished away,
> And they from day to day
> Felt life's burdens grow lighter. . .

Far from their home within the wood,
Once Rodney went to search for food,
And ready make, for he next day
Must toward the North Star take his way.
Leeona biding, sandals knit
Of fibres from the cypress split,
A basket rude of willows wove,
And gathered fruits within the grove.
Thus wand'ring round, she missed her track,
And lost, could not her way find back. . .

A true heroine of the cypress gloom,
Now there to lie, the Creole saw her doom—

From "Chapter 16":

Canadian farmers came oft to the little green cottage,
To see their new neighbors and hear them tell over their
troubles.
The tales of their pilgrimage e'er to their hearers had new
charms;
And instances, once told, cloyed not in repeating them over.

To relate the subordinate plot of an Indian romance, Whitman
favors unrimed lines, mostly trochaic tetrameters. Such orchestrated
metrical variety helps sustain interest of sorts. His *Drifted Leaves,*
which contains "My Mountain Home," ". . .the first poem that I ever
attempted to write," presents 22 poems of different meters and
forms, including two Negro dialect poems, and other pieces in iambic
heptameter couplet and blank verse. His *Miscellaneous Poems*
exhibits even other forms. His *Twasinta's Seminoles* uses some 257
Spenserian stanzas, and his *Idyl of the South* is conveyed in 235
stanzas of ottava rima. Now such a display is certainly noteworthy,
especially for one who, born in slavery, never had more than thirteen
months of formal education. Faults of occasional pretentiousness,
prolixity, often undisciplined, headlong metrics and all, Whitman is
nevertheless a poet who deserves attention. An edition of his
complete works is in preparation.

from Leelah Misled

I.

Not of imputed heroes, nor of ghosts
That wander o'er fictitious fields of song,
Nor kingdoms won or lost by battling hosts,
Nor ruined castles, nor of rev'lers' throng;
But of our Leelah, come now friendly muse,
Come, touch my lyre of elegiac string:
The narrative with tender thoughts profuse,
To full inspire my waiting heart to sing,
And while our theme, no wrong would justify,
The penalty 'twill justly modify.

II.

Nor sing to me of distant climes, O muse!
Nor foreign cities, groves nor empires great,
But from my own Columbia fair, I choose
A song bearing with it of truth the force and weight,
For who can boast of more than here is seen,
Rich, and profusely rich, on ev'ry hand,
From proud New England's mounts of evergreen,
Down the coasts where Sable's scorching sand
Mirrors the sun's rays, and where ev'ry shore
Is by delicious fruits all crowded o'er?

III.

My fetters broken, I began to sing.
Who hears my strain, then, mark the happy cause
Thus prompting me; and, as my lay I bring,
Think not that I thus come to win applause;
For as a bird just fledged would swell its throat,
Warble a song, and warble it again,
Careless of who mark an imperfect note:
So sing I now, and will I sing again,
But since so many bards have shamed their muse
By aims too high, an humbler course I choose.

IV.

The battling gods of Milton's epic page;
The loftiness of Byron's well wrought rhyme;
The pictured thought of Shakespeare's peopled stage;
The lay of Scott, and Spenser's verse sublime,
Proud Europe have immortalized in song.
These bards wore laurels of unequalled fame,
And bore applause from many a crowded throng,
Kindling in great minds admiration's flame,
And building up poesy to such height
As later bard's have ne'er reached in their flight.

V.

And some were they, which one by one have set,
Guilding their sky with such o'er gorgeous dies,
That others in their zenith seem, as yet,
Not brilliant, or seem waning when they rise;
Yet, since Columbia's fettered sons are free,
May not one from the scenes which gave him birth
Draw forth a lay, the theme of which may be
No mean purport—nor tale of trifles' worth?
And may not he, adverse to slavery, find
Where human institutions gyve the mind?

VI.

O, seems it not to other eyes as sweet
Upon my parent clime to musing look?
Here, where the wild, sublime and pleasing meet
In many an aspect rich, of glassy brook,
Smooth lawns, full harvests, and of forests deep?
Here, where the happy circles, passing gay,
Of rich and poor alike, through pleasures sweep
The paths of life along from day to day.
And this is sweet America, and this
The goal, where people form the people's bliss!

VII.

Full many a time, in life's fair spring, I've strolled
Far 'mong the rocks of mountain solitude,
When, by stern care unsullied, I could hold
Converse with speaking nature; and I've stood
Where o'er the caverns' stony mouth did lean
The vine wreathed hawe, fantastically wild.
And then I've knelt, the moss-clothed stones between,
To quaff the lucent streamlet's dripping mild.
Awe-stricken I, the beetling cliffs beneath,
Have felt a burden on my very breath.

XXI.

I love the symphony of nature's chords,
When to my ear they're wafted, undisturbed
By tread of human, or by babbling words
Ejected by roused passions, hot, uncurbed.
For in the bosom of the forest I,
By the sweet quiet lulled, could long abide,
There on the lap of solitude could die;
Or from the herd of low mankind could hide
There, and then my humble aspirations there,
Could find a Heav'n, a bright, a golden sphere.

XXII.

Away from this toward fair Georgia's plain,
O'er Missionary Ridge, through pine woods deep;
And down the Chickamauga we again
Move on, our theme and course to wistful keep.
Music, awake! and touch my lyre, O muse!
My song must change, a story to narrate.
And now the scene bursts on my sight. Just views
In me, O now, Eternal God, create!
To truth, let moderation lend her grace,
While I the course of rising thoughts may trace.

XXV.

Clothed with the rich aspect of this fair clime
There lies a pleasant farm—a country seat,
On which once dwelt the subject of my rhyme—
A sweet young blonde, of form and feature neat.
Excellent of mind, graceful in her mien,
And tender as the early budding flow'r.
Devoted in affections, and as clean
At heart as a blown rose after a shower.
Cheerful as the lark o'er a bow-gilt spray,
And mild as the peep of Autumnal day.

XXVI.

Extravagantly rosy her fair cheeks,
Serenely beautiful her soft blue eyes,
Of that expression full which ever speaks
Of brain abundant, and which magnifies
The blaze of admiration; small her feet,
Shoulders pointed, gracefully round her arms,
Bright as the gems of ocean, her teeth neat,
As magic wonderful her curls' rare charms
Were quite enough to worship as divine,
Or more, at least, than any bigot's shrine.

XXVII.

The only child was she of a rich pair,
Descended from grand fam'lies, old and proud;
She was their jewel, she their idol fair,
At which, with all their goods, they jointly bowed.
She was an echo to their wishes fond,
A whisper in their dreams, a ray of joy
Which kept forever bright their nuptial bond,
And tended their high principles to cloy.
Those principles which thirst to be alone
Unequalled, grand and extensively known.

XXXVIII.

There lived a dashing gentleman of worth,
(However, little moral;) Christian reared,
In this fair centre of the South, where mirth,
From time to time, in long, long spells was heard.
He was a man that might be termed grandee,
His mein was knightly; of appearance fine,
His countenance expressive, open, free;
And in this unaffected did combine
Entreaty and command; and then he wore
And air which made these pow'rs impressive more.

XXXIX.

Not beautiful, but very prepossessing,
Among the ladies, he stood first in rank;
For, much indeed, they fancied his fine dressing,
And much relied on what he had in bank.
And then they liked his style of calling, too,
Which was, I think, an unbecoming style,
That is, to never call except to woo,
And then sit on the door-step all the while.
Of, fathers, chaste! rub well your nose-glasses,
And eye such men when wooing your lasses.

XL.

From Macon out, 'twas just a "pleasant ride,"
'Till you arrived at Leelah's mansion quite,
Broad fields and meadows green on either side,
The way did one to often pass invite.
Our hero "liked the travel," for you see,
Physicians said, "Twas splendid for his health,"
And then, again, indeed the fact may be,
He sought thus to exhibit his great wealth,
Be this, or that the case, one thing I know,
A little wealth may thus make a great show.

XLI.

But why he'd "ride" so certainly each eve,
Out to this farm, and only out to this,
Is easy quite to guess, for I believe,
If I remember rightly; some "fair miss,"
Was most he talked about on his return.
And then the "chat" was much the same in town,
Old women said that "wedding light would burn"
Ere long, at Leelah's, and her "bridal gown,"
Some lasses "thought" that they "had seen her busy."
But that some doubted, you may well judge why.

XLII.

When he, his heart had pledged, to full fifteen,
'Mong whom were some old maids, say five or six,
Who all avowed that "coquettes they had seen,
But with such company, would never mix,"
Old maids, learn one thing, and 'tis well to learn
It, all ye maidens who are "setting out."
That is, to disappointment's barbed end turn
Upon him, whose false heart brings it about,
'Twas thus, when our hero forsook these,
All with a sigh, said, "Ah! I'm hard to please."

XLIII.

Back to our theme, McLambert's "ev'ning rides,"
For here my hero's name I now disclose,
But, e'en his name, there is a fact besides
That's prominent; though, as the "story goes"
So goes my pen, that is, right straight along.
Perchance I'll point this fact to you again,
If it appears some further down my song,
At present my Pegasus on a strain,
Heightens his speed, and to the mansion on,
Gallops, nor finds a scene to look upon.

XLIV.

But now a glimpse of Leelah checks him up,
She meets McLambert at the mansion door,
And here I'll repeat what I've given up,
Such beauty never graced the earth before,
She's not a Hagar nor a Magdalene,
A Scott's Rowena nor the painted glare
Of wild chimeras in the player's scene,
Where Amorous Fancy leaves Chastity bare,
But she is Leelah, beautiful as e'er
Was thought, as pagan monarch's jewels dear.

XLV.

"Stir, cooks," the mistress whispers, in a rage,
While they, the hasty meal are serving up,
"Get the decanter and be quick, my page,
To bring us some old claret, ere we sup,"
The master bids. Soon is the table spread,
And seems beneath its load to almost groan,
Soon the decanter with its contents red
Passes around, untouched by "page" alone,
The wine drunk up, cooks scolded, and tea o'er,
Leelah sits with McLambert in the door.

XLVI.

'Twas said by some, that Leelah was too fast,
But this was wrong, e'en though a preacher said
It, for you will see, ere your three-score be past,
That, when the schemes of "drawing on" are laid
By fine young men, old maids get fast, and then
Cases have been, that married women stray
From pleasant homes, to follow up such men.
Who then concerning poor young girls could say,
"Too fast," when some such man should bear the
    blame?
Girls love deceivers, as true hearts, the same.

XLVII.

Fates, burn these novels that young ladies read,
Of "Rescues," "First Loves," and of "gentle taps"
At "Brown-Stone Fronts"—they only serve indeed,
As preludes to their many sad mishaps.
Aware of this, McLambert would present
A volume such to Leelah, and retain
One too, himself peruse; in this he meant,
A mastery complete, o'er her to gain
And he would study ev'ry part, in fact,
Until the nov'list's hero he could act.

XLVIII.

A servant met him at the outer gate,
From time to time, and held his prancing "bay,"
To, soon as he the saddle could vacate,
Bounce quickly in, and proudly ride away.
And here was joy mutual, all around,
Leelah's to meet the object of her pride,
McLambert's thus to be met, and to bound
Into a saddle fine, and "take a ride."
The slaves' and thus to ridden be, the steed
Enjoyed much, since he went toward his feed.

L.

From time to time, McLambert came and went,
And more, and more, his victim's love engaged.
His fine talk, to his "love" such lustre lent,
That Leelah thought her dreams its truth presaged.
His purpose now began to ripen fast,
And Leelah's parents became satisfied
That all her days of girlhood most were past,
As her they'd giv'n to be McLambert's bride;
And now determin'd to bring to bear his aim,
Once more, the proud false-hearted, lover came.

LI.

I charge you, O chaste lasses! all beware.
A kiss may oft designs most brutal hide,
The human heart itself may be a snare
And set for those, who in it would confide.
The face may, like the skillful players, screen,
Conceal the dirt, and gaudy scenery show.
A sigh, a smile, a bright eye's twinkling keen,
May all preface the plan that brings you low.
Beware, O lasses! you I charge again,
For fancy's men, are seldom men of brain.

LII.

'Twas eve, and far and near deep quiet reigned,
Save where, 'mong myrtles, sighed the winds, "good
     night."
Now weary life, by prompting nature trained,
Sank to repose, lulled by the soft starlight,
But Leelah, with her heart's prized treasure, sate
'Neath creeping vines, beside the mansion door
While such fond thoughts as these retreats create,
Burned in her heart, and ruled her senses o'er,
Those dang'rous thoughts, which lend emotions
     sweet,
And hush the "no," while lips in kisses meet.

LIII.

'Twas eve, ah fatal eve! and no one near,
Save him, who breathed a poison on each word,
No guardian angel bright was watching there,
To check transgression with a flaming sword.
But Leelah prized it thus to be alone,
Quite all this earth could boast or Heaven bestow.
So, 'gainst her idol's breast she leaned, while shone
Her playful eyes, with pure affection's glow;
He heard her beating heart, and knew full well,
What such pulsations in young lovers tell.

LV.

'Twas eve, and there no parent's eye could see
The erring movements of their Leelah fair.
Her soft arm rested on McLambert's knee,
His hand tossed her carelessly-waving hair.
Now, circumfused in all the soul can bear,
Feeling his arm about her gently pressed,
She thought not once his purposes to fear,
But long submitted thus to be caressed;
Caressing's fond submission is divine,
But often harm ensues, when they combine.

LVI.

McLambert now upon Leelah looked down,
And whispered, "Dearest, aren't you mine, all mine?"
Leelah looked vacant on, (sad fact to own,)
And like an echo soft, replied, "All thine."
How moments passed now, friendly muse, withhold.
But, reader pause, and to thy ways take heed,
See dimness now, upon the "gold, fine gold,"
The victim see, with heart destined to bleed;
And though it bleed, and grief be long and sore,
Her doom's unchanged, the spring of joy is o'er.

LVII.

Though slaves, a thousand come at her command,
And wealth in stores uncounted, crowd around,
Though teeming trees and vineyards clothe the land,
The "pearl of price" is lost, to ne'er be found.
No boons hath earth like that kind Heaven bestows—
True happiness from virtue springing out—
'Tis this that in the burning seraph glows
With Heav'nly radiance; this, brings about
That Heav'nly whisper, cheering poor girls, when
Their neighbors, sneering, flaunt about with men.

LVIII.

My muse is mournful, and I turn away,
To leave my reader pond'ring at the scene,
What you will think, is just what I would say.
Then think, while I escape the critic mean,
What e'en I've said, I know that some will think,
"Too this," "Too that," or "not enough" somehow;
Or, "better keep such thoughts than frame with ink,"
But some will be consid'rate I allow.
Though be the case with you, or this or that,
I leave you as you are, and where you are at.

LXV.

Now, reader, this digression you'll excuse,
Since best of poets often ask the same;
You see, we thus contrive to help the muse
Along, when she becomes a little lame,
And then a greater work may thus be done,
We thereby sweep o'er wider fields of thought,
Gath'ring the rare, and touching common, none,
And so, with int'rest our page is fraught;
Then if you're pleased, with what I've gathered here,
Your criticisms will not be severe.

LXVI.

Time passed away, and Leelah downcast grew,
She sought e'en her own mother's face to shun;
Her cheeks of rose began to lose their hue;
Her eyes to lose their brightness, and to run,
At intervals, with burning tears, fast down;
She ceased rising at early morn to vie
In cheerfulness with birds which first had flown
From their dewy cover; but late she would lie,
Weighing the horrid thoughts which came and went,
Causing her heart to rend, and leave it rent.

LXVII.

At times she thought to commit suicide,
Or seek relief in some physician's hell,
But last thought she, "Whatever may betide
The whole affair I'll to my mother tell."
And then, like bleak winds o'er a barren shore,
Lashing the storm-worn rocks, all desolate,
Fear's frightful menaces, as ne'er before,
Began to gloomy make her pending fate
Inextricably linked to nameless shame,
She'd dream of succor, but 'woke doomed the same,

LXVIII.

McLambert long had gone from home away,
To make some speculations, I suppose,
(For that is what such men are apt to say,
When time bids fair some dark deed to disclose,)
And Leelah not a letter could receive,
From him; though long she anxious watched the mail.
And yet herself, she scarcely could believe
That he in such fair promises could fail.
But last, convinced of her forsaken state,
She fell to grieving at a fearful rate.

LXXIII.

'Twill hope and fear, this condition's a war,
Upon the ground that self always assumes,
When circumstance, to pleasure forms a bar,
Or the sun sets that Fortune's sky illumes.
And this as near as I can now express,
Was about the condition of the mind
Of Leelah's mother; she knew that distress
Of deepest seat, and, of peculiar kind,
Approached her child, and while all this she knew,
She feared to think of what must come to view.

LXXIV.

Leelah looked up and, sobbed. "McLambert, ma,"
This was enough, that mother knew the rest,
So crying out, "I thought it, Leelah, ah!
I thought it." She clasped her child to her breast.
The father, hearing this, returned anon,
With fury kindling 'neath his dark-brown brow,
And said, "No more shall you be looked upon
As child of mine; and know it fully now."
Then turning off, he ne'er spoke to her more,
But often wished she'd "keep out side his door."

LXXV.

There's one, who never will her own forsake;
There's one, who always sheds a gracious tear
And kisses pardon for each sad mistake
That in her children's actions may appear,
And e'en when crime its horrid self may show
She'll find a circumstance to palliate
The victim's guilt, and none so well can know
As she, how to "the whole affair relate."
This one is mother, best of friends and first
Since she loves most her child whose faults are worst.

LXXVI.

"In Rama," here was truly heard "a voice,"
"A weeping Rachel" o'er her ruined child;
Refusing comfort.[1] Hopeless grief, (her choice)
Assailed her heart with ravages most wild.
Few months of such were all that she could bear,
With mortal things, whe was forced to part.
Soon Leelah saw her faithful mother dear
Laid in her grave—she died of broken heart—
And now, she of her only friend bereft,
To stroll about from place to place was left.

---

[1]In Rama. . . . A voice was heard in Ramah, lamentation, *and* bitter weeping; Rachel weeping for her children refused to be comforted for her children, because they *were* not. Jeremiah, 31, 15.

LXXVII.

Go, ponder at that mansion desolate,
See, how Decay approaches with long strides:
The slats are broken in the garden gate,
A mother's grave the weeping willow hides,
The gravel walks by thistles are o'ergrown,
The pee-wit[2] builds along the corridor,
The rail fence at the well has tumbled down,
With moss the window-sills are covered o'er,
And noisy vermin play beneath the floor,
While screech-owls cry each night around the door.

LXXVIII.

Go ponder at that faithful mother's grave,
Think of what brought her to its cold confines,
And on the silent marble, thou mean slave
To foul seduction, read these touching lines:
"I loved my child with affection pure,
And she loved me with childish heart, the same,
She was misled, and I could not endure,
To live and know that she must bear the blame;
Mothers and maidens, pause, nor blush to read,
But look well to the life that you daily lead."

LXXIX.

With hands behind him clasped, that father walked
His home, now desolate, about, and wept;
And often to himself he lowly talked,
Or muttered groans of anguish as he slept;
His faithful servants waited at his call
As at his bidding sped with anxious heart,
For truly, he was dearly loved by all,
So, of his grief, they strove to bear a part,
And much did bear, so, he, full many an hour,
Passed calmly on, nor felt the spoiler's pow'r.

_____

[2] "pee-wit." The sandpiper bird.

XC.

"My Leelah's ruined, and her mother's grief
Proved fatal, so I'll seek the distant West,
Perchance in solitude I'll find relief,
Or, fleeing civil'zation, perfect rest.
Out on the plains, I'll dwell 'mong savages,
Nor tortured feel by social joy's decay,
Nor feel bereavement's fearful ravages,
Lest weary of my life, I pass away,
For what is life, when all that's dear is gone?
Or what is happiness, to man alone?"

CXIII.

To care for others is the God in man,
To care for self alone the brute; then we
Should teach ourselves, if teach ourselves we can,
To careful of the good of others be;
Blind instinct teaches lower life to move,
The ass to bray, the hungry wolf to howl,
The hawk to pounce upon the harmless dove,
And the fierce panther at midnight to prowl;
But Reason, proud dictator of man's mind,
Cannot by these low promptings be confined.

CXVI.

Great God! and yet shall feeble man presume
To fix a penalty, when Thou[3] dost clear,
If not by laws, by custom stern to doom
His brother to a torture most severe?—
A torture of the mind, immortal part
Of man, and of Thyself a part; whence flow
Intelligence's springs—nay, may the heart
Of each for others, with forgiveness glow,
Since Christ forgave the woman doomed to die
And took the robber chief to worlds on high.

---

[3]It is characteristic of most of Whitman's thought to argue for mercy, especially, as he would have it here with seduced Leelah, when there are extenuating circumstances and Christian appeals available.

CXVII.

"My shell is broken,"[4] but I once again
Look on my country's scenes, of vales and hills.
These I embrace, and hush my feeble strain,
But that which moved me first to song, yet fills
With musings inexpressible my mind.
I've sung of one who was my country's own,
Then full's my joy, when in myself I find
Rememb'rance not extinct, for I have known
No other motive than her gen'ral good,
Which will be seen, if I am understood.

CXVIII.

Now, reader, pardon me for having sung
Without the polish of much erudition,
And while my tuneless lyre lies unstrung,
Compare with better life, the bard's condition,
Stern poverty, her millions has controlled,
And many an aspiration set at naught.
But, in this thought alone am I consoled:
True eminence by any may be sought,
Obtained by any, and by any held,
Who suffer not ambition to be quelled.

from Twasinta's Seminoles;
Or Rape of Florida

CANTO I.

Invocation

I.

The poet hath a realm within, and throne,
And in his own soul singeth his lament.
A comer often in the world unknown—
A flaming minister to mortals sent;

---

[4] "My shell is broken." i.e., my poem has ended.

In an apocalypse of sentiment
He shows in colors true the right or wrong,
And lights the soul of virtue with content;
Oh! could the world without him please us long?
What truth is there that lives and does not live in song?

II.

"The stuff's in him of robust manliness,
He is a poet, singing more by ear
Than note." His great heart filled with tenderness,
Thus spoke the patriarch bard of Cedarmere[5]
Of me, who dwelt in a most obscure sphere;
For I was in the tents of bondage when
The muse inspired, and ere my song grew clear,
The graceful Bryant called his fellow-men
To mark what in my lay seemed pleasing to him then.

III.

O! shade of our departed Sire of song!
If what to us is dim be clear to thee,
Hear while my yet rude numbers flow along!
If spirit may a mortal's teacher be,
Stand thou near by and guidance offer me!
That, like thy verses, clear as summer blue,—
Bright mirrors of the peaceful and the free,
Reflecting e'er the good, the great and true,—
So mine may be, and I my pleasing task pursue.

IV.

Say, then, of that too soon forgotten race[6]
That flourished once, but long has been obscure
In Florida, and where the seas embrace
The Spanish isles; say if e'er lives more pure
Warmed veins, or patriots could more endure
Around the altars of their native bourne!
Say, when their flow'ry landscapes could allure,

---

[5] "bard of Cedarmere" . . . William Cullen Bryant (1794-1978), one of several major American poets who so praised Whitman.

[6] "that . . . forgotten race," i.e., Seminole Indians, see pp. 189-190.

What peaceful seasons did to them return,
And how requited labor filled his golden urn!

V.

How sweet their little fields of golden corn!
How pleasure smiled o'er all the varying scene!
How, 'mid her dewy murmurs dreamt the morn,
As Summer lingered in the deep serene!
How nibbling flocks spread on the hillsides green,
And cattle herded in the vales below;
And how wild meadows stretched in bloom-sweet sheen,
Beneath unconquered shades, where lovers go
When comes the evening star above the dark to glow!

VI.

In this delightful valley of the isle,
Where dwelt the proud Maroon, were not deeds done·
Which roused the Seminole and fierce exile
To more than savage daring? Here begun
The valiant struggles of a forest son;
And tho' by wrong's leagued numbers overborne,
His deeds of love and valor for him won
The envied wreath by heroes only worn,
And which from manhood's brow oppression ne'er hath torn!

Part II.

from The Southland's Charms
and Freedom's Magnitude

Stanza I.

Far in a vale among the mountains blue,
    Close by a stream where roving cattle stray,
Where grand old sylvans darkly crowd the view,
    And towering summits brush the clouds away;

Down where the water, wildly rushing through
　　The rocks, enchant the scene with song and spray,
There round my childhood home, a cabin rude,
Wild Nature taught me Freedom's magnitude.

2

There I have stood upon the precipice
　　That hovered awful space, and heard the leap
Of waters downward with a fearful hiss,
　　To thence rush onward in their angry sweep,
Like fiends contending in the fierce abyss;
　　And musing there in meditation deep,
I learned to reverence the Almighty Force,
Which rends the hills and shapes the water-course.

3

And there I've mused among the wood-haunts deep
　　When Silence told her secrets in my ear;
When Echo startled from her midday sleep,
　　Would flee and mock, and flee and—disappear.
I've heard the harp-strings of the wild breeze give
　　Such music sweet as only poets hear;
While floods of bird-song filled the vibrant boughs
With meanings which no vulgar soul allows.

4

Here I have heard the all-consoling speech
　　Of mystery which fills the solitudes,
When leaves with velvet pleadings do beseech
　　The pensive winds to linger in the woods;
And here I've found the depths beyond my reach—
　　The depths of feeling o'er which Silence broods—
And out upon which, as upon a sea,
The Soul would venture to meet Deity.

5

Dear land of many a classic wood and stream,
   The proud birthright of ancient families,
With mountains whose blue robes have been my dream,
   In glorious compass ranged 'neath charming skies;
Thou art a fit retreat, I fondly deem,
   For those romantic loves which brave men prize,
Which clothed a wigwam with historic grace,
And charmed the cabins of an injured race.

6

Hail, Native land! first-born of Freedom, hail!
   Maintain the foremost rank of pow'r and pride!
Thy far-ranged mountains rich with wooded vale,
   And classic waters rolled in crystal tide,
Adjure thee loftily now to prevail.
   Oh! Let thy sons in New World light decide
To plant for aye on Freedom's glorious heights
The standard of triumphant equal rights.

from Miscellaneous Poems
Hymn to the Nation

When Science, trembling in the lengthened shade
Of monster superstitions, and menaced
By raving Bigotry, a dream embraced
Of prosperous worlds by mortal unsurveyed,
Genoa's seaman and a daring few,
Wide Ocean's stormy perils rent and brought her
    bounds to view.

Who then had thought that with the Eternal mind,
That in vast Future's covered bosom bound—
Shut up—by these sea-roamers to be found,
Was this green home of poor, abused mankind,
This land of exiles, and the peaceful borne,
Where Babel's scattered tongues shall yet to one
    great speech return.

Fair Freedom travailed 'neath an unknown sky,
And tho' the tyrant shook his envious chain,
And tho' the bigot reared a gloomy fane,
She bore our darling of the azure eye;
Baptized its childhood in brave blood and tears,
But trumpted her independence in Great Britian's ears.

Astonished kingdoms heard of the new birth,
And royal vengeance drew her warring blade,
And bloody strokes upon Columbia laid,
To smite the young offender to the earth;
Colonial hardships shivered where she went,
And border horrors thro' the years a thrill of sadness sent.

But patriotism bold sustained the blow,
Returning deeper wounds with daring might —
For Freedom ever steels the stroke of right —
And cool determined Valor's proud arm so
Dismayed the imperial hosts, that baffled George
Saw he could ne'er enslave the men who withstood
        Valley Forge.

A century has spun around the wheel
Of ages, and the years in noiseless flight
Have heaped their golden tributes to the right;
Till now religion in her heavenly zeal,
To mend life's ills walks hand in hand with lore,
Where clank the chains of slaves in Law's offended
        ears no more.

Here honest labor trembles at the nod
Of no despot; and penury no more
Must with her gaunt and withered arm implore
Scant life at Charity's closed hands; but God
Doth lead the bounteous thousands as a flock,
And Peace's happy voices echo from the Nation's Rock.

Tho' at the name Republic tyrants mocked,
Columbia has lived a hundred years
Thro' trials, triumphs, hopes, and doubts and fears,
And still she lives, tho' often tempest-rocked.

Republic yet, united, one and free,
And may she live; her name the synonym of Liberty!

Go forth, ye children of the valiant land,
Go, sound the timbrel of her praises loud!
Ye Alleghenies, in your ascent proud
Thro' cloud-surrounded realms, the winds command
That revel in your soaring locks, to raise
One harmony, and mingle all their hoarsest notes in praise!

Ye Rocky mountains, as with awful glee,
Or icy scorn, ye stare against the sun
Whose shafts glance harmless your strong front upon,
And splintered fall, awake the Western Sea
To join the thunders of your snowy reign,
And speak responsive to your neighbors tow'ring
        o'er the plain!

Stride on, thou dread Niagara, stride on!
Thou lord of waters, in thy mighty wrath,
And thy earth-rocking leap into the bath
Of thunders, stride on! Omnipotent, alone!
And from thy stony lungs her praises sound,
Till Mexic's potent Sea reply and Oceans shout around!

The Lute of Afric's Tribe

To the memory of Dr. J. McSimpson, a colored Author of Anti-Slavery
Ballads. Written for the Zanesville, O., Courier.[7]

When Israel sate by Babel's stream and wept,
The heathen said, "Sing one of Zion's songs;"
But tuneless lay the lyre of those who slept
Where Sharon bloomed and Oreb vigil kept;
For holy song to holy ears belongs.

---

[7]*The Emancipation Car/ being an/ Original Composition/ of/ Anti-Slavery Ballads,/
composed exclusively for the/ Underground Railroad,* by J.M.C. Simpson (Zanesville, Ohio,
1874). Several of Simpson's songs were designed to be sung by escaping fugitive slaves. See
p. 268 n.

So, when her iron clutch the Slave power reached,
And sable generations captive held;
When Wrong the gospel of endurance preached;
The lute of Afric's tribe, tho' oft beseeched,
In all its wild, sweet warblings never swelled.

And yet when Freedom's lispings o'er it stole,
Soft as the breath of undefiled morn,
A wand'ring accent from its strings would stroll—
Thus was our Simpson, man of song and soul,
And stalwart energies, to bless us born.

When all our nation's sky was overcast
With rayless clouds of deepening misery,
His soaring vision mounted thro' the blast,
And from behind its gloom approaching fast,
Beheld the glorious Sun of Liberty.

He sang exultant: "Let her banner wave!"
And cheering senates, fired by his zeal,
Helped snatch their country from rebellion's grave,
Looked through brave tears upon the injured slave,
And raised the battle-arm to break his gyves of steel.

But hushed the bard, his harp no longer sings
The woes and longings of a shackled mind;
For death's cold fingers swept its trembling strings,
And shut the bosom of its murmurings
Forever on the hearing of mankind.

The bird that dips his flight in noonday sun,
May fall, and spread his plumage on the plain;
But when immortal mind its work hath done
On earth, in heaven a nobler work's begun,
And it can never downward turn again.

Of him, whose harp then lies by death unstrung—
A harp that long his lowly brethren cheered,
May'nt we now say that, sainted choirs among,
An everlasting theme inspires his tongue,
Where slaves ne'er groan, and death is never feared?

Yes, he is harping on the "Sea of glass,"
Where saints begin, and angels join the strain;
While Spheres in one profound, eternal bass,
Sing thro' their orbs, illumined as they pass,
And constellations catch the long refrain.

Written for the Zanesville (O.,) Courier.
Custer's Last Ride[8]

Forth on the fatal morn,
Proud as the waves of Horn
Rode the cavalier;
Followed by gallant men,
Far in a rocky glen
To disappear.

"Halt!" bands of Sioux are seen
O'er all the dark ravine,
Crouched in numbers vast;
"Halt!" and a hush, "Prepare!"
"Charge!" and the very air
Starts at the blast.

Long waves of horsemen break,
And hoofy thunders wake
On the steep glen sides.
Back roll the columns brave,
Back in a smoky grave,
Each hero rides.

"Ready!" their chieftain cries,
Steady his eagle eyes
Sweep the dark ground o'er.
Slowly the lines re-form,
Slowly returns the storm,
Yet dreadful more.

---

[8]Custer—George Armstrong Custer (1839-1876) dashing cavalry officer who refused a lieutenant-colonelcy with the newly-formed Negro Ninth Cavalry and accepted the same rank with the newly-formed Seventh Cavalry, with an entire command of which he was slaughtered by Sioux Indians at Little Big Horn, Montana, June 25, 1876.

"Charge!" is the proud command,
Onward the daring band
Like a torrent dash;
On heaving gorges long,
On groaning rocks among,
With tempest crash.

Up from their ferny beds
Dart fields of pluming heads,
As if hideous earth,
Out of her rocky womb,
Out of an army's tomb,
Doth give them birth.

"Rally!" but once is heard,
"Rally!" and not a word,
The brave boys, rallying, speak.
Lightnings of valiant steel
Flash fast; the columns reel,
Bend—reel and break!

"Stand!" cries their Custer proud,
"Stand!" in the battle cloud
Echoes high around.
Answers the sabre's stroke,
Tho' in black waves of smoke
His fair form's drown'd.

Fierce hordes of painted braves
Melt down, for well behave
Horse and cavalier:
As round their chief they fall,
Cheered by his clarion call,
From front to rear.

No more their leader calls,
Pierced 'mid his men he falls,
But sinks breathing, "Stand!"
And where the hero lies,
Each soldier till he dies,
Fights hand to hand.

Ye Bards of England

England, cannot thy shores boast bards as great,
And hearts as good as ever blest a State?
When arts were rude and literature was young,
And language faltered with an uncouth tongue;
When science trembled on her little height,
And poor religion blundered on in night;
When song on Rome's vast tomb, or carved in Greek,
Like epitaphs with marble lips did speak,
Thy Chaucer singing with the Nightingales,
Poured forth his heart in Canterbury tales,
With rude shell scooped from English pure, and led
The age that raised the muses from the dead.

And gentle Thompson,[9] to thy mem'ry dear,
Awoke his lyre and sang the rolling year.
The dropping shower the wild flower scented mead,
The sober herds that in the noon shade feed,
The fragrant field, the green and shady wood,
The winding glen, and rocky solitude,
The smiles of Spring and frowns of Winter gray,
Alike employed his pure and gentle lay.
The wrath of gods, and armies' dread suspense,
Celestial shouts and shock of arms immense.
In all his song ne'er move us to alarm,
But earth's pure sounds and sights allure and charm.

To Missolonghi's chief of singers too,
Unhappy Byron, is a tribute due.
A wounded spirit, mournful and yet mad,
A genius proud, defiant, gentle, sad.
'Twas he whose *Harold* won his Nation's heart,
And whose Reviewers[10] made her fair cheeks smart;

---

[9] Thompson, i.e., James Thompson (1700-1748) English poet, widely known for his four part poem, "The Seasons" (1726-1730).

[10] Reviewers, i.e., *English Bards and Scotch Reviewers* (1809), a retaliatory piece of neo-classical satire by George Gordon, Lord Byron (1788-1824). Exiled since 1816, Byron wrote *Don Juan* (1818-1824), which became an immediate "best-seller," a feat which, Whitman suggests, Englishmen would rather have had created on English soil, as was the case with much of the poet's *Childe Harold* (1812-1817): "*Mazeppa*" appeared in 1817.

Whose uncurbed Juan hung her head for shame,
And whose *Mazzeppa* won unrivaled fame.
Earth had no bound for him. Where'er he strode
His restless genius found no fit abode.
The wing'd storm and the lightning tongued Jungfrau,
Unfathomable Ocean, and the awe
Of Alpine shades, the avalanche's groan,
The war-rocked empire and the falling throne,
Were toys his genius played with. Britain, then
Urn Byron's dust—a prodigy of men.
But Shakespeare, the inimitable boast
Of everybody and of every coast;
The *man* whose universal fitness meets
Response in every heart of flesh that beats,
No tongue can tell him. One must feel his hand
And see him in his plays, to understand.
All thought to him intuitively's known,
The prate of clowns, and wisdoms of the throne,
The sophist's puzzles and the doctor's rules,
The skill of warriors and the cant of fools.
When Shakespeare wrote, the tragic muse saw heights,
Before nor since ne'er tempted in her flights.

Stonewall Jackson, 1886[11]

Defiant in the cannon's mouth,
I see a hero of the South,
    Serene and tall;
So like a stonewall in the fray
He stands, that wond'ring legions say:
    "He is a wall!"

He heeded not the fiercest onsets
From bristling fields of bayonets;
    He heeded not
The thunder-tread of warring steeds,
But holds his men of daring deeds
    Right on the spot.

---

[11] At Chancellorsville, Virginia, May 2, 1863, Jackson, who once taught slaves in Lexington, Virginia, 1851-1862, was shot by mistake by his own men and died May 10.

And is it insanity?
Nay, this is but the gravity
        Of that vast mind,
That on his Southland's altar wrought
And forged the bolts of warrior thought
        Of thunder kind.

An eagle eye, a vulture's flight,
A stroke leonine in might;
        The man was formed
For that resolving deep inert
Which sprang stupendously alert,
        And, sometimes, stormed.

And so, his mount to the charge,
Or led the columns small or large,
        The victor rode;
Till over danger's castle moat,
And in the cannon's silenced throat,
        His charger trode.

And so, with fierce for speed, or near
To right and left and in the rear,
        His fury fell
Upon the foe too much to meet.
For Jackson's soul abhorred retreat,
        Except from hell.

But comes the saddest at the last,
As sad as life's ideal past—
        And, oh! how sad!—
That, in his pride, the Stonewall fell
By hands of those he loved so well—
        The best he had.

How sad that dark and cruel night
Should fold her mantle on the sight
        Of those tried, true
And valiant men, who followed where
Their leader went, despising fear
        And darkness, too!

But sometimes triumph is sublime
The most when on the brink of time,
     And his was so;
A shady hope beyond he sees,
And asks for rest beneath the trees,
     And it was so.

And do you ask, can he whose sweat
Hath clods of weary slave soil wet,
     The praises sing
Of one who fought to forge the chain
That manacles the human brain?
     Do such a thing?

I answer, yes, if he who fought,
Fought bravely and believed he ought,
     If that can be;
If manhood in the mighty test
Of manhood does its manliest
     Believingly.

Then poet songs for him shall ring,
And he shall live while poets sing;
     And while he lives,
     And God forgives,
The great peculiar martial star,
In old Virginia's crown of war,
Will be her Stonewall, proud and sad,
The bravest that she ever had.

       * * * * * * *

IV

Dialect Poets

Negro Dialect Poetry

Because America is, whatever else, a conglomeration of peoples from all over the world, it is not surprising that there are almost as many different dialects as there are ethnic groups, and yet, for reasons that seem clear enough, it is not surprising either that Negro dialect has flourished more than the others. The vogue was established among white Southern writers (who failed to appreciate their own amusing dialects) with Irwin Russell (1853-1879) whose popular pieces were collected and published posthumously as *Poems by Irwin Russell* (1888) with a loving preface by Joel Chandler Harris, also popular for his Uncle Remus and Brer Rabbit prose tales in Negro dialect. Other white writers of the form, and they are plentiful, include Thomas Nelson Page, A.C. Gordon, but almost always they used the genre to parade the stock Negro, contentedly servile on the plantation or comic in his favorite pursuits of eating and bumbling with polysyllabics at his religious or romantic affairs. The black man in the hands of most white dialect writers is a subject for ridicule, and served to document the learnings and expectations of white readers in need of repeated confirmations of their psychological and social notions about superior and inferior races.

A few Negro dialect writers also produced similar creations, but there were those who, like Paul Laurence Dunbar (1872-1906), recognized that such language, although limiting, might be used for more than the usual characterizing purposes. While none of his characters did anything overtly to disturb the racist status quo, several of them do achieve a measure of reality and genuine pathos which other dialect writers did not care to delineate. Dunbar was launched into a curious fame when William Dean Howells praised his early *Majors and Minors* (1895) and wrote an introduction for his *Lyrcis of Lowly Life* (1896). But, as Dunbar soon saw, he was praised for the wrong reasons. His home in Dayton, Ohio, is a national shrine, his works are as available as those of most other American poets, he is regarded as the Folk Negro Poet Laureate—all of this despite the fact that about two thirds of his *Complete Poems* (1913) have nothing at all to do with dialect. Although he is the most famous Negro writer of such verse, he is not the first and is certainly not the only one. Frances E.W. Harper (q.v.) produced clumsy attempts at dialect with her Aunt Chloe pieces in *Sketches of Southern Life* (1872, and in enlarged later editions); James T. Franklin wrote several dialect things in *Midday Gleanings* (Memphis, 1893). James E. McGirt declared as early as 1899 in his *Avenging The Maine, a Drunken A.B.* (Raleigh) that he, for one, would not use dialect as much as he might because Negroes themselves, moving from the plantation in droves, were no longer using it extensively. But study and versified practice of Negro speech and folklore has persisted, producing an everswelling library unto itself (see, for instance, pages 439-448 in Alain Locke's *The New Negro*, New York, 1925; reprinted by Antheneum, 1968).

With radical differences, obvious relationships exist between Negro dialect poetry and the modern militant black poetic uses of "black ghettoese" language, city-paced spontaneous rhythms, vivid atavistic images. Owing much to Leroi Jones, they would include, to mention a very few, David Nelson, *Black Impulse* (New York, 1968); Etheridge Knight, *Poems From Prison* (Detroit, 1968); Don Lee, *Think Black* (Chicago, 1968) and *Black Pride* (Detroit, 1968). Although there is common use of such language, rhythm and imagery, the poets of dialect and "ghettoese" differ in their views of themselves and the world around them. The selections that follow should give some indication of the diversity of thought and skill as presented by early black American poets. Born in Richmond, Virginia, in 1862, Daniel W. Davis was a long time Richmond educator and popular platform personality; he was awarded an honorary M.A. degree by Guadaloupe College in Seguin, Texas, 1898. His books include a collaboration with Giles B. Jackson and W.W. Davis on *An Industrial History of the Negro Race in the United States* (Richmond, 1908) and two volumes of verse, *Idle Moments* (Baltimore, 1895) and *'Weh Down Souf* (Cleveland, 1897), which includes a reprinting of much of *Idle Moments,* from which his selections below are taken. Born in the early 1860's in Pomeroy, Ohio, where he attended public schools, James Edwin Campbell later attended Miami College in Ohio, wrote for several Chicago newspapers, co-edited a literary publication, *Four O'Clock Magazine,* and two books of verse: *Driftings and Gleanings* (by 1888) and *Echoes from the Plantation and Elsewhere* (Chicago, 1895). His mother dying at his birth in 1816 in Cass County, Michigan, and rejected by his father, James D. Corrothers knocked about in a variety of odd jobs, including shoeshining where a customer, impressed by his bookish conversation, helped him to attend Northwestern University 1890-1893; a restless man, he later attended Bennett College in Greensboro, North Carolina, and was successively a minister in the Methodist, Baptist and Presbyterian churches. He relates even more in his autobiography, *In Spite of The Handicap* (New York, 1916). He wrote for several Chicago newspapers, cullings of which, below, help make up his *Black Cat Club* (New York, 1907). J. Mord Allen was born in Montgomery, Alabama, and moved, with his family, when he was seven years old, to Topeka, Kansas, where he apprenticed for and became a boilermaker, except for a three year stint, 1889-1892, with a travelling theatrical group, for which he wrote some otherwise unknown stage pieces. Selections are from his single volume, *Rhymes; Tales and Rhymed Tales* (Topeka, 1906). Elliott B. Henderson was a prolific author of at least eight volumes of verse, mostly dialect pieces. The selections, following, are from his early *Plantation Echoes* (Columbus, Ohio, 1904), but the titles of some of his later works may prove illustrative: *Darky Meditations* (Springfield, Ohio, 1910); *Uneddykated Folks* (Author, 1911); *Darky Ditties* (Columbus, 1915).

James Edwin Campbell *(Echoes from the Plantation)*
Ol' Doc' Hyar

Ur ol' Hyar lib in ur house on de hill,
He hunner yurs ol' an' nebber wuz ill;
He yurs dee so long an' he eyes so beeg,
An' he laigs so spry dat he dawnce ur jeeg;

He lib so long dat he know ebbry tings
'Bout de beas'ses dat walks an' de bu'ds dat sings—
                    Dis Ol' Doc' Hyar,
                    Whar lib up dar
Een ur mighty find house on ur mighty high hill.

He doctah fur all de beas'ses an' bu'ds—
He put on he specs an' he use beeg wu'ds,
He feel dee pu's' den he look mighty wise,
He pull out he watch an' he shet bofe eyes;
He grab up he hat an' grab up he cane,
Den—"blam!" go de do'—he gone lak de train,
                    Dis Ol' Doc' Hyar,
                    Whar lib up dar
Een ur mighty fine house on ur mighty high hill.

Mistah Ba'r fall sick—dee sont fur Doc' Hyar,
"O, Doctah, come queeck, an' see Mr. B'ar;
He mighty nigh daid des sho'ez you b'on!"
"Too much ur young peeg, too much ur green co'n,"
Ez he put on he hat, said Ol' Doc' Hyar;
"I'll tek 'long meh lawnce, an' lawnce Mistah B'ar,"
                    Said Ol' Doc' Hyar,
                    Whar lib up dar
Een ur mighty fine house on ur mighty high hill.

Mistah B'ar he groaned, Mistah B'ar he growled,
W'ile de ol' Mis' B'ar an' de chillen howled:
Doctah Hyar tuk out he sha'p li'l lawnce,
An' pyu'ced Mistah B'ar twel he med him prawnce
Den grab up he hat an' grab up he cane
"Blam!" go de do' an' he gone lak de train,
                    Dis Ol' Doc' Hyar,
                    Whar lib up dar
Een ur mighty fine house on ur mighty high hill.

But de vay naix day Mistah B'ar he daid;
Wen dee tell Doc' Hyar, he des scratch he haid:
"Ef pashons git well ur pashons git wu's,
Money got ter come een de Ol' Hyar's pu's;

Not wut folkses does, but fur wut dee know
Does de folkses git paid"—an' Hyar larfed low,
Dis sma't Ol' Hyar,
Whar lib up dar
Een de mighty fine house on de mighty high hill!

Uncle Eph—Epicure

You kin talk erbout yo' 'lasses an' yo' steamin' buckwheat cakes,
'Bout yo' eisters fried in crackers, an' yo' juicy hot clambakes;

'Bout yo' beefsteak fried wid inguns, an' yo' ros'n yeahs ob co'n,
But ol' possum wid sweet taters beats dem all, des sho's you bo'n.

Tek erway yo' Floyda eiange, tek erway yo' fig and date,
An' bring erlong my 'possum on dat bigges' ol' tin plate.

Turnip greens all biled wid bacon an' er co'n pone smokin hot,
I gwi' nebber scratch *dat* ticket caze it retch ur tender spot.

An' hot biscuits wid hot coffee mek ur mighty han'som pa'r,
W'ile ol' hen biled wid dumplin's, O yes, dat's parsin' fa'r.

But tek erway yo' greens an' bacon, tek erway yo' chicken biled,
An' bring 'possum an' sweet taters—hesh yo' mouf, dey sets me wild!

Sta't him out'n pawpaw thicket, chase him up er 'simmon tree,
W'ile de music ob dat houn' pack sets de woods er-ring wid glee.

Roun' de hill an' troo de bottom, up de holler by de spring,
Ow! ow! ow! ow! des a whoopin'! how dat ol' lead-houn' do sing!

An' you hurry troo de briahs an' you tumble ober logs,
Nebber knowin', nebber cyarin' ez you chyuh dem blessed dogs.

An' w'en dey all sees you comin', how dem dogs sing wid new grace,
Fum de young houn's sweet, cla'r tenah ter de ol' houn's mighty bass.

An' dar on ur lim' er grinnin' wid his tail quoiled mighty tight,
Hangs my fren', ol' Mistah 'Possum—how dem dogs howl wid delight.

An' you crawl out furder, furder, twel you hyuh dat ol' lim' crack,
An' you shake er loose his tail holt, an' you put him in yo' sack.

Den you tote him home an' feed him twel he fat des ez you please,
Den you kill him an' you hang him out er frosty night ter freeze.

Den you stuff him wid sweet taters an 'put butter all ur roun',
Den you put him in de oven an' you bake him twel he's brown.

Oom! all swimmin' in his graby an' ur drippin' in his fat—
Talk erbout yo' milk an' honey, wut's de hebbenly food ter dat?

Let dat show-ban' play its loudes', let dat 'cession des march on,
I wouldn't stop my eatin' ef ol' Gab'ul blowed his horn!

De Cunjah Man

O chillen run, de Cunjah man,
Him mouf ez beeg ez fryin' pan,
Him yurs am small, him eyes am raid,
Him hab no toof een him ol' haid,
Him hab him roots, him wu'k him trick,
Him roll him eye, him mek you sick—
    De Cunjah man, de Cunjah man,
    O chillen run, de Cunjah man!

Him hab ur ball ob raid, raid ha'r,
Him hide it un' de kitchen sta'r,
Mam Jude huh pars urlong dat way,
An' now huh hab ur snaik, dey say.
Him wrop ur roun' huh buddy tight,
Huh eyes pop out, ur orful sight—
    De Cunjah man, de Cunjah man,
    O chillen run, de Cunjah man!

Miss Jane, huh dribe him f'un huh do',
An' now huh hens woan' lay no mo';
De Jussey cow huh done fall sick,
Hit all done by de cunjah trick.
Him put ur root un' 'Lijah's baid,
An' now de man he sho' am daid—
    De Cunjah man, de Cunjah man,
    O chillen run, de Cunjah man!

Me see him stand' de yudder night
Right een de road een white moon-light;
Him toss him arms, him whirl him 'roun';
Him stamp him foot urpon de groun';
De snaiks come crawlin', one by one,
Me hyuh um hiss, me break an' run.
    De Cunjah man, de Cunjah man,
    O Chillen run, de Cunjah man!

* * * * * * *

'Sciplinin' Sister Brown

Shet up dat noise, you chillen! Dar's some one at de do'.
Dribe out dem dogs; you 'Rastus, tek Linkum off de flo'!

Des ma'ch yo'se'f right in sah! (Jane, tek dem ashes out!
Dis house look lak ur hog-pen; you M'randy, jump erbout!)

W'y bress my soul, hit's Ef'um—w'y, Ef'um, how you do?
An' Tempie an' de chillen? I hopes dey's all well too.

Hyuh, M'randy, bresh dat stool off; now, Ef'um, des set down.
Wut's de news f'um off de Ridge an' wut's de news in town?

Now doan' you t'ink dem niggahs hed Susan 'fo de chu'ch
'Bout dawncin' at de pa'ty—dey call dat sinnin' much.

Dey up an' call ur meetin' ter 'scipline Sistah Brown,
But de night dey hol' de meetin' she tuk herse'f to town.

Dey sont de Bo'd ob Deacons, de pahstah at de head,
Ter wait urpon de sistah an' pray wid her, dey said,

But Susan mighty stubbo'n, an' wen dey lif' ur pra'r
She up an' tell de deacons she des wawn' gwine ter cyar.

An' wen de Reb'ren' Pa'son prayed 'bout ur "sheep wuz los'."
An' 'bout de "po bac'slidah," she gin her head ur toss!

I seed de debbil raisin' in de white ob Susan's eyes—
Fyeah she blow dat deacon-bo'd ter "mansions in de skies,"

I des tuk down my bawnjer an' den I 'gins an' plays;
"Come dy fount ob ebbry blessin', chune my ha't ter sing dy
praise."

De pa'son an' de deacons dey jined me pooty soon;
Lawd! Dat bawnjer shuk itse'f ur-playin' ob de chune!

An' wen dey mos' wuz shoutin', I tightened up er string,
Drapped right inter "Money Musk" an' gin de chune full swing.

De "Debbil's Dream" come arter—de debbil wuz ter pay,
Dem niggahs fell ter pattin'—I larf mos' ebbry day!

Deacon Jones got on his feet, de pa'son pulled him down;
I played ur little fastah, an' sho's my name am Brown,

De pa'son an' de deacons jined han's right on dis flo',
Su'cled right and su'cled lef'—it sutny wiz er show.

Dey 'naded up an' down de flo' an' w'en hit come ter swing,
De pa'son gin hisse'f a flirt an' cut de pidgin-wing!

An' we'n urfo' de meetin' dat 'mittee med its 'po't
'Bout Sistah Susan's dawncin', dey cut it mighty sho't.

De Chyuhsman, Mr. Pa'son, said in tones so mil' an' sweet:
"Sistah Brown wa'n't guilty, caze—SHE NEBBER CROSSED HER
FEET!"

* * * * * * * *

Daniel Webster Davis ('Weh Down Souf)
Miss Liza's Banjer

Hi! Miss Liza's got er banjer;
    Lemme see it, ef yo' please!
Now don' dat thing look pooty,
    A-layin' 'cross yer kneeze,
Wid all dem lubly ribbins,
    An' silber trimmin's roun'.
Now, mistis, please jes' tetch it,
    To lemme hear de soun'.

'Scuze me, mistis, but dar's sumfin'
    De matter wid dem strings;
I notis it don' zackly
    Gib de proper kinder ring;

An' den de way yo' hol' it
    Ain't lik' yo' orter do.
Now, mistis, won't yo' lemme
    Jes' try a chune fur yo'?

Now lis'n to de diffunce;
    I'se got the thing in chune,
An' de music's lik' de breezes
    Dat fills de air in June.
Fur a banjer's lik' a 'ooman—
    Ef she's chuned de proper pitch,
She'll gib yo' out de music
    Dat's sof', melojus, rich.

But when yo' fail to chune her,
    Or to strike de proper string,
Yo' kin no more git de music,
    Den mek' a kat-bird sing.
An' 'taint always de fixin's
    Dat makes a 'ooman bes',
But de kind ub wood she's made un
    Is de thing to stan' de tes'.

I s'pose yer plays yer music
    Jes' lik' yo' hab it wrote,
Or—what is dat yo' call it—
    A-playin' by de note?
Yo' kin fill yer head wid music
    Ez full ez it kin hol',
But yo' nebber gwine ter play it
    'Tell yo' gits it in yer soul.

T'ain't de proper notes dat makes yo'
    Feel lik' yo' wants to cry,
But de soul dat's in de music
    Dat lif's yo' up on high;
An' 'taint always de larnin',
    'Do' a splendid thing, I kno',
Dat lif's de low an' 'umble
    To higher things belo'.

Keep larnin', den, Miss Liza,
   An' when yo' wants ter know
Ef yo' kin play de banjer,
   Jes' kum to Uncle Joe;
Jes' fill yer head wid music,
   Ez full ez it kin hol'
But de music from de banjer
   Must fust be in de soul.

Aunt Chloe's Lullaby

Hesh! my baby; stop yer fuss,
I's 'fraid yuz gittin wuss an' wuss;
Doncher cry, an' I gwy mek'
Mammy's baby 'lasses cake.
Hesh! my lubly baby chil',
I gwy rock yo' all de whil';
Nuffin gwyne to ketch yo' now,
'Cause yer mammy's watchin' yo'.
Sleep! my little baby, sleep!
   Mammy's baby, Lou!

How dem dogs do bark to-night!
Better shet yer eyes up tight;
Dey kan't hab dis baby dear;
Mammy's watchin', doncher fear.
Hear dem owls a-hootin' so?
Dey shan't ketch dis baby, do'.
Jes' like mistis lub her chil',
Mammy lubs dis baby too.

* * * * * * * *

From James D. Corrothers *(The Black Cat Club)*
"Sweeten 'Tatahs"

I

"I has always laked good eatin's,
   F'om de minute I wah bo'n,
Plum' up 'tel de present writin'—
   An' I *will* 'tel Judgment mo'n!

Nothin' good I draws de line on;
  But I's happies', it seem,
When I's eatin' sweeten 'tatahs,
  An' I shet ma eyes an' dream.

II

"Bake a 'tatah good an' mealy,
  In de ashes, ef you please—
'Way dese No'then people cooks 'em
  'S' nuff to make a chicken sneeze!
Kivver it wid coals an' ashes—
  Le'be 'it in dah foh a while—
Draw it out an'gin it to me—
  Take keer, honey, lemme smile!

IV

" 'Ca'se you see a-eatin' uv it
  Makes me thaink uv ma ole home—
'Way down yondah in ole Dixie,
  Whah I deahly longs to roam
'Mongst de cotton-fields an' flowahs,
  Roun' de ole home place once mo',
Happy, munchin' sweeten 'tatahs,
  Is I did in days uv yo'.

V

"I kin see de little cabin
  Whah our fambly libbed, an' whah
Putty vines an' mo'nin' glories
  Shed dey fragrance on de a'h,
An' de mockin'-bird sung sweetly,
  An' de squirrels sassed an' run;
'Ca'se dey wanted sweeten 'tatah,
  An' I wouldn't gib 'em none.

VI

"I kin heah de rain a-fallin'
     On de cabin roof once mo',
An' de lonely tree-toad callin'
     F'om de gum tree by de do',
An' I sees us chillun settin'
     Roun' de fiah-place, at de feet
Uv our mammy, smilin' at us,
     Is we eats de 'tatahs sweet.

VII

"An' I 'membahs how us chillun
     Used to set aroun' de fiah,
Uv a wintah, roas'in' 'tatahs,
     An' I allus did admiah
De way ma stomach helt 'em so—
     Wy'y, it use to seem I hid
Mo' uv dem precious 'tatahs
     Den a bushel basket did!

VIII

"Co'se I owns dey's othah eatin's'
     At is putty *middlin'* fine;
But dey cain't compah wid nothin'
     In de sweeten 'tatah line!
Yo' highfahlutin' 'a la mo's'
     Soun's mighty chahmin' like;
But 'at 'ah ain't de kine o' grub
     Foh a hongry man to strike!

IX

" 'Watahmillun'?—You mus' keep it
     On de ice, an' lak o' dat—
Sweeten 'tatah's *sweeten 'tatah,*
     Make no diffunce whah you's at!
You kin eat 'em in de pahlah,
     In de kitchen er de wood—
Europe, Asia, San Domingo—
     Anywhahs!—dey's des' az good.

X

"Watahmillun's mouty temptin'
    'Long about de mont' o' June—
On de hillside, winkin' at you,
    At de settin' uv de moon;—
But, in Aprile er December,
    Whah's a't millum to be foun'?—
Lemme hab ma sweeten 'tatahs,
    Ca'se dey's good de whole yeah 'roun'!

XI

"Whut would 'possum be widout 'em?—
    Nothin' whutsomevah, 't all!
Cook it widout sweeten 'tatah,
    An' you'll see how flat it fall!
Pie an' cake am common eatin's—
    An' ice cream am white folks' muss—
Ham an' cabbage, co'n-pone, nothin'
    Hit's de spot lak 'tatah does!

XII

"I lubs peaches, too—I's eat 'em
    Ripe an' fresh, right off de tree;—
Dey is juicy, dey is mellah,
    Dey is sweet as sweet kin be—
An' dey's rosy, an' dey's yellah—
    Yit an' still dey nevah seem
Good as eatin' sweeten 'tatahs,
    When I shets ma eyes an' dream.

XIII

"Evahthaing is 'dulterated
    By de white folks, nowadays—
Eben chime bones,* when you buys 'em,
    Dey ain't wo'f de cash you pays.

---

*Note.—The ribs, neck, and back-bone of a hog are called "chime bones" by Negroes, and are considered delightful eating—especially if the hog has been freshly killed by themselves or a neighbor. J.D.C.

W'y', dey's sellin' cats foh possum!—
   Buttah's nothin' but beef fat!
But de Laud makes sweeten 'tatahs—
   White folks got no han' in dat!

XIV

"An' when I eats sweeten 'tatahs,
   Seem lak trouble, grief, an' sin,
An' ma aches an' pains goes f'om me,
   An' I ain't got nothin' 'g'in'
Ma wo'ses inamy! Ma soul
   Lets Heben's own glory stream
Plum' th'u' an' th'u' it, is I eat,
   An' jes' shets ma eyes an' dream!

XV

"Oh, I tell you sweeten 'tatahs
   Is de pleasah uv ma life!
An' I'm allus boun' to hab 'em, too!
   An', ef I had a wife'
At couldn't cook a 'tatah *right,*
   'At ah'd settle it wid me—
I'd go ma way, an' she'd go hern;
   Jes' you watch me now, an' see!

XVI

" 'Ca'se dey's heaps o' memories
   Sweeten 'tatahs brings to me—
W'y, I nevah thainks about 'em
   But ma mammy's face I see—
An' ma mammy sho'ly lubbed 'em,
   An' ma little brothah Joe,
At died, craved foh 'em awful bad—
   Jes' 'fo' he had to go.

XVII

"As his little eyes wah closin',
   An' we stood aroun' his bed,
While de sunset, th'u' de windah,
   Shed its glory 'roun' his head,

Mammy drawed him to huh bosom,
  Tendah, knowin' Death had won,
An' he whispahs—'Please to wake me
  When de sweeten 'tatah's done.'

Der Rabbit's Foot

I

"Foun' dis rabbit's foot, you see,
Uddah day, fuss thaing I knowed—
Rabbit shuck it off foh me,
's he run'd across de road;
Change ma' luck right dah an' den!
Evah foe become mah fr'en!
No use talkin', gen'l'men,
Virtu' in dis foot hab growed!

II

"Rub it th'ee times 'cross ma face—
Hol' it so, in mah lef' han'—
Put it back into its place—
Make a wish, an' own de lan'!
Take de hoss shoe f'om de do'!
Let de fo'-leaf clovah go!—
Nevah need 'em any mo',
'Ca'se dis rabbit's foot am gran'!"

* * * * * * * *

Elliot B. Henderson *(Plantation Echoes)*
Good Bye, Honey—Good Bye

Gwine to leeb dis dear ol' place,
  Good bye, honey; good bye!
Time's er flyin', I mus' make has'e,
  Good bye, honey; good bye!
Hate to go, but I kain't say no,
It gives mah hea't er pang o' woe,
Yo' all's mah fren', not one's mah foe,
  Good bye, honey; good bye!

Sistah Jane, an' uncle Joe?
  Good bye, honey; good bye!
I hope we'll see us all sum mo',
  Good bye, honey; good bye!
We's gittin' ol', we's gittin' gray,
Ah days am dun' fo' makin' hay,
Ah steps cum slo', we's wastin' 'way,
  Good bye, honey; good bye!

We's had good times on dis ol' place,
  Good bye, honey; good bye!
We's frollic'd in de possum chase,
  Good bye, honey; good bye!
We's picked de cotton, hoed de co'n,
We's picked de berries spite o' thorns,
We's wocked at night, we's wocked at morn,
  Good bye, honey; good bye!

Hain't dat Miss Linndy, obeah dah?
  Good bye, honey; good bye!
Sho' it am; well, I declah!
  Good bye, honey; good bye!
Cum an' shake de ol' man's han',
Gwine to leeb ol' massa's lan'
'Deed, Miss Linndy, yo' look gran',
  Good bye, honey; good bye!

Rastus? little Rastus, chile,
  Good bye, honey; good bye!
Look ee dah, jes' see him smile,
  Good bye, honey; good bye!
Jes' ez natshul ez his paw,
De bes' chile dat I ebbah saw,
Got de mannahs ub his maw,
  Good bye, honey; good bye!

Whah is Massa, is he 'roun'?
  Good bye, honey; good bye!
'Pears' I koch his footstep soun',
  Good bye, honey; good bye!

I 'fess it's hard to leeb him now,
To say good bye, I doan' kno' how,
I'll shake his han', jes' make er bow,
    Good bye, honey; good bye!

Mockin' bird up in de tree?
    Good bye, honey; good bye!
Yo's sung er manny day to me.
    Good bye, honey; good bye!
Er manny day dis hea't o' mine
Yo's cheered it wid yo song divine,
An' made de sunlight brighter shine,
Goodbye, honey, goodbye!

Git on Board, Chillun

De Gospel train am er scootin' down de rail!
    Git on board, chillun!
Fas'ah den er ship wid er ruddah an' er sail!
    Git on board, chillun!
De Lawd in heaven am de steam an' de pow'r!
He run dat train forty millun miles an' hour!
Jes' es stroke ub de throttle
Sends her clah to heaben's tow'r!
    Git on board, chillun!

No sinnah tribe kin ebbah ride on dat train!
    Git on board, chillun!
De debil ner his imps ef day's cut loose fum dey chain!
    Git on board, chillun!
None but de lams ub de good Lawd's fol'
Kin ride dat train to de streets o' gol',
Wid de 'liggun lak an' ocean obeahflowin' in yo' soul!
    Git on board, chillun!

She's jes' lak lightnin' an' de quibbah o' de eye!
    Git on board, chillun!
Ez she's puffin' an' er steamin' in er trabblin' to de sky!
    Git on board, chillun!

She's limited, too, an' she goes clah th'ew!
She's got no time fo' to fool wid yo'!
Yo' mus' git on board, when de time cums, doo!
    Git on board, chillun!

Dat train hain't skeddul fo' de secun' time.
    Git on board, chillun!
Fo' to cum an' fotch yo' to de heabenly clime!
    Git on board, chillun!
She goes straight on an' she doan' tarn back!
When she once git start why she hain't gwine to slack!
Till she runs in heab'n on de right side track!
    Git on board, chillun!

De debil ner his imps kaint wreck dat ol' train!
    Git on board, chillun!
Ez she's dashin' an' er steamin' o'er de mountains an' de
plain!
    Git on board, chillun!
She sticks to de rail lak de hyah on yo' back!
An' she nebbah was known fo' to jump fum de track!
Kaze de Lawd's at de throttle an' he sho' got de knac'!
    Git on board, chillun!

Uncle Ned an' de Mockin' Bird

Bruddah Mocking Bird,
Yo's moighty lazy.
Yo' doan' do nufin'
    But sing dat song,
    Till de daylight's gone
    An' de night cum 'long.
Er coon has got to hoe an' hoe,
Till de sinkin' sun
    Tells de day to go.

Lawd, but yo' sing
    So pow'ful sweet!
Perched up dah,
    In yo' leafy seat.

Is yo' lonesum?
Does yo' hea't feel sad?
'Pears to me
    Dat yo' soul feels glad.

Ez Ise wockin' hard,
    Sweet ez de cloveah
Yo' song
    Floats obeah,
Way in de co'nfield
    Whah de medlark sings,
Up in de bough
    Ub de tree it clings.

Yo' nebah wock
    But yo' bread is sho',
Out in de yahd;
    'Fo' ebbry do',
Sum kine han'
    Th'ows de little crum!
Kaze dey kno' fo' sho'
    Dat yo' boun' to cum.

De good Samaritan
    Part dey play.
    Let yo' go 'way?
Hungry? No!

Trussy's Visit

Bress mah life! why, dis hain't Trussey?
    Go 'way Chile! whut dat yo' say?
Yo' hain't fiddlin' Peedah's sonny—
    Who'd er tho't it, any way!

Ax me ef I knowed yo' daddy—
    Knowed each uddah yeahs ergo.
Me an' him hab bof togeddah,
    Hoed er many 'taytah ro'.

Res' yo' duddin's! take de sofa,
   Make yo'se'f jes' lak yo' home.
'Cep' mos' free mah hooskerpalty,
   Plenty time eroun' to roam.

See, hyeah, Dina, am dem chittlins
   An' dem hog feet th'ew er bile?
Who yo' think we got fo' dinnah?
   Ol' fren' Fiddlin' Peedah's chile!

Well, sah, I hain't seed yo' daddy
   Since dat fight at Possum Trot.
Dog mah socks, we bof togeddah,
   Whoop'd de debbil on de spot!

Still er libbin' down in Guinea?
   Why, dat's my ol' rompin' groun'.
Hain't er spot, ner nook, ner crebbice
   Dat I doan' know 'bout dat town.

Ready, Dinah? Bress de Lawd! umph!
   Mah ol' lady am er sight.
Kin she cook? Whut? Doan' yo' staht me!
   She kin sho' put things up right!

Walk out, Trussy; go pertaykin'
   Ub de bes' de ol' man's got!
Kose tain't much, but prob'ly sumfin's
   Dah will kinedah tech de spot!

Go 'head, say de bressins, Trussy,
   Fo' de Lawd sakes cut 'em short.
Lemme pos' yo' fo' yo' staht in,
   Doan' yo' preach an' try to e'ort—

"Make us thankful, Heab'nly Faddah,
   Fo' dis hyeah pussipyus spread;
Hyeah deez few mos' feeble 'spreshyuns
   Dat yo' umble sahvunt shed.

"Gibb us wid ah daily bread, sah!
   Chicken, an' all sech ez dat!
Th'ow in now an' den er possum,
   Coon wid plenty lean an' fat!

"Po' dy bressins on dis family—
    Put mo' chickens on dey roos';
Things git skace, dey needs er he'pin',
    Len' er han', gibb 'em er boos'."

Jump in, Trussy; git to business!
    Ebbry fellah fo' himse'f.
Whut's hyeah fo' us on dis table's
    Nuf to take er possum's bref.

Ha! ha! Trussy, dem ol' hog feet
    Sots dis ol' soul all er chune!
Ha! ha! Dina? look at Trussy
    Kock dat lef' eye at dat coon!

Yo' hain't full kin to yo' daddy
    Ef yo' doesn't lak de coon;
Possum, chicken, sweepahtaytahs,
    An' de sumpshus musherroon.

Tell us 'bout ol' Tootsy Tadpole,
    Slipshod Beebe, Feeby Scott!
Susan Rhinehole, Sukie Slowup,
    Husky Botts, de res' de lot.

Does I 'membah Slimmy Twostep?
    Who? dat dah ol' onry cuss?
Usetah hug de stove when happy,
    In church raised all kine o' fuss?

Gibb him mo' coon dumplin's, Dina!
    Sakes! he's jes' fell into eat.
Tote him few dem frizzlin' passnups,
    Lecktrifies yo' to yo' feet!

Whah's ol' Susan Peecock, Trussy?
    Is de debbil got her yet?
Sakes o' lie! she's got mo' husban's
    Den yo's fingers got, I'll bet!

Cum on wid dem pig tails, Dina!
    Doan' be primpin' in de glass!
Mussen' make de ol' man wait so,
    Yo' look poody nuf to pass.

Bress de Lawd! whee! glory! glory!
  No joke, dem am sizzlin' hot!
Lissen at de res' dem fellahs
  Prayin' an' singin' in de pot!

Go 'way, Fido! see hyeah, Dina!
  Kick dat debbil out de do'!
Ebbry time he sniffs dem chittlins
  He's er hangin' 'roun' hyeah, sho'.

See hyeah, chile! yo' hain't th'ew eatin',
  Rake mo' dumplin's on yo' plate!
Go dem flapp jacks, sum dat grabey,
  Eat 'long in de mopein' gait.

Pass de ol' man few dem biskits;
  B'lieve I'll take sum poke chops, too!
Little mo' dat drap down coffee,
  Nuddah dose dat bullyun stew.

Go on in de pollah, Trussy,
  Ef yo' got ernuf to eat.
I'll be th'ew in jes' er minute,
  Den we'll go an' thrash sum wheat.

* * * * * * * *

J. Mord Allen *(Rhymes, Tales and Rhymed Tales)*
The Devil and Sis' Viney

Dar ain't no use o' talkin': when er man lets loose o' evil
En sets out in de narrer path, he's got ter whup de devil;
Who knows jes' how ter tempt er man—who knows jes' whut'll
  ketch yer—
Who knows jes' whut ter 'proach yer wid, ef anything'll fetch
  yer.
Yer got ter look out mighty sharp, wid er prayerful eye en
  humble,
En step high wid de foot o' faith; er else, yer gwine ter stumble.
Dese thoughts come ter me years ergo, when I fell out wid
  sinnin'
En parted wid Ole Satan at de gospel path's berginnin'.

So, knowin' dat Ole Satan wuz ergwine ter try ter git me,
I watched de bricks he flung at me ter see which nighes' hit me.
I hadn' been er dodgin' long berfo' de thought come to me
Dat Satan had mah medger [measure] en wuz ergwine ter ondo
me.

Bekaze I looked inter mah heart—wid prayerfulness en meek-
ness—
En seen dat 'lovely woman' wuz mah bigges', stronges'
weakness.
So, right dar, I made up mah min' ter fight ergins' de yiel'in'
[yielding]
In all things, tetchin' woman-kin', ter any tender feelin'.
Likewise I 'termined after dat, when I fust started preachin',
Ter foller in de *steps* o' Paul, en not live by his *teachin'*,
Wharin he seen dat man wuz weak. (Dat's why he writ dat letter
Dat says dat women ain't so bad—but shunnin' 'em is better.)
Yit, any preacher'll tell yer, ef de sisters only backs 'em
Dey'll git erlong wid any church; en so, o' co'se, dey laks 'em.
En Proverdence has fixed things so—ter make 'em right en
fittin'—
Dat er elder draws de sisters lak er warm brick draws er kitten.

Ole Satan seen how I wuz fixed. I bet he poked de fire
Er heap o' times right after church, when I wuz in de mire
O' yiel'in'; when some sister'd come en take mah han' en tarry
En joke wid me, en say she wondered why I didn' marry.
But now end den, bertwixt dey smiles, I seen Ole Satan grinnin',
En den I'd hyeah de 'Postle say, "Wid women, losin's winnin'."
O' co'se I'd take ernuther holt, when I hyeahed Paul er callin',
En so, by hol'in' [holding] tight ter him, I barely kep' f'um
fallin'.
Me en Ole Satan kep' it up fer years, suh; him er tryin'
Ter ketch me wid de women-folks ersmilin' en ersighin'.
But while de fight wuz sometimes close—'kaze he knows how
ter rassle [wrestle]—
I kep' mah foot right on his neck en helt on ter de 'Postle.
I flung him down so much, ontell at las' I got ter feelin'
Dat he mout keep on tryin', but he'd never ketch me yiel'in'.

One Ap'ul Sunday mawnin', while de sun laffed at de showers
Dat couldn't ebem stop de birds f'um singin' 'mongst de
    flowers,
I wuz settin in de pulpit, readin' f'um mah fav'rit author,
"So live, dat men may see yer works en glorify yer Father."
Er passel o' folks wuz comin' in, en, happenin' ter look up,
I seen er sight dat took mah breath en made me shet de book
    up.
Er pair o' modes' downcast eyes—er gown cut plain en simple—
Er little han'—er little foot—er half-smile en er dimple—
Shucks! I kain't tell yer how she looked; but while I set
    erwaitin'
Fer time ter start de op'nin hem [hymn] I clean fergot Ole
    Satan—
Fergot de sermon—en de tex'—almos' fergot mah 'ligion,
Er gazin' at dat lady, settin' lookin' lak er pigeon.
I drapped back down ter earth in time ter hyeah de las' bell
    ringin',
Give out "Er charge ter keep I have" en set de flock ter singin'.
But th'ough de hem, en after, th'ough de sermon en collection,
I couldn' keep mah eyes f'um turnin' 'roun' in her derection.
I meant ter preach ter sinners, too, ter talk erbout damnation;
But, 'stid [instead] o' dat, I tole erbout de joys o' salvation.
En Heab'm en Heab'm's blessin'—never said er word o' evil—
Fergot de brimstone en de dire, de pitchfo'k en de devil.
I said de benerdiction wid er kin' o' cu'is [curious] notion
Dat, ef she wuz good ez whut she looked, she'd git er double
    po'tion.

When church wuz out some sisters come (it always is dey failin'
Ter shake han's wid de elder en ter talk ercross de railin')
En stood er talkin' ter me, when I seen er deacon takin'
Her han' en leadin' her right up ter whar I stood er shakin'.
En den I kin' o' 'member hyeahin', "Dis is our preacher,
Sis' Viney": en den, mighty sof', "I'm r'aly glad ter meet yer."
En den, er pair o' eyes met mine—en things wuz gittin' hazy:
En den, er sof' han' drapped in mine—en I wuz stone-blin'
    crazy!

I never hyeahed er single word o' whut she wuz er sayin';
Jes' stood en watched de dimples dat erroun' her mouf wuz
playin',
En hyeahed her laff—de sweetes' laff!—en seen her eyes
ergleamin',
En reck'ned dat ef I *wuz* sleep, I'd jes' keep on er dreamin'.

But oh, dat night! When I got home, mah conscience 'gin ter
'buke me;
Ole Satan flung right in mah face how fur temptation took me.
I drapped down on mah knees en sez, "O Paul, yer know I'm
human.
I'm trustin' you ter stan' twix' me en dis hyeah awful woman."
Him en de 'Postle had it den—er agernizin' rassle;
Sometimes he had de underholt, de other times, de 'Postle.
Ole Satan helt Sis' Viney up in all her temptin' beauty:
En Paul sez, "Goodness gracious! Ain't I p'inted out yer duty?"
Ole Satan sez, "Dem han's o' hern—dey's mighty sof' en givin:"
De 'Postle sez, "I'd lak ter know how dat he'ps righteous livin?"
Ole Satan sez, "Yer know yer'd give de worl' ter make her love
yer:"
De 'Postle sez, "But is yer gwine ter give de Heab'm erbove
yer?"
Ole Satan kinder laffed en sez "De sweetes' in creation;"
But Paul, he stomped his foot en sez, "Don't yiel' ter no
temptation.
Dis hyeah's de cross yer got ter tote whilst on dis earth yer
tarry—
Ter put in *yo'* time fightin' sin. Let other people marry."
En den I riz up in mah might, wid no mo' hesitatin',
En sez, "I'm gwine ter stick ter Paul. So, git berhin' me, Satan."
Proud in mah strength, I said mah prayers wid nary stop ner
quiver;
But, hadn' mo' en got in bed en settled 'neath de kivver
En shet mah eyes, when Satan come en kotch me layin',
dreamin',
En fetches up Sis' Viney wid her teeth en eyes er gleamin'.
I dreamp erbout dat woman clean up 'tell de day wuz breakin';
En when I woke wid empty arms, mah heart wuz sho'ly achin'.

Fer fo' long weeks mah feelin's nachully wuz in er riot:
I never knowed er hour er er minute's time o' quiet;
'Kaze when I seen mah heart wuz he'pin' Satan in de rassle,
Dar ain't no use o' talkin', I almos' give up de 'Postle.

En so it wuz. Mah 'termination kep' er gittin' thinner
Ontell, one Sunday after church, she axed me 'roun' ter dinner
On Chuesday. Den I knowed de en' wuz comin' nigh en nigher,
En 'magined I hyeahed Satan, jes' er pokin' up de fire.
Dat night I fit ernuther fight erginst Ole Satan's trappin'.
Ole Satan he slipped up on me en almos' kotch me nappin';
'Kaze I'd jes' been erthinkin, "She *kain't* be so mighty harmful—
De blessed Paul hisse'f sez so. En she's er 'lishus [delicious] armful."
But Paul, he kinder he'ped me out when things wuz giting' sort o'
Disheartenin', by showing whut I *might* en whut I *ought* to.
I argied [argued] en I argied 'tell I got sick o' debatin',
En at de las' I 'termined I wuz gwine ter fool Ole Satan—
Wuz gwine ter Sis' Viney's house, mah min' sot on de 'Postle—
Wuz gwine ter meet Ole Satan dar en give him one las' rassle.
Ef he thought I wuz shyered [scared] o' him, dis wuz de time ter show him.
I'd grab him fo' Sis' Viney's face, en once fer all I'd th'ow [throw] him.
En den I tried ter drap ter sleep; but dough [though] I tried mah hardes',
I couldn' think o' nothin' 'cep'n Viney, plump en modes'.

De day come 'roun'; en 'roun' I went ter dinner wid Sis' Viney,
Dressed in mah new Prince Albert coat en plug hat, high en shiny.
(I don' know ez I tole yer, but Sis' Viney wuz er widder
Wid two small chillun, ez she said, ter work fer en consider.)
O' co'se er lump wuz in mah th'oat 'fo' I'd been dar er minute.
En ez fer talkin'—dar'd been none, ef she'd let me bergin it.
But she—ez cool ez Chris'mus—got ter talkin' 'bout mah preachin';
En how 'twuz strange ter her dat all de sinners wuzn't eachin' [itching]

Ter git inter de gospel road: dat she knowed *she'd* git nervous
Ef she wuz boun' de other way en hyeahed *me* hol'in' service.
Now dat wa'n't hardly fightin' fair—I felt I needed rightin'.
Jes' den, Paul whispered in mah year [ear], "I'm hyeah. J'ine in
    de fightin'!"
I felt mah strength er comin' back—en, ez de talk got warmer,
De lump it went back down mah th'oat; en so, I got some
    ca'mer [calmer].

Well, dinner-time it come at las'. But I ain't no ways able
Ter give yer de leas' notion o' whut all wuz on de table.
I jes' kin 'member chicken, baked, wid gravy, en mashed 'taters,
En collards, en some col'b'iled ham, en egg-bread, en termaters.
Well, in dat kitchen, Ev'ything, suh, 'minded me o' Viney—
De clean, white flo'—de table-cloth—de tin-pans en de chiny—
De frush [fresh] newspapers on de shelves—de chillun fat en
    smilin'—
De dish-pan, hangin' hime [behind] de stove—de big brass
    kittle, b'ilin'.
Dey all looked jes' lak home ter me de fust time dat I seen 'em:
Dey showed dat Viney lakked things clean en wa'n't erskyered
    ter clean 'em.
En right ercross de table, too, ersayin' she wuz sorry
De dinner wa'n't no better, but dat she'd had so much worry,
Whut wid de butcher en de stove en her two little sinners
(Dem's her two boys) she reck'n'd dis erbout de wust [worst]
    o' dinners,
Sis' Viney set. It would er warmed er heart made out o' leather
Ter see Sis' Viney *en* de grub er settin' dar tergether.
My heart wa'n't leather. Ez I set, er eatin' en er gazin',
I seen whar I wuz gwine ter feel de need o' grace amazin'
Ter keep mahse'f f'um gwine whar Ole Satan tried ter shove
    me—
Ter keep f'um grabbin' Viney's han' en beggin' her ter love me.
Er dozen times, ez I sot dar, Ole Satan fetched me to it:
Er dozen times I promussed Paul I wa'n't ergwine ter do it.
I riz up f'um dat table jes' erbeggin' Paul ter save me
Er strack [strike] me wid lockjaw 'fo' I could ax her would she
    have me.

Now always, after dinner-time, I'm mighty fond o' smokin';
En I guess Sis' Viney knowed it, kaze she said, half shy, half
   jokin',
"I'd offer yer er pipe, but I'm erskyered I might offen' [offend]
   yer.
Mah husban' uster smoke de one I'd be so proud ter len' [lend]
   yer."
Now, her two boys wuz gone ter play (I hyeahed de lambs er
   blatin' [bleating];
De room wuz empty, 'cep'n Paul, Sis' Viney, me en Satan.
So, when she brung dat pipe en sack en I seen her eyes glimmer,
I knowed de 'Postle's chances wuz er gittin' slim en slimmer.
I sadly filled de pipe. But when she lit er strip o' paper
Fer me ter light wid, den Ole Satan cut his cutes' caper.
When she bent down ter hol' de light, I felt her gentle breathin'
Right on mah neck; en lak er flash—mah blood wuz b'ilin'—
   seethin'!
I grit mah teeth en tried ter puff ter start de pipe ter burnin';
But ter save mah soul, I couldn' keep dem eyes o' mine f'um
   turnin'
Ter whar hern shined. Our heads nigh tetched! Den I give up de
   rassle.
Right dar Ole Satan flung me down—en likewise flung de
   'Postle.
I jes' had breath ernuff ter say, "Sis' Viney, will yer have me?"
En couldn't er said ernuther word ef dat word wuz ter save me.
Nex' thing I knowed, Sis' Viney's head wuz layin' on mah
   collar,
En de nex' bes' place ter Heab'm wuz right in Sis' Viney's
   parlor.

Appendixes

Appendix A

At times there were efforts to educate young black Americans, either privately, as with Phillis Wheatley, or publicly, when sometimes white mob resistance reacted violently, as it did against Miss Prudence Crandall in 1831 by attacking her schoolhouse for Negro girls in Canterbury, Connecticut, and causing her imprisonment for violating a state law against such teaching. But, unlike the more fortunate Phillis, even when blacks received an education they usually learned that often such education could be meaningless, indeed almost a liability instead of an asset in a racially prejudiced society. The New York African Free School was organized in 1787 and incorporated in 1808 by the New York Manumission Society, featuring a distinguished Board of Trustees that included John Jay and Alexander Hamilton; General Lafayette was made an honorary member in 1788, and was welcomed on his visit to the school in 1824 by an address from an eleven year old student, James D. Smith. Supported by patrons and the cooperation of Negro organizations like The African Dorcas Association, which procured and made clothes for the destitute black students, the school overcame fires, and relocations and developed from a forty student roster to a roll call of over six hundred pupils by 1830. It utilized the monitorial system, an extensive vocational curriculum, and stimulated some fine young minds, but competitive and racial realities would prove frustrating to most graduates, and the students recognized as much. Said one student, in his valedictory of 1819:

Respected Patrons and Friends

. . . We have been the objects of your care, and I still earnestly solicit your sympathy. Had I the mind of a Locke, and the eloquence of a Chatham, still, would there not be in the minds of some an immeasurable distance that would divide me from one of a white skin? What signifies it! Why should I strive hard, and acquire all the constituents of a man if the prevailing genius of the land admit me not as such, or but in an inferior degree!. . .Pardon me if I feel discouragement to oppress me to the very earth. I am arrived at the end of my education, just on the eve of setting out into the world, of commencing some honest pursuit, by which to earn a comfortable subsistence. What are my prospects? To what shall I turn my hand? Shall I be a mechanic? No one will employ me; white boys won't work with me. Shall I be a merchant? No one will have me in his office; white clerks won't associate with me. Drudgery and servitude, then, are my prospective portion. . .

Nevertheless, the school did graduate several men who became successful, some going on to graduate from various colleges: John Russwurm, the first Negro to graduate from Bowdoin College, 1826; Theodore Wright, from Princeton Theological Seminary; Edward Mitchell, from Dartmouth; Edward Jones, from Amherst; Charles L. Reason (q.v.); and William Brown and William E. Smith were students at Columbia University's Medical school as of 1830. There were others.

The intellectual quality of some of the boys as students is noteworthy. One youngster composed and delivered an essay in which he says,

"I am but seven years old, and I think I have learned considerable since last examination. I was then entirely ignorant of writing; I now present you with these humble specimens of my attainments in that art. I was then also unacquainted with the use of figures; I have since gone through simple addition, subtraction, multiplication and division; I have some knowledge of the compound rules. . ."

Another boy, ten-year old George R. Allen, carried on a recorded discussion of astronomy with a Dr. Samuel Mitchell, who happened to visit the school. Some example of the versification ability can be found in the following brief pieces. Every three months, the school held a fair, at which students exhibited their various creations, the best work entitling the manufacturer to fifty school tickets. Andrew R. Smith offered (a) "Lines on the School Fair." Representing the school's versifying training at the American Convention in Baltimore in 1828 were two very young boys, one of whom, George R. Allen, was instructed to take his slate and pencil and, closeting himself behind a locked door for no more than a half an hour, produce a piece of poetry on any subject he pleased. In less than half an hour, he composed (b) "On Slavery." A fellow student, Thomas S. Sidney, took longer, one hour, to produce fewer lines, (c) "On Freedom."[1]

A. Lines on the School Fair
(by Andrew R. Smith)

The work of children here you find,
The fruit of labor and of mind,
Three months are past, the day is come,
And he that gains shall have the sum.
   Although our minds are weak and feeble,
   Some can use a knife or needle:
   If fortune by my side will stand,
   I mean to join the happy band.
   A girl can make a frock or coat,
   A boy, a pretty little boat;
   Another girl, a pretty quilt,
   A handsome cap, or gown of silk.
T' excel we all will work and strive,
Till to perfection we arrive;
Many will work and strive in vain,
The fifty tickets to obtain.
Our little fair to us is great
As any other in the state;
It is a cheerful time to some,
Though idle scholars will not come.

---

[1] See Charles C. Andrews, *The History of the New York African Free-Schools*, etc., (New York, 1830).

The child that comes to this good school
Should never rest an idle fool;
Though there are many, once were so,
We mind them daily wiser grow.
The beauties of our little fair
You will not know, if you're not there;
It will be taking too much time,
To enter all the things in rhyme.
You'll find mistakes I do not doubt,
And if you do, please leave them out.

B. On Slavery

Slavery! oh, thou cruel stain,
Thou dost fill my heart with pain:
See my brother, there he stands
Chained by slavery's cruel bands.
Could we not feel a brother's woes,
Relieve the wants he undergoes;
Snatch him from slavery's cruel smart,
And to him freedom's joy impart?

> George R. Allen, aged 12
> years, October 21st, 1828.
> New York-African Free
> School

C. On Freedom

Freedom will break the tyrant's chain,
And shatter all his whole domain;
From slavery she will always free,
And all her aim is liberty.

> Thomas S. Sidney, aged 12
> years, October 21st, 1828
> New York-African Free
> School

Appendix B

To indicate something of the social and poetical contacts made by some of these early Negro poets, the following might be helpful. A sampling of the uninspired verse of Mrs. Josephine D. (Henderson) Heard, *Morning Glories* (Philadelphia, 1890-1891), is, perhaps, not necessary, an example being supplied in the poem below. She is included here for the information she affords in her dedication and in several appended commendatory letters. Born 1861 in Salisbury, North Carolina, of parents who were only nominally slaves, she moved with them as they hired themselves out in Charlotte, where she began a long period of study that took her to Scotia Seminary in Concord, North Carolina, to Bethany Institute in New York, and, as a teacher, in schools in North Carolina, South Carolina and Tennessee. She married the Reverend William H. Heard in 1882, who was himself an author, *The Bright Side of African Life* (Nashville, 1898), and travelled widely. Her dedication to her husband, for instance, is "further dedicated to Sir Walter Wilkins and Lady Wilkins, Lord Mayor, Lady Mayoress of London, England, with whom I dined, and through whose courtesy I was presented to England's greatest sovereign, Queen Victoria, in 1896." An exchange between her and John Greenleaf Whittier, the Quaker poet, records an old man's sincerity and a young lady's youth. Her poem to him, his written reply and her florid reply to his reply follow:

To Whittier

In childhood's sunny days my heart was taught to love
Thy name, all other poets' names above,
And when to womanhood at last I came,
Behold the spark was fanned into a flame;
Nor did I dare presume that I should live,
And to the honored, white-haired poet give
My sentiment in rude constructed rhyme;
O, wondrous change wrought by the hand of time!

When he who came the slaves among to dwell,
From frigid Idaho (we loved him well),
A—thirst for knowledge I stood at his side,
With quickening thoughts and eyes astonished, wide.
He nightly read, and held me on his knee,
From Whittier's "Snowbound" filling me with glee.
The seed sown by his hand in infant heart,
Has lived and grown, and cannot now depart.

Now to the sunset thou hast set thy face,
And silvery crown thy head doth grace;
The mind of fertile thought doth not decline,
Preserved yet from ravages of time.
Since I can never hope my first desire,
To shake thy hand, which would my soul inspire,
Now ere yet "the chord is loosed or pitcher broken,"
Grant me with thine own hand this little token:
Ere yet that hand by feebleness grows lame,
With condescension write for me thy name.

Letter from John G. Whittier

Massachusetts, March 24, 1890

My Dear Friend:
Our mutual friend, Miss Higginson, has written me enclosing a
Poem, which gives me credit for much more than I deserve, but
for which I thank thee. It is a pleasant gift to express, as thee
can, thy thoughts in verse among thy friends and acquaintances.
In this way poetry is its own great reward—it blesses and is

blest. *I am very glad to give the "token" asked for in thy little poem by signing my name, with every good wish from thy aged friend.*

John G. Whittier

Letter from Mrs. Heard to Whittier

Philadelphia, Pennsylvania
April 2nd, 1890

To My Esteemed and Honored Friend:
I now assume the pleasantest duty of my life, that of acknowledging the cordial receipt of your most inestimable favor of recent date.
Cognizant of the weight of years you bear, I will not burden you with a long letter, while my heart out of its fullness dictates to me faster than my fingers are able to trace; but my joy is **full**; *my gratitude* **unbounded.**
I should certainly have congratulated myself upon being so favored as to have obtained even your name from thine own hand, and **a letter,** *such as thee wrote me, freighted with rich advice and kindly recognition, is priceless.*
God Bless Thee, *and may thy passage to the land of the blest be upon a calm sea with zephyrs laden with the perfume of thy noble life's deeds to waft thy spirit's bark onward and over Jordan.*

Gratefully Thine,
Josie D. Heard

Appendix C
Francis Williams (1700?-1773?)

Francis, the youngest of three sons to free-born John and Dorothy Williams of Jamaica, was selected, as part of an experiment by the Duke of Montagu, to determine whether or not an educated black person could be as capable of abstract literature as a white person. Accordingly, he was sent to an English grammar school and Cambridge, where he was concerned with mathematics, but, upon his return to Jamaica, he was denied the opportunity of a political career on the Governor's Council. He then opened an elementary school in Spanish Town and taught reading, writing, Latin and elementary mathematics. The information about Williams is found in a biographical note by an historian, Edward Long, who was an admitted racist, "I have ... alledged (sic) ... to prove an inferiority of the Negroes to the race of white men," and we may regard him accordingly. If Williams were as arrogant and vain as described, wearing a periwig, a sword and ruffled shirt, and proclaiming that he was really "a white man acting under a black man's skin," he does not extend such views into his Latin dedicatory poems, an example of which he wrote for each governor of his homeland. He is said also to have composed a popular ballad, beginning, "Welcome, welcome brother debtor, etc." Long, who supplied notes for his translation of the ode, (q.v.) finds the work "highly labored; designed, modeled, and perfected, to the utmost stretch of his invention, imagination, and skill," but has to admit the obvious strength in versification. Although Williams was born and reared on Jamaica, educated in England and flourished on his homeland, because he was a black early poet, he was regarded by many white persons to be about as Jamaican or West Indian as any black American early poet would be considered American. In the light of that reality, he may be included here as an example of one black man's poetic uses of Latin.

Integerrimo et fortissimo viro
Georgio Haldano, armigero,
Insulae Jamaicensis gubernatori;
Cui, omnes morum, virtutumque dotes bellicarum,
In cumulum accesserunt.

CARMEN

Denique venturum fatis volventibus annum,
Cuncta per extensum læta videnda diem,
Excussis adsunt curis, sub imagine clarâ
Felices populi, terraque lege virens.
Te duce, quæ fuerant malesuada mente peracta
Irrita conspectu non reditura tuo.
Ergo omnis populus, nec non plebecula cernet
Hæsurum collo te *relegasse* jugum,
Et mala, quæ diris quondam cruciatibus, insons
Insula passa fuit; condoluisset onus,
Ni vixtrix tua Marte manus prius inclyta, nostris
Sponte ruinosis rebus adesse velit.
Optimus es servus regi servire Britanno,
Dum gaudet genio Scotica terra tuo:
Optimus herôum populi fulcire ruinam;
Insula dum superest ipse superstes eris.
Victorem agnoscet te *Guadaloupa,* suorum
Despiciet merito diruta castra ducum.
Aurea vexillis flebit jactantibus *Iris,*
Cumque suis populis, oppida victa gemet.
Crede, meum non est, vir Marti chare, *Minerva*
Denegat Æthiopi bella sonare ducum.
Concilio, caneret te *Buchananus* et armis,
Carmine *Peleidae,* scriberet ille parem.
Ille poeta, decus patriæ, tua facta referre
Dignior, altisono vixque *Marone* minor.
Flammiferos agitante suos sub sole jugales
Vivimus; eloquium deficit omne focis.

Hoc demum acccipias multâ fuligine fusum
Ore sonaturo; non cute, corde valet.
Pollenti stabilita manu, Deus almus, eandem
Omnigenis animam, nil prohibente dedit.
Ipsa coloris egens virtus, prudentia; honesto
Nullus inest animo, nullus in arte color.
Cur timeas, quamvis dubitesve, nigerrima celsam
Cæsaris occidui, scandere musa domum?
Candida quod nigra corpora pelle geris!
Integritas morum *Maurum* magis ornat, et ardor
Ingenii, et docto dulcis in ore decor;
Hunc, mage cor sapiens, patriæ virtutis armorque,
Eximit è sociis, conspicuumque facit.
Insula me genuit, celebres aluere *Britanni*
Insula, te salvo non dolitura patre.
Hoc precor ô nullo videant te fine regentem
Florentes populos, terra, deique locus!

Translation of Latin Ode

To that most upright and valiant man, George Haldane, Esq.,
Governor of the Island of Jamaica; upon whom All military and
moral endowments are accumulated.

An Ode

At length the revolving fates th' expected year
Advance, and joy the live-long day shall cheer,
Beneath the fost'ring law's auspicious dawn
New harvests rise to glad th' enlivened lawn.
With the bright prospect blessed, the swains repair
In social bands, and give a loose to care.
Rash councils now, with each malignant plan,
Each faction, that in evil hour began,
At your approach are in confusion fled,
Nor, while you rule, shall rear their dastard head.
Alike the master and the slave shall see
Their neck relieved, the yoke unbound by thee.

Ere now our guiltless isle, her wretched fate
Had wept, and groaned beneath the oppressive weight
Of cruel woes save thy victorious hand,
Long famed in war, from *Gallia's* hostile land,
And wreaths of fresh renown, with generous zeal,
Had freely turned, to prop our sinking weal.
Formed as thou art, to serve *Brittania's* crown,
While *Scotia*[1] claims thee for her darling son;
Oh! best of heroes, ablest to sustain
A falling people, and relax their chain,
Long as this isle shall grace the Western deep,
From age to age, thy fame shall never sleep.
Thee, her dread victor *Guadaloupe* shall own,
Crushed by thy arm, her slaughtered chiefs bemoan;
View their proud tents all levelled in the dust,
And, while she grieves, confess the cause was just.
The golden *Iris* the sad scene will share,
Will morn her banners scattered in the air;
Lament her vanquished troops with many a sigh,
Nor less to see her towns in ruin lie.
Fav'rite of *Mars!* believe, th' attempt were vain,
It is not mine to try the arduous strain.
What! shall an *Aethiop* touch the martial string,
Of battles, leaders, great achievements sing?
Ah no! *Minerva,* with th' indignant *Nine,*
Restrain him, and forbid the bold design.
To a *Buchanan*[2] does the theme belong;
A theme, that well deserves *Buchanan's* song.
'Tis he, shall swell the din of war's alarms,
Record the great in council, as in arms;
Recite each conquest by the valor won,
And equal thee to great *Peleides'*[3] son.
That bard, his country's ornament and pride,
Who e'en with Maro might the bays divide:

---

[1] *Scotia.* Mr. Haldane was a native of North Britain [Long.]

[2] Buchanan. George Buchanan (1506-1582), Scottish satirist and composer of tragedies and Latin verses.

[3] Peleides' Son, i.e., Achilles.

Far worthier he, thy glories to rehearse,
And paint thy deeds in his immortal verse.
We live, alas! where the bright God of day,
Full from the zenith whirls his torrid ray:
Beneath the rage of his consuming fires,
All fancy melts, all eloquence expires.
Yet may you deign accept this humble song,
Tho' wrapped in gloom, and from a falt'ring tongue;
Tho' dark the stream on which the tribute flows,
Not from the skin, but from the *heart* it rose.
To all of human kind, benignant heaven
(Since nought forbids) one common soul has given.
This rule was 'stablished by th' Eternal Mind;
Nor virtue's self, nor prudence are confined
To *color;* none imbues the honest heart;
To science none belongs, and none to art.
Oh, Muse, of blackest tint, why shrinks thy breast,
Why fear'st approach the *Caesar* of the *West!*
Dispel thy doubts, and with confidence ascend
The regal dome, and hail him for thy friend:
Nor blush, although in garb funereal dressed,
Thy body's white, though clad in sable vest!
Manners unsullied, and the radiant glow
Of genius, burning with desire to know;
And learned speech, with modest accent worn,
Shall best the sooty *African* adorn.
A heart with wisdom fraught, a patriot flame,
A love of virtue; these shall lift his name
Conspicuous, far beyond his kindred race,
Distinquished from them by the foremost place.
In this prolific isle, I drew my birth,
And *Britain* nursed, illustrious through the earth;
This, my loved isle, which never more shall grieve,
Whilst you our common friend, our father live.
Then this my pray'r—"May earth and heaven survey
A people ever blessed, beneath your sway!"

                                                       Francis Williams

* * * * * * * *

Bibliography
Early American Negro Poets

The number of single poems by Negroes of the eighteenth and nineteenth (perhaps even the seventeenth) centuries is unknown, for reasons such as desire for security, affectation or specialized training. Some of them were fugitive slaves, and if they wrote and wished to protect their precarious freedom, they might sign their works with initials, pseudonyms or no names at all. Thus, in the relation of his death house confession in 1788 to a (white?) moralist amannuensis, a convicted Negro murderer revealed that he escaped from slavery in Delaware and when once in Woodbury, New Jersey, he changed his real name of Benjamin to that of his (deceased?) brother Abraham Johnstone. In the early years of the *Liberator,* William Lloyd Garrison published poems by a certain Ada from Philadelphia, identified only as "a young lady of color." Other Negro poets (e.g., Ann Plato, q.v.) professed not to be concerned with racial matters, while still other such versifiers were so educated that they had genuine difficulty trying to utilize their mastery of classical mythology and poetic apparatus for Negro readers who had not been so educated. These poets are sometimes identified as Negroes by descendants or acquaintances. When they wrote verse enough to fill a volume, they usually let their race be known, often proudly. Several of the following poets published more than one volume of verse, but the listing, below, is confined to volumes of verse published by Negroes, other than those represented with selections, of the eighteenth and nineteenth centuries.

Maria and Harriet Falconar, *Poems on Slavery* (London, 1788)

James Montgomery, James Graham, E. Benger, *Poems on the Abolition of the Slave Trade* (London, 1809)

Anonymous, *The West Indies and Other Poems* (1811)

John Bull, *The Slave and Other Poems* (London, 1824)

Rev. Noah C. Cannon, *The Rock of Wisdom. . .To Which Are Added Several Interesting Hymns* (New York,? 1833)

Anonymous, *"The Commemorative Wreath: In Celebration of the Extinction of Negro Slavery in the British Dominions* (London, 1835)

Anonymous, *Slavery in the British Dominions* (London, 1835)

Anonymous, *Anti-Slavery Melodies* (Hingham, Massachusetts, 1843)

George Whitfield Clark, compiler, *The Liberty Minstrel* (New York, 1844)

William Wells Brown, *Anti-Slavery Harp* (Boston, 1849)[1]

"A West Indian," *Charleston, South Carolina: a satiric poem showing that slavery still exists in a country which boasts, above all others, of being the seat of liberty.* (London, 1851)

Sam ⸺ *Darkness Brought to Light* (Derry, New Hampshire,? 1855)

George W. Clark, *The Harp of Freedom* (New York, 1856)

Abel Charles Thomas, *The Gospel of Slavery* (New York, 1864)

Jacob Rhodes, *The Nation's Loss* (Newark, New Jersey, 1866)

Islay Walden, *Miscellaneous Poems* (Washington, D.C., 1873)

J. Willis Menard, *Lays in Summer Lands* (Washington, D.C., 1879)

Sam Lucas, *Careful Man Songster* (Chicago, 1881)

Rev. H.M. Turner, *The Conflict for Civil Rights* (Washington, D.C., 1881)

George C. Rowe, *Thoughts in Verse* (Charleston, South Carolina, 1887)

⸺, *Our Heroes* (Charleston, South Carolina, 1890)

William J. Vandyne, *Revels of Fancy* (Boston, 1891)

Frank B. Coffin, *Coffin's Poems and Ajax's Ordeals* (Little Rock, 1892)

[1] As their titles suggest, some of these collections contain song lyrics and even music; Simpson's *The Emancipation Car,* including lyrics and appropriate "airs," also contains some interesting autobiographical information and a rollicking satire in prose, "A Consistent Slaveholder's Sermon."

James T. Franklin, *Mid-Day Gleanings* (Memphis, 1893)

Cupid Aleins Whitfield, *Poems of To-Day* (Quincy, Florida, 1893)

J.M.C. Simpson, *The Emancipation Car* (Zanesville, Ohio, 1893)

F.S. Alwell, *The Open Door* (Winfield, Kansas, 1895)

Eloise Bibbs, *Poems* (Boston, 1895)

Alice Ruth (Dunbar) Nelson, *Violets and Other Tales* (Boston, 1895)

Charles H. Shoeman, *A Dream and Other Poems* (Ann Arbor, Michigan, 1895)

Mary Weston Fordham, *Magnolia Leaves* (Charleston, South Carolina, 1898)

Aaron Belford Thompson, *Morning Songs* (Rossmoyne, Ohio, 1899)

James T. Franklin, *Jessamine/ Poems* (Memphis, 1900)

George H. Temple, *The Epic of the Columbus Bell and Other Poems* (Reading, Pennsylvania, 1900)

Priscilla H. Thompson, *Ethiope Lays* (Rossmoyne, Ohio, 1900)

Benjamin Wheeler, *Culling from Zion's Poets* (Mobile, Alabama, 1907)[2]

---

[2] Originally prepared for publication in 1890 as *The Harp of Zion,* this volume, greatly expanded, was obliged to find its present title when some one else used the first proposed title.

Index